Errislannan

First published in 1993 by
THE LILLIPUT PRESS LTD
4 Rosemount Terrace, Arbour Hill,
Dublin 7, Ireland

A CIP record for this
book is available from
The British Library

ISBN 0 946640 83 1

Acknowledgments
The Lilliput Press receives financial assistance from
An Chomhairle Ealaion/The Arts Council, Ireland

Jacket design by Elizabeth van Amerongen
Set in 11 on 13 Garamond 3
by Koinonia Ltd of Manchester
Printed in Dublin by
Betaprint of Clonshaugh

Errislannan

SCENES FROM A PAINTER'S LIFE

Alannah Heather

THE LILLIPUT PRESS

Contents

Illustrations between pages 86 and 87 and 118 and 119

CHAPTER 1

The Fall of the Loft

'There was things which he stretched, but mainly he told the truth.'
Huckleberry Finn, Mark Twain

If one thing more than another made me write this book it was the fall of the loft over the coach-house in the stable yard. All the beams gave way at once and down came sacks of letters and diaries, trunks of clothing and linen, crates of honey, boxes of china and broken furniture. Regimental flags wrapped in old corsets, dozens of sermons, my great-grandmother's will and a huge block of wood on which mutton had been chopped up. All this, draped in cobwebs, fell on the carriage (known as the coach), which took six inside and three on the box, the side-car and the trap. The sacks of letters and diaries were put in a dark wet outhouse in the yard. Ranging in date from 1790 to the 1960s, they give fascinating glimpses into the lives of the last five generations living in Errislannan, Burmount Manor (the previous family home in Co. Wexford) and the Dublin house. To read them one needs a magnifying glass, and they are so full of biblical quotations that they are tedious except for the unusual or tragic event.

Connemara, that land of mountains, lakes and bogland, stretches out into the Atlantic protected by many small islands. The high rocky fingers of land are divided by bays which wind far back nearly to the foot of the mountains. One of these fingers is the peninsula of Errislannan, which is almost an island, so close do the seas come at its neck. The Manor in the centre is beautifully situated, with the lawn – a hayfield in summer – running down to a small lake, Loch Nakilla. It is sheltered from the north by a horseshoe of trees which slopes down to the lake on each side of the house. Its stone plastered over, with three small dormer windows and one big one facing out across the lake to the distant line of sea and the beam of Slyne Head lighthouse, the house is half covered with ivy and takes its place among the trees.

Among the papers of the 1790s I found the sad story of my great-great-grandmother, Jane Wall (*née* Frayne), written on bits of paper sewn together to form a little diary. 'I was married in Furlonge Cornmarket in the presence of … and was remarried in the Church of Castlebridge on 24th June 1790 in the presence of … ', and here followed a list of officers and titled gentlemen and

– 1 –

their ladies. Obviously the second wedding was a respectable one. 'Sarah was born in October 1790, Richard Henry Wall' – my great-grandfather, who bought Errislannan – 'born 1793'. Then, 'Parted with my dear mother to return to Dublin being near lying down of my Dear Little Daughter, and met a very unfriendly welcome from her father at my return, which Alas! was often the case with me.' That baby, little Mary Jane, died when she was three 'and was buried in Carnolway Graveyard in the County Kildare near the big thorn bush on the off side of the Church about a yard from the thorn, the side next to the Church'. Later 'My Sarah and Richard were taken away from me by their father and left in the County Kildare. I parted with them beyond Ballareen Church ... that day miserable! May the Lord protect them and grant me a happy sight of them in this world and in the world to come, Amen.' Perhaps it was being taken away from his mother as a child which made my great-grandfather so difficult to live with and accounted for there being none of the usual expressions of regret when 'Papa left us.'

There is a photograph of him – 'The Rev. Richard Henry Wall D.D. and his wife and daughters' – posing on the lawn at Errislannan among the haycocks; the women in crinolines, the men in top hats. My great-grandfather is sitting on the only chair, hand on stick. The women stand meekly round with smooth hair parted in the middle; beautiful gentle faces caught by the camera for future generations to see. Their brothers were far away; Henry, whose fascinating naughty diary I found, was killed in the Indian Mutiny; George was an army surgeon and was killed in India. James, in the navy, died, with all his shipmates, of yellow fever in Jamaica and was buried under a palm tree on the beach. Walter died unmarried though he was a great 'ladies' man' and spent much time dressed in wrinkled stockings and knee-breeches at the Viceregal Lodge.

Of the girls in the photograph, Great-aunt Sarah was extremely musical, playing the harp and singing the famous Tom Moore's Irish Melodies with Tom Moore playing her accompaniments to 'Oft in the stilly night' and 'Believe me if all those endearing young charms'. She longed for Dublin and did escape to Paris, but made the mistake of letting her father know where she was. He wrote saying she was insane, and her defiant reply has survived the years: 'Dear Papa, I am not insane but on the Seine.' He forced her to return to Errislannan, where she literally pined away and died of misery. I found her harp in the attic of Drinagh covered in mould, with the strings lying on the ground like seaweed.

Then came Great-aunt Rachael, who was loved by everyone and was the mainstay of Errislannan. Then my grandmother, Henrietta.

The West of Ireland does not breed husbands. George Moore's book about the maidens of the West of Ireland, *A Drama in Muslin*, gives a tragic picture. They were pretty, healthy girls, but all their brothers went to school in

England and then into the British army or navy, and their sisters were left pining for young men. Mercifully when my grandmother was about to pine, a young clergyman called George Heather came along and asked her to marry him. On the wedding day in 1866 a full gale was blowing. The rain fell, the wind blew and howled around the church for this, the first wedding to be celebrated there since it was built in 1855, and the last for over a hundred years.

Henrietta kept her bridegroom waiting at the church for two hours as a bridesmaid's dress had not come from Clifden. One can imagine the bridegroom's cold feelings, both physical and mental, and the shivering of the guests until the bride was seen to enter the churchyard. Then the storm took over and her veil went sailing over the tower until another gust blew it down tangled in the gorse. The wedding guests had to retrieve it and were soaking wet before the laughing bride passed up the aisle.

Great-aunt Alice was a memorable character, though I only knew her when she was over eighty. She then had a mass of white curly hair, cut fairly short so that it stood out round her head like a halo, and magnificent bright blue eyes, under which she smeared in with her finger a large patch of black grease-paint. Alice would walk fifteen miles when she was eighty-two, dressed in a flowered kimono and an old felt hat, gone to a point with the rain, and carrying a long black stick with a silver knob – not for support, but to tap the road and poke at people and things. She was very deaf so did all the talking, and would make up witty limericks and rhymes about people as she approached them; then, flourishing the stick, she dramatically recited her piece, reducing the victim to silent hate. One farmer got the full treatment over a period of years: up came the stick and a deep voice intoned, '*Who* stole the pig?' referring to an embarrassing episode of the past. A plain cousin staying with us got this at the dinner table:

> M stands for Mabel,
> Who sat at the table
> And tried to eat more
> Than she really was able.
> With the lean kine of Egypt
> She dared to compete
> And vox populi thundered
> Her success was complete.

From then on she and her sisters were always referred to as the 'Kine'.

I remember my brother and me cowering behind walls when Great-aunt Alice passed, we were so afraid of her. Once I sat on a bag of eggs and she heard the crunch. Her black-ringed eyes appeared over the wall and we flew away over the hill, working ourselves up into nightmare fears, which were quite groundless.

She built two stone bathing-boxes on a high rock from where one could dive into the deep green sea. She considered our bathing-dresses indecent and herself wore a long gown of butcher-blue with slits for arms, tied only round the neck. She mounted the rock, put back her shining white head, raised her arms and took a spectacular leap into the air, sailing down with the gown acting as a parachute. It was then our turn to be embarrassed.

Great-aunt Alice's diaries are much livelier than the others, even as a child in 1854: 'We made Paddy get up early and catch our ponies for us. Very cross. We saw the sun rise over the mountains and saw it set, coming home from Ballyconneely, over the Atlantic.'

I have managed to trace some love affairs, but they were very one-sided as all the local men were married or about to have weddings, after which she always wrote RIP. 'Walked home in the dark arm in arm. Ecstasy ... delicious ... exquisite ... he talked to me for a long time.' Or, 'He did not speak to me. Miserable and agony of mind. Could not sleep for thinking of Capt. P. Went skating with Capt. P. and fell in. Very cold and wet. Nearly died.' The next day 'very ill'. But the following day, 'Rode Capt. P's horse into town and walked home.'

The next year, 'Called on Mr C. and he would not notice me. Stayed late with Irelands, in Clifden, sea rough and nearly dark; tide too far out for boat.' 'Went by long car 40 miles to Westport and on by carriage to Cahille. Janie and the children well [Heathers]. Ben cruel to me. I don't like him any more. Do not break the bruised reed.'

'Wedding day of Francie Robinson to Dick Pelley. Cried a lot. Mr Paddon proposed to Kathleen. Mr Corry married to Sec. Awfully depressed.' ('Sec' was the disparaging name always given to Mrs Corry, who had been a secretary.) 'Capt. P. said I would be in a lunatic asylum yet.' 'Illuminations for Daniel O'Connell. Sec was there. He only said good-night to me and he is going to Dublin tomorrow. Tired to death.'

Then among the texts and biblical quotations, some blasphemous hand has written in a different ink, 'Went to Errismore races and lost £5. I drowned my sorrows in eight pints of beer. Johnnie took me home and put me to bed.'

Great-aunt Alice finally married a clergyman much younger than herself: Charles Heaslop, who had come as a curate to Mr Corry, the Rector of Clifden, the earlier object of Alice's love. Charles proposed and was refused, but Great-uncle Walter, who was hidden under the table, ran after him and brought him back. The superstition that it is unlucky to return to a house without sitting down was fully justified. He stood and found himself engaged, to rue many the day.

Alice and Charles had two very beautiful, saintly daughters, Phedora and Viola, but their mother put an end to all their love affairs. I found their love letters stuffed into a dressmaker's dummy in the Drinagh attic – and they died spinsters. They are the only members of the family to be in the peerage, under the heading of Lord Byron, of all people. Phedora, who comes into this story later on, was born with difficulty at Letterfrack, a few miles from Errislannan; Great-aunt Rachael describes the dramatic event. Her father, the son of an Admiral Heaslop, had an intense love of the sea and removed himself from domestic disharmony in Errislannan by taking to a half-decked boat, with a cubby-hole in which he slept.

After Viola's birth Charles left home for seven years, discarding his family. He became a chaplain in the navy, where he was tutor to King George and the Duke of Clarence as young boys. Charles is important to me only because he built a boat-house, which fifty years later I used as a studio and sometimes slept in. After leaving the navy he had twenty-seven parishes, driven on by his eccentric wife. When Great-aunt Alice thought she was about to die she returned to lay her bones with the family. She pounded on the piano with great vivacity until the day she died and was buried exactly as planned, in her beloved Errislannan. Perhaps her best memorial was the letter-box in the stone wall near the lodge. She disliked government green, so took any paint she had by her and produced ever-changing works of art to delight anyone going to post a letter. Animals, flowers, all very cheerful.

That generation were more active, happier and far better educated than later ones. The local schoolmaster came before breakfast to teach them Latin, Greek and astronomy. They also learned excellent French and German: Great-aunt Rachael taught my aunts French to such a high standard that they were moved to the top class for languages in their English boarding-school. They learned historical dates and geographical facts in rhymes that were never forgotten, and fascinating jingles came out at meals when they were over eighty.

The most important thing in the life of the family was the church, which was built partly by the Irish Church Missions – one of whose founders was my great-great-grandfather – but mostly by my great-grandfather, with the donations he extracted by sending round the following letter in 1853.

'Therefore we His servants will arise and build.'
All ye who feel a desire that Protestantism should take root in our land, – all ye who would wish to see the blessings of CIVILISATION, INDUS-TRY, CONTENTMENT, LOYALTY AND PEACE grow up in this remote and unvisited peninsula, instead of BARBARISM, SLOTH, DISCON-TENT, DISAFFECTION AND TURBULENCE, a change which a know-ledge of God's Blessed Word and the inculcation of its principles, are eminently calculated to produce ... It is twelve months since, relying on Him who can use weak instruments as well as strong, I laid before the public the spiritual wants of the truly primitive and interesting people of Errislannan ...

I will spare you the rest, it was a long letter. What incredible conceit! And what a vivid picture those few lines give of the attitude of the Protestant land-owner fired with missionary zeal. The tragedy of the Famine was only four years behind them; Connemara was dotted with ruined houses; thousands of acres were going back into bog; landlords were being murdered and the Irish Republican Brotherhood was to start its long bloody fight for freedom only eight years ahead, but families like ours survived with their eyes shut. My youth was enclosed in this pious and contented atmosphere, and it has taken a lifetime and extensive reading to discover what was happening in Ireland in this century.

The church was finished in 1855 and consecrated by Lord Plunkett, Bishop of Tuam, on July 31st. The next day in the diary has the entry, 'George gone to the Crimea in *Imperatrice*,' and inserted later, '6th Gibraltar, 11th Malta. Close to Constantinople, Balaklava – Genoa'. But brother George died later in India.

In the seventh century there was a village on the site of the Manor, near our good spring well. St Flannan is said to have come from the Aran Islands one day driving a cow, and asked where he could spend the night. Only on the island in the lake, he was told, the lake at that time extending to the foot of Look-out Hill. In the morning he was ensconced on what had been an island and the lake had retreated to its present level. Flannan built a small beehive church of stones and a beehive hut beside it, in which he lived. In 1684 Roderick O'Flaherty wrote, 'No bodies are to be buried in it, or they will be found above ground in the morning,' but the Morris family from Ballinaboy are still buried there and seem to rest peacefully. By it is a holy well with a bullaun – a hollowed-out stone – where coins, Rosaries, buttons are still placed after prayers and walking clockwise round the well. Long ago I used to draw groups of women kneeling there. There must have been a religious house on the site of the Manor, as small bits of carved stone have been found in the walls.

The family diaries indicate the astonishing amount of social life in Conne-mara between 1850 and the turn of the century: the calling, dining, dancing and parties; tennis with thirty-four players, picnics and boating expeditions. They drove in the carriage and pair as far afield as Westport – forty miles – visiting friends and staying the night; 'The gentlemen walked part of the way.' Also to Boffin Island, spending the night with the Hildebrands: 'We danced and then slept eight girls to one room.' Next day, 'Back to Cleggan in rough seas, but transferred to the Adamsons' boat and on to Kill, where we dined and stayed the night . . . Called on the Irelands on our way home.' The next day, 'We rode to Roundstone [twelve miles] to the Robinsons and called on the Hazells on the way home.' And so on, day after day, calling or being called on. Men came to fish or shoot – 'Hares, partridges and the simple rabbit.' 'Captain Palmer shot a black cat in mistake for a black rabbit.'

My great-aunts thought nothing of walking the five miles into town, or rowing the two miles across the bay. Once they rode their ponies nine miles to Shinenagh for breakfast with the Sheas and then drove to the mountains, which they climbed 'Right to the very top in the rain. Soaked through so we stopped at a farm and sat by the fire and drank tea.' The next day the only entry was 'Very stiff.'

The next generation did none of these things; they could not ride, swim or row boats, which resulted in a very confined life. When my turn came I found I could easily walk into town, or row across the bay and go fishing by myself, but I had no pony or even a bicycle. Great-aunt Alice's diary strikes a sympathetic note: 'Rowed to town, coming home in the dark, it was very rough. Terrified and could not find my way in' – this is exactly what happened to me several times. Nearly a hundred years later I rowed my little boat home in the dark and moored to the same rocks and walked the same path up to the house; this continuity is what makes Errislannan the most loved place in my life.

In the middle of the nineteenth century the D'Arcys were at Clifden Castle across the bay and later moved to the dower house, called Glenowen. Their descendants, the Eyres, came to the castle and were friendly enough until one night Great-uncle Walter drove Miss Eyre home in the 'coach' very drunk and handed her in to her angry father.

There were Blakes at Renvyle who had to leave because of poverty; the last, Miss Julia Blake, died in London of starvation. There were Mansfields at Faule, Kendalls at Emlanabehe, Hazells, Morrises, Armstrongs, Corrys, Palmers, Irelands, Browns, and, on Errislannan, Byrnes at Boat Harbour. Most important for the family was a large family of Irwins in our rectory (Drinagh) near the church. Ben was greatly fancied by Aunt Jane when they were in their teens, and Alfred was for generations a much-loved doctor in Connemara. Now all those houses are empty, ruined, or turned into hotels owned by foreigners.

Great-aunt Rachael's diaries cover the greatest span. She tells of all the children being sent to England during the Famine, the journeys by canal boat across Ireland and later: 'Trelford [the coachman] is very angry at doing the churning. May [the cook] has fled. Gone to America I think.' And when her loved young cousin died at Burmount, 'Aunt Rachael and Louisa bowed to the earth with grief, but John is happy in Heaven with Jesus in the Blood of the Lamb.'

Years later, when the Manor was being sold, I plunged my hands into those sacks in the yard at Errislannan and drew out, among nineteenth-century deeds and trivia, letters from those two great protagonists, the Duke of Wellington and his victim, Daniel O'Connell: a strange find for our stable yard. That from the Duke was to one of our ancestors, General Munro, a Waterloo friend, inviting him to breakfast 'between one and two o'clock to meet their Royal Highnesses the Duke and Duchess and Princess Augusta of Cambridge, and the princess Sophia Matilda ... at Walmer Castle.' Daniel O'Connell's letter was to my great-grandfather on a business matter, but his signature was thrilling to me. In 1843 he had held one of his 'monster' meetings in Connemara in the fight for Catholic emancipation and the repeal of the Union. One hundred thousand people gathered round Clifden, but he stayed the night with the Martins at Ballynahinch Castle and many travelled there to meet him. There were no proper roads then so the people must have come on horses and donkeys or by sea in their curraghs or puchauns. An amazing sight it must have been, like a modern refugee camp without any of the helpers or suppliers. Our now empty harbour must have been crowded with boats. A year or two after this, Daniel O'Connell was defeated in his most glorious hour by the Duke of Wellington; he had cannons trained on one of these 'monster' meetings, and to avert slaughter O'Connell ordered his followers to disperse. He died a few years later during the Famine in 1847.

Another find in the sack was the notice fastened to our wall at the time of the Fenians, about 1870 when many landlords were murdered; we received only the following:

To you who pay rent by work and labour in Errislannan to Mr Wall or any other unmerciful land jobber, this manifestly proves your determination to stand antagonistic defiantly to the voice of the nation and the public press. You need not expect to prevaricate us – if you attempt to shroud in distant solitudes in crevices of rocks, in the bowles of the earth, you shall be detected. You parcel of infernal vipers we notify you to desist, desist, desist.

    John Conneely Dan   Val Conneely Martin

The families of the two signatories still live in Errislannan. The notice shows to advantage the vocabulary taught by the local schoolmaster. One tenant brought a calf down from the back of the hill as a present to my great-grandmother as he dared not pay rent.

With the collapse of the loft floor, the 'coach' was sent to be mended, but it was left out in the rain until it fell to pieces. After a century of use its loss was felt very much, not only for its shelter coming over the hill on dark nights and in bad weather; its musty blue felt seats and mirrors were tangible reminders of the past generations who wore lovely dresses and went to dances and parties; while all we knew were dreary entertainments in the parish room, dressed in black woollen stockings.

Before the coach is forgotten for ever, I must tell of one stormy night when we arrived home to see the cook, Mrs Keegan, in the light from the carriage lamps, waving her arms and screaming in at the window: 'Murder! Murder! Pat has cut Tommie's throat and he's bleeding in the sink. Oh! Glory be to God I saw him, I saw him.' The blood flowed into the sink all right but Tommie was still standing. The boy Pat was sitting at the table with the bread-knife still in his hand, his eyes like black buttons in his white face. In the dimly lit kitchen the cook was walking up and down gesticulating and shouting: 'He called him a bastard, and why not? Isn't he Big Biddie's bastard found under the garden wall by Miss Edyth?'

Aunt Jane plastered Tommie's throat and threatened him with death if he moved during the night. The next morning Pat had gone. We were very worried about him as we knew he had no money, but he found his way to Galway and joined the band of the Connaught Rangers, who were just off on their ill-fated trip to India. This must have been about 1920. The men were mostly from the West of Ireland, and when they heard of the terrible things being done to their families at home by the Black-and-Tans, fifteen of them mutinied, refusing to obey orders until the British army left Ireland. They were treated with barbaric cruelty and one, Jim Daly, was shot by firing squad: the last British soldier, I believe, to suffer this penalty. The other fourteen, by order of the court martial, were sentenced to penal servitude for life and sent, under harsh conditions, to Portland. The feeling was so strong in other Irish regiments that those in Dorset had to be confined to barracks while the prisoners were being taken through. Mercifully our Pat was not in trouble and came back to us for his leaves. Many years later Uncle George found him working as a porter at the Waldorf Astoria Hotel in New York.

CHAPTER 2

Journeys to Dublin by Bianconi Car and Canal Boat

When winter came, my great-grandparents and the family went to Dublin, and to dances at the Castle and the Viceregal Lodge. A photograph shows Great-uncle Walter in court dress and the girls in white satin long dresses with tiny waists. There were plenty of army officers for partners, but the season was short, Connemara a long way off and they never met again. Everything at the Castle was on a fantastically lavish scale and they seem to have been unaware of the starvation and dangerous unrest that surrounded them as they made their leisurely way across Ireland in safety, though threatened at home from time to time.

These journeys were made by Bianconi car to Ballinasloe near Galway. This was a double-length side-car drawn by two horses, with a third horse waiting at steep hills to help it to the top. It carried nine or ten people, according to width, and there was a deep well between the seats for luggage. The road from Clifden to Galway must be one of the most beautiful in Ireland, winding round the foot of the mountains, among the lakes, over heather-covered moors, between banks of flaming yellow gorse, but in the last century it was little more than a track. Even in my youth I have been held up by raging waterfalls across the road, so it must have been quite perilous in the heavy four-wheeled side-car. Maria Edgeworth gives a horrifying description of the road and how the wheels had to be taken off the carriage and the whole thing carried across the streams, when she paid a visit to the Martins at Ballynahinch in 1834 at the age of sixty-seven. She describes it as the 'haunt of smugglers, caves, murders, mermaids, duels and banshees', and refers to 'the wonderful ways of going on and manners of the natives'.

I remember the road being frightening, lit only by the flickering light of the candles in the carriage lamps. On a grey day when the mountains are purple, the moorland seems dark and threatening; the solitary scarlet holly and rowan trees, wings spread, seem to try to fly from the west wind, but are anchored to the ground by their slender silver trunks. Black-faced sheep stare and run away; little dark figures of men, far away, dig their turf: the silent clouds sail over the hills casting fingers of light like searchlights, turning the land to rusty red, and the gulls' bellies shine white against the sky. All this must have been exactly the same when the family travelled that road in the middle of the last century.

Reaching Ballinasloe after the sixty-five mile drive, they went on board a canal barge which they hired to take them to Dublin; once, they shared it with the Martins of Ballinahinch. The journey took three days and was enjoyable if the weather were fine and they could walk along the tow-path with the horses. They must have been an attractive sight in their crinolines and the circular scarlet hooded cloaks which hung in the porch at the Manor for seventy years; I always slipped one on for wandering about Errislannan.

Those journeys across Ireland by canal were not as Spartan as they sound. For sixty years of the nineteenth century canals were the best form of transport; the Grand Canal Company had large comfortable hotels along their quays – at Portobello, Robertstown, Tullamore and Shannon Harbour on Lough Derg. Some had handsome Georgian façades and the one at Portobello was described in an 1821 guide-book as

> a very fine edifice situated on the banks of the Grand Canal ... a very fine portico and the interior is fitted up with great elegance for the accommodation of families and single gentlemen. [Note, no single ladies!] The beauty and salubrity of the situation, enlivened by the daily arrival of the canal boats, renders it a truly delightful summer residence.

The entry in my great-great-aunt's diary refers to canal barges but most of their journeys must have been on the 'fly-boats', which travelled at eight miles an hour, including the time spent on the locks. The cabins were comfortable with stoves for warmth, cushioned seats, a kitchen and pantry. The slow boats had two horses; the fast ones, three. Two postilions rode on the horses armed with pistols and blunderbusses to protect the boat, and the crew comprised a captain, a steerer, a stopman, a barmaid and cabin-boy. The boats were a magnificent sight when travelling fast.

In the last half of the century the passenger services were largely given up except for the hire of barges, but freight was profitable, especially when they began to carry coal for the railways.

After the Famine, when emigration was draining the life-blood of the country away to America, the emigrants travelled west in their thousands from Dublin to Shannon Harbour by canal. The people of Shannon baked them large oaten cakes to feed on during their voyage across the Atlantic. In one year the canals carried 110,000 passengers and thousands of tons of freight; hence the great ruins of warehouses all along the way. One little item was the carrying of illegal fighting cocks and bantams, for which the company charged 6^{1}/$_{2}$d per stage.

By 1830 the rival canals – the Royal and the Grand – had come to an agreement to run a through service without changing boats, from Dublin to the west and back. During the 1798 insurrection in Ireland, Lord Cornwallis embarked an army in barges in Dublin and moved it to Tullamore in a day and a night. They were to meet a French force that had landed at Killala in Co. Mayo.

Wolfe Tone had persuaded Bonaparte to send troops to Killala. Only one thousand arrived, who distributed arms to unwilling Irish on the west coast, and marched on Castlebar with seven hundred men. The British were three to one against the French, but, after pillage and outrage, were in no state to fight and ran like rabbits: this became known as 'The Races of Castlebar'. The Franco-Irish army later were overwhelmed by ten thousand British at Ballinamuck in County Longford

The old Shannon Harbour on Lough Derg is now derelict, but was used in 1913 for cargoes. Now the waters of the great lake run south down the Shannon to work the hydroelectric dam at Ardnacrusha before reaching the ocean. A plaque on the wall of the last lock leading to the Shannon reads:

> The extension of the Grand Canal from Tullamore to the River Shannon being a distance of eighteen Irish miles, consisting of ten locks, three large aqueducts and fifteen small aqueducts or tunnels and twenty bridges, commenced on January 1st 1802 and opened, complete for navigation, on 25th October 1803.

A very rapid bit of work.

It is strange to think that Ireland owes its canal system to the Huguenot refugees, who were good businessmen and had come to Ireland from southern France with a knowledge of the Languedoc Canal, built in 1681. Work had been started on a canal from Dublin to Tullamore in 1756, but failed in 1771 due to bad engineering. The new company, the Grand Canal Company, first pushed one branch southwards and then in 1803 connected Dublin with the Shannon at a cost of two million pounds. It was very successful in spite of competition with the Royal Canal, which ran almost parallel a little to the north. Country districts were well served with 'lorries' or wagons for delivery. They were one of the first to introduce steam- – and later diesel- – driven barges. Now all is gone; until its recent restoration the Royal Canal was silted up and many of the branch lines were invisible.

So the family travelled in comfort for the greater part of the journey, but the long drives on the Bianconi cars must have been a trial of endurance – especially when it was raining and cold, with none of the mackintoshes we know today. Perhaps it was while sitting on those cushioned seats in the barges that they wrote their diaries: hopefully, going to town; sadly, returning with no rings on their fingers.

Judging by the diaries, my great-grandparents and their eight children thought nothing of this difficult journey, and divided their time between Errislannan and 6 Hume Street, Dublin, although some members of the family remained until the middle of the century in the previous family home, Burmount Manor on the river Slaney in Co. Wexford, where the Errislannan relations often joined them. Burmount was a beautiful house and the writer of one diary continually bemoans the fact that Errislannan was ever heard of. Jane Heather's diary describes its tragic history:

Our ancestress Jane Worth, who lived in the early seventeenth century, was also ancestress to the Arran family. A great deal of money has been spent trying to get back some of the Wexford property that we feel convinced belongs to the Frayne side of the family. My great-great-grandfather, Major Frayne (whose uniform button and wife's wedding ring I have), raised a contingent of men in the troubled times for England. He was thrown off his horse and drowned crossing the River Slaney at Ferry Carrig. (There is a bridge there now.) His little widow and two sons were at Burmount when the rebellion of 1798 started. The rebels came to Burmount and took the eldest son out of bed where he was ill of a fever. They dressed him in a rebel coat and held him up on a horse, and so to the Battle of Ross. Here they threw him down with a pike beside him, and owing to the rebel coat he was killed by his own side.

The second son was put in jail at Wexford, and three times he was brought out on to the bridge to be piked and thrown into the river, and each time he was saved by a Roman Catholic priest, the Rev. Father Michael Healy.

Then the boy's mother devised a way to get him out. In those days there was a lot of illicit spirits made, which went round the country in small barrels, dressed like a woman in a red cloak, riding pillion behind a man on a horse. Mrs Frayne dressed like this, and, carrying clothes for her son, got into the jail and they came out together. When they got near Burmount they heard great lowing of cattle, and saw that the rebels had cut steaks out of the live cattle. It is hard to believe but they did worse. At Sculla Bran they put the women and children inside and set fire to the barn. The women threw out the babies but they were caught on pikes and thrown back into the flames. At Vinegar Hill they had barrels lined with nails, into which they put the people and rolled them down the hill.

These things really happened and it should be told, as those people are now held up for veneration and have monuments erected to their memory.

It was from Burmount and the Fraynes that most of our silver and better furniture came, including the famous Nelson chairs, of which more anon.

The rigours of the Dublin journey were alleviated at the beginning of this century when a railway was built from Galway to Clifden, but now there is hardly a trace left of that great engineering feat except where portions turn into a fine new road. In my youth I travelled on it many times and had to witness the heart-breaking scenes of parents saying goodbye to their children for the last time on earth as they left for America. The men clung to each other and cried aloud; the women in their big black shawls collapsed on to the ground swaying and weeping, raising cries like the keening at a funeral. The emigrants, having spent the previous night at parties, looked like death and heaven help me if they came into my carriage! Some of our Errislannan parents have parted with seven or eight of their children in this way, mostly bound for San Francisco, but now they part with the hope that the emigrants will fly back one day for a holiday, and more and more go to England and return to help with the turf and the hay.

CHAPTER 3

The Great Famine and
Queen Victoria's Visit

Before advancing further into this century, I must go back to the Famine of 1845–9, as it had such lasting effects. The ruins of the houses that were emptied in those years are dotted all over Errislannan.

Reading my family's diaries of those terrible years, one realizes that it was a time of starvation of the poor – chiefly those in the country districts – while the rich went almost unscathed; the country landlords suffered financially but did not go really hungry. In one day-by-day diary written in Dublin by my Great-aunt Rachael, there is not one mention of famine or shortage, but in others, written in Errislannan, one reads of the terrible isolation, the helplessness to relieve horrifying distress on a small peninsula without even a horse to ride and everyone too weak to walk. My grandmother and all her brothers and sisters had been sent to England, but my great-grandmother in Errislannan collected what food she could, and some Indian corn came from the depot in Clifden, brought in carts under armed guard. She boiled it in the copper of the old laundry on the back drive and distributed it to whoever could come, but they were often too weak to leave and lay on the ground in the laundry garden, where some died.

My great-grandfather planted turnips in the meadow that encircles the graveyard by the lake. Unfortunately starving people ate them raw and died round the field. There was no one strong enough to bury them and so they remained.

In the winter of 1846–7 snow fell in November, and later there was such a heavy frost that the Errislannan lake froze over. Terrible icy winds blew over the desolate land; people had been too weak the year before to save the turf for warmth and cooking and this was not taken into account when supplies such as raw maize were sent. It was not only our people, but islanders and those from nearby headlands, that came, and lay dying along the roads. On Clare Island there were 576 deaths. Digging ditches in the years to come meant finding bones. In 1969 a grave with about fifty skeletons in it was uncovered. In all the houses on the back of our hill, only one old woman remained alive and she eventually came down to live with us. The dogs they were unable to catch and eat eventually ate them when they were dead, and these dogs were one of the worst horrors, prowling about the woods howling like wolves.

One diary entry for 1849 describes how the ladies went out in a boat to see a ship laden with 'three hundred paupers bound for America'. The fact that it was in Clifden Bay shows that it was too small to reach America with that number of people crowding the decks; but drowning must have seemed a merciful death compared with that awaiting them at home. The great granaries on the quay in Clifden were full of corn, which was loaded under military guard and sent to England while people died of hunger in the streets.

In Clifden the Union or workhouse and the lane leading up to it were full of people, packed together, dying of starvation, the relapsing fever, typhus and pestilence. Eventually the bodies had to be burned. In 1847 the Union went bankrupt and people were living in caves, in holes in the bogs – probably the warmest homes – and shelters put over ditches. In other parts of the country, houses were pulled down by soldiers for the landlords, for non-payment of rates or rent, but I think the houses round us were deserted because they had dead people in them. In one house near the church, Rockstrow, a sow being kept for her litter ate the baby in the cradle.

The people had no savings to fall back on; the men had been paid wages of 7d a day and the women 4d , and then it was only casual work such as building out-walls round Errislannan. With no potatoes and no turf it is strange that there were any survivors. Road-works were started and the south road was built on Errislannan running out to Coronagh Harbour, but the men were too ill to continue and soon gave up altogether; I remember it being referred to as the Famine Road. The Famine also ruined nearly all the land-owners in the West. Their houses emptied and the land went back into bog.

All over Ireland from these years onwards wholesale evictions were taking place as by constant division the farms had become too small to be economic. In 1879 6000 were evicted, in 1880 10,457; and then in four years 23,000 were made homeless. I remember an old song that ran something like this:

> 'Oh rise up Rory darlin' for there's knocking on the door.
> We must leave the little cabin that we built in days of yore ...
> There's no place for us in Ireland, the place is ours no more.
> We must go now Rory darlin' far away across the sea ... '

and across the sea they were sent, under most unhuman conditions; many in the holds of the ships that had just unloaded wood at Cork.

On Errislannan, being a small place, only one family was evicted, and they had two houses; one in Clifden and one on the spit of land that is almost an island. Here they had dug out a cellar where they made poteen. They thought they were safe from the police as they could see any boat coming up the bay, and the smell was carried away by the wind. They had a big black pot for a still and when the police did eventually arrive they threw this pot into the channel; we used it for many years as a turf container. The house was pulled down and the evicted family camped on our back drive in tinker-like shelters to extract pity. It was very unpleasant, but in the end they retired to their town house.

Much has been truly said about the cruelty of the absentee landlords and their agents, but not enough about the landlords who lived on their land and were fathers to their people. The D'Arcys of Clifden Castle, our next-door neighbours, suffered financial ruin through their generosity; the Martins of Ballynahinch and the Gore-Booths of Lissadill in Sligo were famous for their humanity to their tenants, but such landlords were few in numbers. In Errislannan it was taken for granted that help would be given, even after the Land Commission had taken over all the tenants in the 1920s. They were still our friends; they might want something we had, and in return do a day's work, or bring endless presents. One common request was for 'the loan of a shirt for the corpse', so Aunt Jane always kept a supply – ostensibly 'Master John's' – for the occasion, and every grave was lined with flowers from the Manor garden. I think this last was a mistake and not always appreciated; it spoilt the natural simplicity of the funerals. The loss of the big houses after the Famine meant loss of livelihood and great hardship for many of the people.

Errislannan survived because the family had resources other than land, but from that time on mortgages were to strangle the place and make life difficult for the future generations.

One good thing that survived for seventy years were the boys' and girls' orphanages, started by my great-grandmother and Mrs D'Arcy, who went round the stricken houses and collected the babies whose parents had died during the Famine. The boys were housed in a large building at Ballyconree at the end of the next peninsula; now it is a gaunt ruin, burned down by the Republicans in 1922. It was an excellent orphanage, which I knew well as I used to stay with the Master's daughters. They did all their own farming, turf-cutting up on the mountain, and had a boat for fishing. The girls' home, which reminded me of the school in *Jane Eyre*, was in the D'Arcy dower house, Glenowen, in Clifden. The girls were dressed in maids' uniforms and were sent into service at fourteen, with no knowledge of where they had come from. As these were Protestant homes, sometimes Roman Catholic relatives kidnapped the children off the side-car on their way to Ballyconree.

The Famine reduced the population from over eight million to less than five million; mostly by starvation and disease, the rest by emigration – forced or voluntary. In five years from 1846 a million people emigrated. From the workhouses were sent the old and infirm and many children while their places were filled by men who were worth feeding so that they could work: shades of the Germans' gas-chamber selection. Everyone went who could reach a port and take ship to Canada. Diseased, naked and destitute, they were very unwelcome when they arrived, and in 1848 Canada passed legislation forbidding entry to paupers. Then good-class farmers who could pay a fare started emigrating, a new disaster for Ireland. From Cork, a thousand a week were leaving; just walking out of their unsaleable farms, leaving unpaid rates which would be levied on any purchaser. In Ballina (I quote Woodham-Smith in *The Great Hunger*)

> thousands of acres looked as though they had been devastated by an enemy; in Erris seventy-eight townlands were without a single inhabitant or four-footed beast. The landlords could not deal with the farms abandoned and large arable tracts were either deserted or squatted on by paupers living in a hut or a ditch and with no chattels whatever distrainable for poor rate.

This taking of any chattel was the final cause of collapse, as without even a spade a man cannot dig turf or plant seeds or potatoes. Although no rents came in, landlords were responsible for rates and this it was that caused them to be sold out under the Encumbered Estates Act. In Connemara the last of the Martins of Ballinahinch had a rates bill of £11,000 which he could not pay after all his generosity to his people, and so the family were driven out.

Even the big towns such as Athlone were being deserted, and many streets in Dublin and Cork were empty and derelict. In Mayo a landlord wrote, 'Thousands are brought to the workhouse *scream*ing for food and cannot be relieved.' The starving people became violent and even armed police could not control them. In 1848 there was an insurrection which was put down quickly and martial law declared. 'In Westport, 26,000 people are destitute of food, fuel and clothing and 200,000 people are crowded into workhouses built for less than 100,000.' Fever, typhus and relapsing fever were still prevalent and then came cholera, which spread from Belfast all over Ireland. There were also 13,812 cases of opthalmia, which took its greatest toll among the young: it became common to see one-eyed children.

Children and young people were committing crimes in order to get into prison or be deported. The Quakers were the best helpers but eventually their funds ran out. The English government had helped in the first two years to the tune of eight million pounds, when it was sorely needed at home, but this had dried up by 1848 and the people, by the Poor Law Act, were thrown back on the bankrupt workhouses, many of which were shut.

By 1849 Ireland had reached rock-bottom in misery, but there were 10,000 British troops in Ireland, well fed and leading a gay social life round Dublin. At this point it was thought that a visit from the Queen would be an uplift and so, in face of much opposition, it was arranged. Lord Fitzwilliam refused to have anything to do with the visit. He wrote, 'A great lie is going to be acted here ... false impressions are going to be made ... then false government will ensue. I would not have her go now unless she went to Killarney workhouse, Galway, Connemara and Castlebar.' Some hotheads planned to seize the Queen and hold her prisoner in the Wicklow mountains, but when the time came only two hundred men turned up at the rendezvous, not enough to beat the garrison, so they dispersed.

Queen Victoria was then thirty; pretty, vivacious and friendly, and although at first there were many against her, after four days she had won all hearts and vast crowds lined the streets and ran beside the carriage for miles in the country.

On 2nd August 1849 the Queen, Prince Albert and four of their children, with the ladies and gentlemen, made up a party of thirty-six. They landed from the *Victoria and Albert* paddle-steamer near Cork, where there were several 'war-steamers' to escort them. Boats crowded with people swept past the royal yacht cheering and thunders of artillery were heard. The Queen toured the beautiful harbour in the *Fairy* before landing at a gaily decorated pavilion, where she received Protestant and Roman Catholic clergy in equal numbers, judges in their robes and other dignitaries. On the yacht she knighted the Mayor of Cork. She graciously named the place 'Queenstown' and a flag was run up with the name in gold on it. (Since independence it has reverted to its Irish name of Cobh.)

The Queen re-embarked and steamed up to Cork, commenting on the beauty of the landscape. They paused to receive a salmon from the poor fishermen of Blackrock and then the *Fairy* came alongside the Custom House, Cork. The whole side of the building was covered with scarlet cloth embroidered with golden shamrocks, the rose and the thistle; above the entrance the famous Irish greeting which was everywhere during her tour, Céad Míle Fáilte, 'a hundred thousand welcomes'. The steps to the water were covered in scarlet, a triumphal arch had been erected on the quay and a stand for 400 ladies under an awning of scarlet. Flags were flying, bands were playing and the artillery continued to deafen everyone. The Famine was forgotten. Queen Victoria's own account written in her diary ran:

> We landed and walked a few steps to Lord Bandon's carriage. The Mayor preceded us and many followed on horseback or in carriages. The 12th Lancers escorted us and Infantry lined the streets. It took two hours ... the streets were densely crowded, decorated with flowers and triumphal arches ... the heat and dust were great. We passed one of the four college buildings that have been ordered by act of Parliament. The crowd is

noisy, excitable, running and pushing about and laughing, talking, and shrieking. The beauty of the women is quite remarkable; almost every third woman was pretty, some remarkably so. They wear no bonnets, and generally long blue cloaks. The men are often raggedly dressed and wear blue coats, short breeches and blue stockings.

The next day the sea was rough and they put into Waterford Harbour for the night. The Queen and children were very seasick. The following day they arrived at Kingstown. The diary again:

With this large squadron we steamed slowly and majestically into the harbour of Kingstown which was covered with thousands and thousands of spectators cheering most enthusiastically ... We were soon sur-rounded by boats, and the enthusiasm and excitement of the people was extreme.

More addresses and the party reached the train through a covered way where ladies and gentlemen strewed flowers.

In Dublin a miracle of camouflage had taken place. The Viceregal Lodge and Dublin Castle had been done up at a cost of £3400; more had been spent on the decorations and illuminations. Especially magnificent was Nelson's Column at night; the lights had to be turned out at intervals so that the other illuminations could be seen. The Bank of Ireland had spent £1000 on lights. The Queen's secretary had warned that no bills were to come in later. The procession made its way to the Viceregal Lodge among arches, decorations and huge crowds. Victoria was very touched:

At the last triumphal arch, a poor little dove was let down into my lap, with an olive branch round its neck ... a never-to-be-forgotten scene; when one reflects how lately the country had been in open revolt and under martial law.

Dublin was like a city risen from the dead; it was the second city of the empire and possibly the most beautiful. Empty derelict houses were painted; muslin curtains were hung in the windows, and window-boxes full of flowers gave a misleading impression of prosperity. My great-grandfather's Dublin house was on the route of the procession, but tantalizingly my Great-aunt Rachael's diary has four blank pages over the days which would have been so interesting. The children had been sent to school in England during the worst of the Famine, but in 1849 in Dublin the last entry before the Queen's visit was, 'Papa insists that we go to Burmount for our Summer Vacation.' Perhaps dear papa thought of the expense of fitting out so many daughters for the drawing-room at the Castle. They would have received invitations as my great-grandfather was chaplain of the Chapel Royal, and their aunt Sarah

Munro could have presented the girls. One entry just after the visit says that General Munro – friend of the Duke of Wellington – had died and was buried in Dublin; later, by order of the duke, he was reburied in Canterbury Cathedral.

For the levee the Queen wore a dress of green Irish poplin lavishly embroidered with gold shamrocks, the blue ribbon and the star of St Patrick, and a brilliant diamond tiara. The gentlemen were in full-dress uniform. The Queen sat on the great gilt throne and more than 4000 people were present; 2000 were presented. She then returned to the Viceregal Lodge for dinner, an evening party and a concert.

The most popular part of the visit was the great review in Phoenix Park. The Queen left the Viceregal Lodge in an open barouche with her four children. The Prince, in the uniform of a major-general, rode a magnificent chestnut.

Carriages remained in Phoenix Park all night – many had acted as hen-roosts since the Union, when society forsook Dublin. Every carriage, cart or side-car was packed amidst the mass of walkers and horseback riders that filled the streets. Of the 10,000 troops in Ireland at this time – more than in the whole of India – 6000 were at this review. After evolutions by hussars and lancers and other troops, the whole body moved to the far end of the review ground, to the music of their regimental bands. The infantry with fixed bayonets, in double-quick time, charged forward with the Irish yell and British hurrah, until within twenty yards of the Queen's carriage.

The cheers and enthusiasm were tremendous and continued all the evening as the Queen drove through Dublin to the Castle for the levee-room. The next day the welcomes followed her into the country to the Duke of Leinster's home. She noted the raggedness of the people running beside the carriage, remarking, 'they will do anything at a word from the Duke, he is so kind to them'.

At last the four-day gala ended and the Queen and her family embarked on the *Victoria and Albert* at Kingstown Pier, amidst unprecedented cheers. 'Her Majesty paced the deck for a little time until, approaching the lighthouse, she looked towards the crowds, ran along the deck and, with the sprightliness of a young girl and with the agility of a sailor, ascended the paddlebox.' On the summit she was joined by Prince Albert, and, taking his arm, 'gracefully waved her right hand towards the people on the pier'. The Queen wrote, 'I waved my handkerchief as a parting acknowledgment of their loyalty. The night was thick and rainy, and we feared a storm.'

Dublin settled back; poorer but happier. All this! And not two hundred miles away to the west were thousands of men, women and children starving and homeless.

CHAPTER 4

Achill Island and County Sligo

In 1866 my grandparents had a storm-drenched wedding in Errislannan. The first baby, 'Deanie', my uncle, was born within the year. Then my grandfather, being a clergyman, was sent to Achill Island, visible up the coast from Connemara, where my father and two of his brothers were born; one each year. Reaching the island, they were packed into a farm wagon with some of the furniture; other wagons following, they drove right across that wild shelterless island to Dugort on the north coast. It was a deserted valley, apart from the church and rectory at the sea end, where they must have been deafened by the constant roar of the Atlantic on that rock and shingle shore; but they came to love it. In 1970 I went on a pilgrimage to see my father's birthplace and found the church flourishing and the roofless ruin of the rectory entirely hidden in trees. It had a resurrection beauty, as trees had grown up inside and formed a roof of palest green leaves, through which the sun shone with a flickering light into the empty rooms and on to the fireless hearthstones.

In 1871 my grandfather was made Dean of Achonry Cathedral in Co. Sligo. The 'Cathedral' was like a hideous little chapel planted within the ruins of a large and beautiful cathedral of which only one window and the base of the walls remained. My grandmother wept when she saw it and cried, 'Why have we left our beautiful home for this?' The original church was built in 534 on land given by the O'Hara family, who in return were blessed and told that they would stay on their land for ever if the eldest son never walked under a certain arch. They are still there in unbroken succession; my father and I later hunted with Major O'Hara's Harriers.

The journey from Achill Island meant the wagons being loaded up again, but this time there were four small boys, the youngest being a cripple – my favourite uncle, John. In Achonry deanery three girls were born, Jane, Eva and Edyth, again one a year. Jane's diaries, kept from when she was a child, have helped fill in this story. She refers to the lovely stone traceries from the cathedral windows which had been used for generations as tombstones and piled up on graves, invisible in summer under a sea of nettles, but interesting in winter, when she was tempted to take some for her garden, but feared watching eyes and the curse that falls on anyone removing anything from a graveyard, even if it is only dead flowers. The stone chancel roof and the walls had become dangerous, hence the horrid little modern building in which the family had to worship. There were square pews like rooms and one large one with a canopy and mitre waiting for the bishop's throne which never came, so the seven little Heathers and their mother sat watching the congregation, Jane observing and recording every detail of their behaviour and dress.

My grandmother was very capable, and ran her husband's parishes in such a way that she was known as 'the Bishop' while he was only 'a Dean'!

They all had gardens and Jane records that my father's was always the best; he helped his brothers and sisters so that the whole garden was a lovely sight. He also climbed the narrow pointed spire of the church and stuck a cauliflower on the top for a decoration.

The deanery was haunted without a shadow of doubt. A deceased dean, Lord Montmorris, leaned over the gate and frightened the horse so much that my father had to get down and lead it in sweating and prancing. Then there was a servant girl who walked down the stairs and into the basement kitchen, followed by the children. My father was so convinced it was a ghost that he fired a shotgun at her; nothing happened. He showed me the marks of the shot on the wall many years later when the deanery was empty.

During these years the family drove the eighty miles down to Errislannan for their summer holidays and Jane and Eva sometimes stayed on over the winter, when their Aunt Rachael educated them, with the help of the Errislannan schoolmaster, who came before breakfast to teach them Latin and other subjects. These years with their beloved 'Gran' and Aunt Rachael taught them to be magnificent gardeners and cooks and how to care for all the smaller animals on a farm.

The only education my father had was at the little parish school in Achonry where one man taught every child in the neighbourhood in one room, and where the dean expected my father to stay until he was seventeen. At home he rebelled at family life, and at school he turned the cane on the master, then helped himself to his bicycle. After this he went to live on a farm that belonged to my grandfather, ten miles from the deanery, called Knockadoo. He took with him a boy of his own age called William and the two set up house and managed to make a living out of farming and breaking in ponies for polo, and young horses, which they hunted until they were fit to sell as hunters.

Knockadoo was a square block of a house with six bedrooms, and a large stable yard on the south side. There was good farming land, with a trout stream running through it, a fast rocky stream which came down from the Ox Mountains, where forty years later my father and I fished together. My father and William lived a primitive and hard-working life, using one of the bedrooms over the kitchen for everything. Their method of emptying the ashes was to pour them through a hole in the floor, until one day the kitchen door was opened and the pile of ashes reached to the ceiling. The drawing-room was used for storing foodstuffs for the horses, and the dining-room for measuring polo ponies, as an absolutely flat surface was required.

This went on for some years and they seem to have led quite a happy life, living largely on rabbits and fish which they caught themselves. My father often met Constance Gore-Booth out hunting and they became friends. Her family home, Lissadell, was not far away, and she used to come over to Knockadoo and help with the breaking-in of the horses. Once she jumped a cow and the horse fell and broke its leg. We have always chronicled the death of the horse, but lately I read in *The Rebel Countess* – a biography – that Constance also suffered considerable injury. When I scraped a bedroom wall at Knockadoo, I found bands of crude colours and abstract designs which I showed to my father. He laughed and said that thirty years before he had tried to make the walls so distracting for Constance that she would not notice the ruined state of the rest of the house. She had to stay the night when she was riding his horses with Major O'Hara's Harriers.

My grandfather, as Dean of Achonry, met many Sligo families, but my father met only those who hunted, until he was made welcome at the Gore-Booths' lovely house. The only photograph I have of my father before his marriage was taken at Lissadell when he wore an elaborate uniform for a fancy dress ball; he had a finely waxed moustache and wrinkled stockings.

Here in the nineties many young people stayed who were later to become famous. W.B. Yeats, three years older than Constance, stayed with his uncle at Thornhill nearby; he was often at Lissadell and wrote a lovely poem about it. The beautiful Maud Gonne was a great friend of Constance's and was working hard to fight the evictions that were still going on, especially in Donegal. She and her band of helpers rebuilt the houses after the soldiers and police had knocked them down, rescuing the people from the ditches in which they were living. She was the love of Yeats's life until he was middle-aged, but she cared for him only in so far as his poetry and his play *Cathleen ni Houlihan* could be useful in helping Ireland. She played the part of Cathleen magnificently, but finally went to France to be cured of TB and met her lifelong love Lucien Millevoye, another freedom fighter, but for Alsace-Lorraine.

Also at Lissadell my father met 'AE', George Russell, the poet and painter, who really knew and loved the country people as his work took him travelling all over Ireland for the Agricultural Board. He was deeply interested in the theosophical movement, which influenced his work, and was to be an important member of the Irish renaissance of art, poetry, literature and the theatre.

Another guest, whom I was to meet when she was an old woman, was Sarah

Purser, who had painted the picture, now hanging in the Tate, of Constance and her sister Eva in a woodland as children. She became famous first for her portraits and later for her stained-glass works.

The Land Leaguers – founded by Michael Davitt after his seven years in Dartmoor – were very active, waging war on unjust landlords or their agents and the rack-renters. Many were murdered or forced to leave, but the Gore-Booths of that generation had a good name as landlords. My father never had any trouble although he had land in Sligo and Galway. He was a natural socialist always, but completely unconscious of the fact. In 1891 Parnell came to a small village near Lissadell to speak at a meeting which Constance and Eva were forbidden to attend, but they crept out at night and rode to hear him. It was depressing to see the great Parnell so wrecked after four years in Kilmainham jail for his part in the work of the Land League. He had spent his life working for Ireland at Westminster and at home, but he was worn out now and died later in the year.

Constance and Eva Gore-Booth were lively girls who perpetrated some hair-raising practical jokes in which my father joined with zest. He kept this tradition when later he came to live in sober England. Constance inherited her father's courage and adventurous spirit. With him adventure meant going off to the Arctic – Greenland or Franz Joseph land – in a sloop which in those days, with none of the modern aids to survival, required a high standard of imagination and courage.

Constance, after a period at the Slade, went to Paris to paint and there met and married Count Markiewicz, also a painter, from Poland. They returned to Dublin and Sligo and lived a social life until Constance got drawn into the Volunteer movement This culminated in the Easter Rising in 1916 when Constance entrenched herself with her Fianna boys in St Stephen's Green, after asking the onlookers, children and nursemaids to leave. They held out for some days but were eventually taken prisoner and put in jail. From her cell Constance could hear her friends being executed by firing squad and was herself condemned to death, but for her a worse fate waited. She spent some years in English prisons being treated like a common criminal instead of a political prisoner. Her name has gone down in history as the first woman elected to the House of Commons at Westminster in 1918; and although she did not take her seat, being in prison, she was amused later on to see her name on her peg in the cloakroom at the house and to have tea on the terrace. In later years she lived among the very poor in Dublin and was greatly loved by them until her death in 1927. Then she was given a tremendous public funeral in Dublin, the whole country gathering to do her honour. They must have been bitter years with her prison sentences and the death of the leaders of that heroic struggle, but she had lived to see a partially free Ireland.

To return to the early days in Sligo, my father's sisters, who had been sent to boarding school in England, brought back with them for the holidays two beautiful sisters, Margaret and Florence Harrison. Unlike anyone in that primitive countryside, they were first seen at a concert in the parish hall, where they wore white evening dresses and played the violin and the banjo, singing songs that my father never forgot to the end of his days. He fell in love with Florence at once, and that summer the deanery became a very popular place, where nine young people had a lively and romantic time. The next year Florence returned and she and my father became engaged, and the following year they married. This showed blind courage on both their parts, as they were the most fantastically unmatched pair and my father had only untransportable money in his horses, the land belonging to him and his brothers equally.

CHAPTER 5

England, and the Road to Paradise

My father had never left the West of Ireland until he went to England to get married. My mother was training as a painter at the St John's Wood Art School and lived surrounded by artist friends in London. However, being very much in love, they were not deterred by the differences in background. They always got on well together, both spirited and cheerful, retaining a curious quality of youthfulness even when great troubles came to them later on.

My father was six feet two inches and lean, so that he appeared taller. He had good features, with a brown, weather-beaten complexion; his eyes twinkled under shaggy brows, but he did not often laugh aloud. My mother was tall with dark eyes and hair, but illness changed her a lot, though she remained lively and ready for any adventure when she was well. She seemed to be able to turn her hand to anything, but her real talent was for painting. She played the piano, the violin and the banjo and sang in a sweet clear voice. She was a good dressmaker and made nearly all our clothes, even a pair of riding breeches for my father which looked quite professional: she then painted an almost life-size portrait of him wearing them. In spite of her town and country upbringing, she was very good in a boat and taught us to row at an early age, giving us a lasting love of the sea.

After their wedding in 1896, being childlike optimists, they took a hunting box in Warwickshire called The Billet in North Kilworth, a small village in the middle of the hunting country, within reach of the Pytchley, the North Warwicks and Fernies. They proposed to make a living by importing horses from Ireland, riding them with the hunts and then selling them as hunters. My mother had some money of her own and her mother helped with this ambitious undertaking.

The Billet was the scene of my earliest memories; a three-storey stone house with a large stable yard at the back and a garden across the village street in the front. Fifty years later I made a drawing of it and asked the butler if I might walk round the stables and garden, but he was understandably frosty. This was our winter home while we were children, Errislannan our summer one.

The Boer War was being fought when they first went to The Billet and my two uncles, Deanie and George, came to stay while waiting for troop-ships going to South Africa. They brought German measles with them. They were transporting horses for the army, and did not know that the beautiful Maud Gonne had joined the IRA and obtained £2000 from the Transvaal representative in France to pay for bombs being made to look like lumps of coal, which were to be placed in the troop-ships going to South Africa. Mercifully British Intelligence found this out in time. Maud Gonne's unsatisfactory husband, John MacBride, had raised a brigade of Irishmen to fight with the Boers, while an even larger number were fighting with the British. Later MacBride fought bravely in the Easter Rising and was executed with the other leaders.

Summer came and time for Ireland. Five months before I was born, I first ascended the steep rocky hill that forms the gateway to Errislannan. My mother swayed about on the side-car, one arm round a large bundle in a rug on the top of the well. This was my brother, Donald, one year old, the first grandchild, the long-awaited heir.

We had travelled all night from our winter home in Warwickshire; the first ten miles had been by pony trap, then the Irish Mail – with no sleepers – then the boat from Holyhead. How did my pregnant mother survive, even with the help of Rosa, the seasick cook? Having crossed Ireland and arrived on the Atlantic coast, we drove the last five miles from Clifden to the peninsula. The road climbs and twists over the spine-like hill of Ballinaboy and then lies open to the sea far below on both sides and the Atlantic in front dotted with islands. Rocks, heather and gorse give no shelter as the road hugs the skyline all the way. At last we reached the top and I was home for the first time; travelling the little road that my family travelled for a hundred and forty years.

Sometimes I stand on the highest rock and look all round at the miles of moorland rising to the foot of the Twelve Bens of Connemara, that most perfectly formed mountain range, backed by the Maumturk Mountains fading into the distance. Then to the south are the long narrow bays divided by spits of land that reach out to Slyne Head lighthouse. To the north more bays and mountains.

To continue this embryonic journey, the horse must have stopped to pant as everyone does after being turned out to walk up the hill. The white ribbon of road runs downhill another mile; in winter this is the picture of grey desolation, in summer yellow and purple light the dark turf bogs. You breathe the Atlantic wind scented with bog-myrtle and gorse and see the white flags of bog-cotton waving.

At the foot of the hill is the church and in the graveyard my family lie in rows. My great-grandfather, the Rev. Richard Henry Wall, Doctor of Divinity and terror of his family, lies under the only good stone, designed by himself. The others lie under coral sand with cement kerbs, but my brother, now passing by, was to lie twenty-six years later in the Military Cemetery near Baghdad. As often in his life, he was unlucky even then.

A quarter of a mile further on we turned through the big silver gates held open for us by Michael and Lizzie King, the lodge-keepers, waving and shouting welcomes, and so we rocked and bounced down the long drive and the Manor came in sight. The family ran out, their arms up in welcome, agog to see the new baby. Mother turned to undo the rug and a horrified silence fell, before shrieks filled the air. No baby! Only the rug.

The unwilling horse was turned and beaten into a trot. Mother told me later that the worst thing to bear was the slowness of their progress, with the thought that the baby would be lying on the road with a broken skull; the height from the well of a side-car is considerable. The lodge gates were shut but their cries brought Lizzie running out, and there, along the road, lay a white bundle. He was unhurt, thanks be to God, and finally they all settled down to the enormous meal and the comforting warmth of the great turf fires that cheered the summer evenings.

The next summer I was the baby on the well and arrived safely, but I had had my adventures too. My mother, a month before I was born, was thrown out of a trap and the wheel went over her, death missing us by inches.

And so began those long summers in Errislannan for my brother and me, doing everything together as though we were twins. We were the same height and were dressed alike in shorts. My brother was dark, with curly hair, huge eyes and a sensitive face. My hair was long and golden, cut with a fringe, and my eyes were blue. It was always taken for granted that I had been the one to think up some evil deed. We played happily in the woods or by the lake; spending hours each day in the stable yard among the clucking, quacking, hee-hawing, chewing animals.

Winter and back to The Billet.

William, the boy who had gone to Knockadoo with my father, had followed him to Warwickshire. Hunting with the famous packs they found the stone walls of Co. Sligo were no preparation for the fences of Warwickshire; but they became accustomed to them in time and did very well the first few years. Then my mother began having babies and they were one rider short. Donald was born and my mother hardly back in the saddle again when I started on my way. My parents had no name ready for me so they stuck a pin in the stud-book which came between 'Medora', a winner of the Oaks, and 'Cobweb'. My father was all for 'Cobweb', hoping I might catch a rich fly later on, but mother insisted on 'Medora'. My Irish aunts demanded an Irish name, so I am generally called 'Alannah' except by my boarding-school friends and the bank.

When we were three or four we had a large white donkey with a double scarlet saddle on which we went to a meet of the Pytchley. The groom, who was to have brought us home, lost us and we followed the hunt, or rather the donkey must have followed the hunt, and poor Mother lost her day bringing us home; a difficult thing to do on a lively disappointed horse with an obstinate donkey tied to the end of her crop.

Then disaster struck. One day out with the North Warwicks William's horse fell and kicked him in the liver in its struggles to rise, and he died. They had loved him so much that the heart went out of everything and they moved to a farm a few miles away where my father started what came to be known as the Rugby Stud, a great success until the First World War put an end to it and to our home in England. There was always one horse for my parents to hunt and one for us to ride, which also had to draw a curious trap my father had designed. As the horses were off the Sligo mountains or the Connemara bogs we were always breaking them in, and had fearful drives and many accidents. Many a picnic was spoiled for me by fear of getting into that trap. My father would take out the horses at night to face the lights of cars while we waited anxiously for his return. Sometimes he would arrive leading the horse and the remains of the trap would be fetched the next day.

When my mother went hunting alone, Donald and I used to hide behind the yard gates when it got dark, waiting for her. Our fears were justified one evening when the horse returned with no rider. Donald opened the stable door and I was knocked over as the horse hurried in. Then we climbed into the hayloft and pushed hay down into the manger, putting off the evil moment when we should have to tell our father. Finally we went into the study and remained speechless until he forced the truth out of us. Then he ran to the stables, dragged out the unwilling horse and went off with Mother's side-saddle still in place. He found her in a cottage not much hurt and they managed to return on the same horse.

Our worst time with the trap was when we went for a picnic and left the horse while carrying baskets. The horse took fright and dashed away, jumping a gate which the trap flattened behind him; then headed up a lane and tried another gate, with spikes on top of it. He came down on the spikes, and when we got there men were trying to lift him off, but he was too heavy for them. It was a terrible, unforgettable sight and the wait seemed endless until we heard two shots. We never went that way again.

When early summer came, the great pack for Errislannan began. Trunks, an oval tin bath with a lid, and endless baskets came with us, or rather went to the station in a cart while we all packed into the trap. The start from Rugby Station at ten o'clock at night was always thrilling, and even now embarking in a sleeper at Euston is exciting although I have been doing it all my life.

My father came to Errislannan only for short periods, and spent those longing for his horses and good farming. Errislannan methods drove him mad, but produced a quiet peaceful happy household, stepping further and further into debt without a qualm.

The train from Galway to Clifden in those days had no corridors, and wooden slats for seats. Our companions were generally wild-looking country-men and women speaking Irish, with live animals tucked under their shawls, or tied by the legs. Chickens, ducks and once a calf crowded the carriage, and with endless conversations, carried on in loud voices, it seemed the best part of the journey. The women wore little head-shawls, and large enveloping black or maroon shawls over their shoulders, with black skirts over scarlet flannel petticoats. They had put their feet into boots with a bit of cloth instead of stockings for town, a painful business, and now in the comfort of the train took these off and reverted to bare feet. The men wore rough tweed trousers, and either tweed coats or flannel home-made jackets. All wore hats, generally black, and very old.

At Clifden Station the heavy, roomy carriage known as the 'coach' was waiting for us, and an ass cart for the luggage. If it were fine we pleaded to have the hood put down so that we could sit on it and see all around. The coach always stopped on the top of Ballinaboy for the walkers to catch up. Then down the hill to the lodge, for more welcomes from Lizzie and Michael King. On then and down the bumpy drive and the breathless excitement of drawing up at the hall door, and the hugs from Granny, the aunts and Uncle John, before the wild rush round the house into every room to make sure everything was the same.

I remember the special smell of turf fires and the smell of the old house itself, and flowers in the hall and the great bank of blossom in the drawing-room. Off with our travelling clothes and up to the stables, deliberately causing a whirlwind of flying hens, ducks, hissing geese, cows and calves, running madly about to escape us. Then down to the lake, jumping in and out of the boats and running along the shore to Paradise, our make-believe home, until the church bell was banged loudly to bring us in. The exhausted grown-ups had been unpacking and always seemed to have headaches.

CHAPTER 6

The Heather Family

The Errislannan household during my childhood and youth consisted of my grandmother, Aunt Jane, Aunt Edyth and Uncle John. These were the four Heathers who were always beaming a welcome at the hall door as the horse came to a standstill. It was always a horse until 1950, when the family was given a car and my husband was there to drive it, but that was a long time ahead. My father was farming in England and Sligo; two uncles spent the summer months in the militia or away doing nothing, and Aunt Eva was a missionary in India.

My grandmother, whose wedding I have described, had once been a lively girl in Errislannan, belonging to the generation that enjoyed themselves dancing, riding, boating and having parties for seventy people within horse-driving distance.

It is sad that when I remember her in Errislannan she had been forced into a state of complete immobility by her two efficient, kindly daughters and the servants, who bowed down before the 'Mistress' and never allowed her to do anything for herself. I remember her sitting year after year in the 'Nelson' chair in the drawing-room, a Japanese fan protecting her beautiful complexion from the fire, dressed in shiny black, a white widow's cap with streamers perched on her still-brown hair. A white fichu round her shoulders was fastened with a posy of heliotrope, mignonette or a rose that had been sent up on her breakfast tray, freshly gathered from the garden. I sometimes saw her rise up when her daughters were out of the way, and go into the pantry and wash any little thing she could find, or do some dusting. She must have been bored to death and now never said anything, but just wrinkled up her face and smiled if it were expected of her, or said 'Oh Moi!' every time Uncle John pushed her chair in to the table in front of her medicinal glass of whiskey.

'Dear Mimma,' they murmured, as they brushed her hair with eau-de-Cologne, or massaged her legs, kneeling before the bedroom fire, before Bible reading and prayers. Occasionally she sat outside the door in the sun, or went out in a black wicker Bath chair, drawn by the boy Pat, until the day he cut Tommie's throat and ran away. Once, he left her stranded in the chair half-way up the drive because of something she had said to him. Fortunately a man came along and pushed her home and she did not tell her daughters. She was always spoken of as the 'Mistress'; but one small shopkeeper whom we generally avoided elevated her to the peerage. It happened that one day in an emergency Aunt Jane went to the shop for jam. The large dirty fat woman in rags rose to her feet and, wagging her finger at Aunt Jane, intoned, 'Tell her ladyship I have jams, I have jelly jams, I have tracle and honey, but they're fusty and musty and under the bed.'

Most of their shopping was done at home in the kitchen, when 'Mary-the-shop' paid her visits. She was a massive woman in many petticoats; the top one dark red with rows of black braid round the tail. She also wore a black jacket and plaid shawl, and a kerchief over her head. She carried a creel on her back and in it were bread, tea, sugar, tobacco, matches and soap; in fact all the small necessities of life. Her footgear was homespun-wool knitted stockings with no soles, almost like foot mittens; like the rest, she carried boots to put on in town. Somehow Mary-the-shop managed to teach Aunt Jane to knit: a triumph, as none of the girls could sew or make anything for themselves.

Aunt Jane and Aunt Edyth were pretty and lively girls in the 1880s, if their photographs were anything to go by; and in middle age, when they had become stout little bodies, they had beautiful soft skins from washing in rain-water, and pink and white complexions. But, somehow, religion, or their father, the dean, had got the better of their generation. They did not ride, drive, swim, dance, or read books on Sundays; drink and cards were 'The Devil's Visiting Cards'. Any thought of sex was a grievous sin. They fell between two stools, having none of the pleasures of the countrywoman; no husbands or babies; no working all together at the turf; no going into town on market-days or gathering produce from the shore. They did not appear to be frustrated or unhappy, but were always full of talk and laughter. They were verbal inspirationists, but their narrow religious outlook did not affect their spirits, for they were remarkably cheerful, kind and hospitable. Nearly all the houses where the previous generation had had such gay times with dancing and parties were empty, and there were no Protestants left on Errislannan to meet at church, except old Paddy Gorham and his wife, Anne.

Aunt Jane, the elder sister, was golden-haired, short, round and very capable in the kitchen and the flower garden, or among her hens, ducks and turkeys. She was a lively teller of tales and anecdotes, with a sharp eye for the ridiculous and a disarming, genuine piety. The family prayers twice a day were often amusing as with her knowledge of the Scriptures she would on occasion choose a chapter that referred to something topical.

Aunt Jane was an excellent cook who overfed everyone in the house. She loved gardening and was extremely knowledgeable about it. As well as caring for the animals, she made many pounds of butter every week in a huge barrel churn which we all turned. She must have baked thousands of loaves of soda bread in the enormous range, which warmed the whole house and made the kitchen like a furnace. I remember her best in the kitchen, red in the face, kneading the dough and cooking, but always came the welcome 'Sit down now and I'll get you a cup of tea.' Then out came cakes and biscuits and I would sit at the long scrubbed table, telling and hearing the day's news, and being told stories of long ago. If the dinner did not appear until three o'clock, what matter?

Aunt Edyth, the youngest of the family, tried to run the estate, and pay the wages if possible. She ordered fantastic things by post, and advertised the mountain mutton and honey that she hoped to sell. She did this very ineffi-ciently, relying on her prodigious memory instead of books, and perhaps it was as well not to have it all down in black and white considering the way things were financially. I think she suffered more than her sisters from having no love affairs. They never met unmarried men and so sometimes she fell in love with married ones who loved their wives, or with unsuitable men such as the sheperd's son, Tommie, who locked her in the pantry. She would have liked to have done outdoor things, such as riding, driving, and so on, but the weight of custom and opinion was too much for her. She did get a sailing boat built and loved being a passenger, but she never sailed. Once she drove the horse to town and once she rowed across the bay, but what stopped her doing this again? I never knew. Aunt Edyth's domesticity consisted of dusting the drawing-room by taking up the bellows and puffing away quietly when not observed, or spreading wet grass on the floors before sweeping. She worked hard in July getting the five cottages ready for tenants, which meant putting flowers in every room and laying supper ready for them. She had been to Morocco as companion to an old lady, and spent a few years with an aunt in Suffolk, but otherwise she had been enclosed by Errislannan and poverty.

The other sister, Aunt Eva, the missionary, spent most of her life in India and China, but when she returned to Errislannan one would think that she had never crossed the sea. She was taller than her sisters, pretty, with a mass of golden hair. She loved to bathe at Candoolan even into the late autumn, and although she could not swim she let the great rollers knock her over while she laughed and enjoyed herself alone in the sea. She told me quite cheerfully that she had never loved or been loved by a man in her life. A terrible thought it seemed to me.

Whenever she returned from India, following the usual custom of greeting guests, every window was lit up, making an exciting welcome as one came out of the dark trees. It was also enjoyed by the local people across the lake, who gathered to look at the lights, often reflected in the water. One return was memorable, as the men arranged to give her a fiery welcome, and to this end soaked sods of turf in paraffin and stuck them on sticks. When the carriage drew near, the sods were lit. One went out, producing a cry of consternation from Aunt Edyth, but she quickly whipped off her petticoat, lit it and draped it over the sod. The horse reared on his hind legs and made off into the night taking the shafts with him. Nothing daunted, the men drew the carriage with ropes: a difficult thing to do with a four-wheeler, and it got bogged down on the way. Aunt Eva's kind heart was worried about the horse, but one man assured her that 'He will find his way home when the bit starts biting him.'

After the first excitement of return had died down, Aunt Eva found that she was quite superfluous in the running of the house, so she took to cleaning the silver every Friday with great enthusiasm. I remember Aunt Jane looking sadly at the Sheffield plate trays and candlesticks, bereft of their silver and with the copper shining through, saying, 'She had to do a thorough job with God pushing her elbow!' Aunt Eva would go to fantastic lengths to give people pleasure, and once she carried a large costume box of oysters from Connemara to me in London. I was away from my lodgings that weekend and on my return complained of a gas leakage. The gas man said it was not gas he smelt and the landlady pulled out the box of oysters. She assured me furiously that there was no room in her dustbin for them, and so I had to leave them surreptitiously on Hampstead Heath. How empty the world must be for those with no aunts!

Uncle John, the youngest of the four sons, was the most loved person in Errislannan. He was tall and thin like my father, with good features and twinkling eyes almost hidden beneath bushy eyebrows. A shaggy man, with rather long hair, he dressed in rough Connemara tweeds that rain and long wear had moulded into an unnoticeable covering. He was very intelligent but it was his kindness and good humour that endeared him to everyone. His tragedy was that he had a withered leg and was very lame. With one leg in irons he limped round the house and farm with the aid of a stick, and whatever bitterness he must have felt at having to live his whole life in the family home with no money or possessions of his own, he never allowed it to appear. The Manor was always inherited by the girls. It was taken for granted that, because of his lameness, he would never go away to school or be trained for any profession – and in fact there had never been enough money to send him away. That he might want to marry never entered anyone's head. He had educated himself by reading every book he could find, and by reading *The Times* he kept in touch with what went on in the world. He had five beehives in the orchard and sold a little 'Heathers' Heather Honey' to visitors. He had the horrid job of packing up joints of mutton which went off by post, but made hardly any profit. He was very knowledgeable about birds, insects and small animals, which he watched happily as he lay about in the woods resting his leg.

John was the mainstay of the family, doing all the chores such as washing up, trimming the many oil lamps, filling hot-water bottles and making up parcels; and whatever the weather he drove the horse into town to do the shopping, twisted round on the uncomfortable side-car. One winter drive I remember, when I went with him to meet a new cook arriving on the evening train. A real storm was raging, making it impossible to keep a rug round one's legs, and before we reached Clifden we were soaked through and the cushions were like sponges. The wind, coming in from the sea, blew us up Ballinaboy Hill; the side-car swayed perilously and I was afraid Uncle John would be tipped off with his hand on the reins. He laughed now and then at our predicament and we gave up trying to keep dry. Our lamps had blown out, but streaks of light between the thundery clouds lit the white road.

At last we reached the gloomy station, with no crowd of onlookers, owing to the weather. There was only one passenger, our cook, a tiny old woman looking scared to death. I took her canvas bag and felt extremely sorry for her as I thought of the five miles we were taking her into unknown country. I had to strap her on or she would have plunged forward off the car. As we went over Ballinaboy her terror increased and before reaching the Manor she was gibbering about how she was a 'real hard worker', although she looked like 'a singed cat'. Uncle John leaned over and patted her on the shoulder and said, 'You'll suit us fine, Mam, we'll soon have you home and dry.' And so the singed cat came to stay and sometimes said that if it hadn't been for Mr John's kindness she would have died of fright. When we arrived at the hall door, Uncle John could not walk at all and nearly fell. It was the only time I ever saw him accept help.

He was such a relaxed, cheerful, kindly man that one did not realize he was practising iron self-control even to walk. Many an hour he spent rowing hale and hearty fishermen round the lake although sitting up tired him. Unknown to him I often saw Uncle John fling himself down on the horsehair sofa in the dining-room, his face screwed up with pain. Later on, Aunt Edyth's stinking dogs took possession of the sofa, and uncle had nowhere to stretch out.

These were the people who made a home for me for most of my life, and when I came over the hill and looked down on it all, there was always the comforting certainty that there would be love and welcome and that everything would be in the same place. With my mobile, insecure existence elsewhere, this was doubly precious. I knew that the Lake Room would be ready, with flowers still wet from the garden, and, in later years, that Uncle John would have cleared part of the loft – at great inconvenience – to make a studio for me. He would have whitewashed the floor to give more light and arranged my easel and table. But from then on none of them ever showed the slightest wish to see my work, and I would feel depressed because their opinion mattered.

A Heather Family Tree

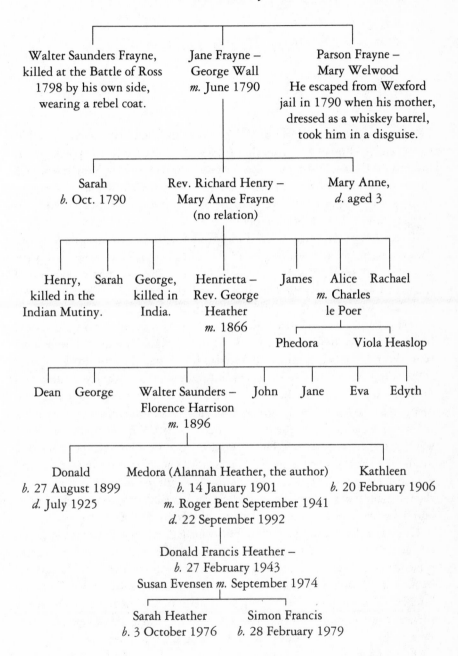

Walter Saunders Frayne, killed at the Battle of Ross 1798 by his own side, wearing a rebel coat.

Jane Frayne – George Wall *m.* June 1790

Parson Frayne – Mary Welwood He escaped from Wexford jail in 1790 when his mother, dressed as a whiskey barrel, took him in a disguise.

Sarah *b.* Oct. 1790

Rev. Richard Henry – Mary Anne Frayne (no relation)

Mary Anne, *d.* aged 3

Henry, killed in the Indian Mutiny.

Sarah

George, killed in India.

Henrietta – Rev. George Heather *m.* 1866

James

Alice *m.* Charles le Poer

Rachael

Phedora

Viola Heaslop

Dean

George

Walter Saunders – Florence Harrison *m.* 1896

John

Jane

Eva

Edyth

Donald *b.* 27 August 1899 *d.* July 1925

Medora (Alannah Heather, the author) *b.* 14 January 1901 *m.* Roger Bent September 1941 *d.* 22 September 1992

Kathleen *b.* 20 February 1906

Donald Francis Heather – *b.* 27 February 1943 Susan Evensen *m.* September 1974

Sarah Heather *b.* 3 October 1976

Simon Francis *b.* 28 February 1979

CHAPTER 7

The Manor Interior

I must now describe the interior of the house – the shell that enclosed us all. It hardly changed in all the years that I knew it. One entered the porch by the east or west door according to the way of the wind. Here were hung the old red cloaks made for my great-aunts for the drives from Galway on the Bianconi long-car. By the south window were the fishing-rods, the telescope and field-glasses, gumboots and some gardening tools.

To the left of the hall was the dining-room with its two big windows, but dark owing to the red wallpaper and the oil paintings of ancestors, all grave and conceited, squeezed into every available space. They watched me wherever I sat, even when I jerked round hoping to catch them out. I felt like a murderess years later when I had to cut them out of their frames and roll them up, and they still lie in my dark attic waiting for the resurrection morning. Over the black marble mantelpiece was a black marble clock that had never been known to work, and a large gilt mirror flickered as it reflected the light from the lake.

Next to this was the hatch – a constant source of trouble, as everything said in the dining-room could be clearly heard in the kitchen and Aunt Jane said plenty that she hoped would be heard, and a snort or grunt and the shutting of the door proclaimed that the hint was taken. The hatch was useful to us as a way of escape from visitors. How I groaned my way through the hour-long meals with the sun shining invitingly outside. The chairs were more than well known to everyone, as twice a day after meals we turned and hid our tails under the table-cloth and rested our elbows on the leather seats to pray. How every button became embedded in the memory, and the pattern of the wooden backs.

One day a clergyman was with us but Aunt Jane was not dethroned and read prayers. The clergyman supported himself on the chair next to the hatch, presenting his broad shoulders to the cat which hurtled through like a tiger, its mouth dripping with its prey, followed by a blood-curdling yell from the kitchen: 'The divil take his bloody soul! he has me "innards".' A moment's silence, the clergyman's neck was draped with 'innards', then came Aunt Jane's calm voice, 'Thanks be to God the chicken is safe. And now may God be with us all and bless us. Amen.'

To return to the hall. On the right was the drawing-room, which had only one window, but again a large gilt mirror over the white marble mantelpiece gave a trembling light as it reflected the lake. The wallpaper was white and shiny, making a pretty room and a good background for the numerous water-colours. My joy was the flower table, which I was sometimes allowed to arrange. There was some beautiful furniture, including the tulip-wood sofa table with its brass inlay and four-footed pedestal with brass claw feet. In the little drawers were kept the latest letters and photographs. Then there were two Hepplewhite armchairs, which were always referred to as the 'Nelson' chairs, as, with two others belonging to my cousins, they were supposed to have been on the *Victory*, and came to us as an inheritance from our ancestors, the Fraynes of Wexford. When sold at Christie's the Nelson association was not mentioned in the catalogue but I attached a label under the seat telling the story and I hope the new owner believes it and calls on Nelson sometimes. Aunt Jane always invited Nelson to guide her when engaged in battles with the creditors as she sat here. In a corner was an Adam-period half-moon table, richly inlaid, and on this a tall alabaster oil lamp, the only light in the room, so not surprisingly the family would sit round in the firelight talking instead of reading.

The thing I liked best was a Sheraton curio cabinet containing a strange collection of junk and valuables: miniatures of the family long ago; snuff-boxes in silver or enamel; pocket Bibles; a minute doll in a walnut shell; an alabaster model of the Taj Mahal with a light inside it, and many more tiny things. The larger curios – strange souvenirs from India and China – were in the cupboard in the wall, which was opened only on wet days. The top shelf was given up to twenty-five pieces of a Coalport breakfast service with bands of deep crimson and gold; and there were thirty-five pieces of an antique Chelsea tea service and two very large Waterford glass bowls.

All this hidden away, when selling even a little with some of the silver would have given the aunts a measure of peace and comfort in their old age, but I never dared to suggest it. They knew that God would see they got by. Their creditors were not so fortified and the battle kept Aunt Edyth at the top of her form. On floor level were some Dresden figure groups, wooden el-ephants, and the coffee-pot belonging to Oliver Cromwell when he sacked the east coast of Ireland. We were showing this pot to a friend, Da Barnett, a very knowledgeable person, and she just dropped the question, 'Did people drink coffee then?' I made enquiries in England, and to our sorrow the ugly little pot had to be put away, of no further interest.

The drawing-room was occasionally used for a rather macabre function: the lying in state of deceased members of the family. Head to mantelpiece they lay for three days, but it took longer than that to dispose of them and sit with any comfort in the armchairs. Protestants do not have the helpful wake which keeps the bereaved busy over the first few days of loss. We compromised by laying out the dead, decorated with flowers; then all the local people filed past saying a payer and finished up in the kitchen with cups of tea.

When Uncle John died suddenly in 1940, Colonel Frere, not having heard the news, enquired for him at the front door. The maid silently opened the drawing-room door and instead of the warm welcome expected, he found himself holding out his hand to the corpse.

From the drawing-room a door led through to the study, a pleasant room with a bow window facing the lake and an ever-open window into the vine-clad greenhouse. All our rooms were sunny and bright, but the kitchen, the pantry, the cloakroom and the servants' hall were dark, damp and cold as they faced into the hill. From them, peering upwards, one saw no sky but a forest glade, as the hill rose so steeply behind the house.

Out of the study one entered a room with glass-fronted bookcases, but it was not a library, rather an all-purpose room where the lamps were trimmed, and it was crowded with trunks containing a lifetime's collection of objects from India and China. There was nothing to read in the bookcases except large leather-bound tomes teaching the Protestant how to floor the Roman Catholic in argument. Great-uncle Henry's diary, written in India, I found horrifying and enthralling, but it was snatched from my hand and burned in the kitchen range when Aunt Jane took a look at it. I ached for something to read, but unless the tenants discarded a book there were none.

The servants' hall came into being one summer, when tenants were expected who were sending a cook, a butler and lady's maid in advance. We were so impressed by this, we thought we had better provide them with somewhere to sit. The dairy was the most suitable room because the churn and all the apparatus had gone down to St Flannan's cottage, where we spent our 'seaside' holidays. So we got a red carpet, chairs and a round table, and, with its big open fireplace, it made too good a room to spoil when we returned, so we built another dairy outside. Across one corner there was a very large cupboard, the top shelf of which was crowded with glass, including some Waterford and twelve beautiful Bristol purple wine-glasses at least a hundred and fifty years old. (I can put the minimum age on anything of value, as since my great-grandfather's time no one has been able to buy anything good.) The next shelf down was occupied by the Rockingham tea and coffee service, about forty pieces of a beautiful green, white and gold.

The dairy was always a ballroom for cockroaches and rats. The cockroaches we drowned in soup plates of porter, to which they were very partial. The rats, which came across the meadows at certain times like a host of the enemy, we met in dark passages, their little eyes sparkling, causing many a scream. One hid in the cushion-cover of an armchair and was gently squeezed to death when my stout Aunt Jane spent an evening there. We chased others from behind bookcases and under tables, and some died beneath the floorboards, making a horrible smell. In fact they livened up what would have been very dull winters.

On mounting the stairs, to the right was the Fuchsia Room, so called because of the scarlet bush which made it almost completely dark. Here Lizzie King, the lodge-keeper's wife, came to have her babies. One being delicate and the mother past caring, Great-aunt Alice let her artistic leanings direct the baptism and called the baby Michael Angelo, thus adding a new name to the limited repertoire of Errislannan. He grew up to be a good fiddler.

On the left was Aunt Jane's room and then came the Lake Room, always my favourite as it overlooked the water, though I remember it once darkened by a swathe of bats that hung across it like a curtain. One stormy night the roof lifted and banged down again and was held in place for months only by a boat-rope flung over it, anchored by the mangle and the garden roller. It was here I made my first tentative attempts to draw and paint. The results were always hidden as I was ashamed of them and of the horrid effects produced by hard little blocks of dried-up water-colour paints, but I had nothing else to use. My mother must have given up painting in oils by then and she seemed to be away ill a great deal of the time.

Along the back of the house was a long passage ending in wide steps which led to my grandmother's room, with its great canopy bed, on which was laid a magnificent nineteenth-century patchwork quilt made of silks, satins and velvets arranged in elaborate patterns outlined in scarlet. This ceremonial décor was always one of the welcoming features, laid on for visitors and, later, for me and my husband and child; used the first day and then put away. It was made by my great-great-aunts in Errislannan, and I could picture them sitting round the drawing-room creating this lovely thing. I have it still. The other large room had no name, but had another canopy bed with beautiful curtains and a more elaborate quilt, all made of patchwork, but not so exquisite, being made of cottons joined together with tatting.

Returning down the wide stairs we come to Uncle John's room, a very dark place, but he would not move to any other. Next to this was the bathroom, which I remember being built; it was an exciting novelty, although there had been a flush lavatory for many years. A hip bath, in which one sat with cold legs hanging outside, was carried into each bedroom in turn, and the maid laid out a rug and brought two enormous cans of hot and cold water, which looked like tea as it came from the bog. The maids' room was next, dark and cold, facing north up the hill and into the trees. The maids saw the sun only when they went down to the well by the lake for spring water.

Our lighting came from oil lamps and candles. A tall lamp flickered in the draught of the hall and one stood in the drawing-room; there were four silver candlesticks on the dining-room table, a small lamp lit only half the kitchen, and for the rest we carried silver chamber candlesticks with snuffers to our bedrooms, with little lamps perched precariously on brackets over the stairs. Turf fires were lit in the bedrooms in winter, but fire-guards were unheard of.

A terrible thing happened once, when the laundrywoman's little girl found her way into the house while the family were away at the cottage. As they came home, they saw across the lake a light going from room to room. They hurried back and found the little girl burned to death on the kitchen floor. The mother left the laundry on the back drive and no one has lived there since. It was where my great-grandmother had boiled food in the copper at the time of the Famine, and the tragedy seems to hang about it still as we pass by on our way to the boats.

We nearly lost this heritage in 1850 as my great-grandfather had thoughts (which mercifully came to nothing) of selling Errislannan, and to this end had a leaflet printed and distributed describing it in great detail. I cannot do better than quote this laudatory advertisement.

Peninsula of Errislannan
To be sold

A portion of Errislannan of 1,100 acres, half of which is under cultivation and the remainder consists of pasture, bog, and mountain ... it extends from Ardbear Bay to Mannin Bay ... an excellent natural harbour runs up into these lands and is almost landlocked (Crumpaugn). It has natural advantages for fishing both sea and lakes.

There is a commodious staunchly-built stone house comprising hall and porch, 3 sitting rooms, 8 bedrooms, housekeeper's room, dairy, kitchen, scullery, pantry, laundry, turf house, water closet, etc., all constructed in the most permanent manner.

The offices are extensive, comprising stables, coach-house, piggery for five brood sows, barn, fowl-house, steward's rooms, and extensive storage – all covered with the best ton slates.

... has also formed a garden, which is well stocked with fruit trees; besides upwards of 20,000 trees have been planted and are in a thriving state – the site being well sheltered.

Errislannan is four (Irish) miles from Clifden a good market town, by road; and a little over a mile by sea.

After a hundred years hardly anything has changed except for weathering and decay. The stable yard looks shabby but is a much-loved place, and the house itself has grown in beauty and fits harmoniously into its wooded surround. Partly creeper-covered, with flower-beds under the windows, it has become mellow. Half the old orchard-house at one end is still standing, which Jack Heaslop, before he died of TB at twenty-seven, built out of great balks of timber washed up by the sea and cut in the sawmill that used to be in the barn yard. It had peach and plum trees, and a vine which even now shows through, and it had hotbeds where Great-uncle Walter grew cucumbers and tomatoes.

CHAPTER 8

Tinkers and Tenants

During my early years the Manor was sometimes let for August and September, and Grannie, the aunts and Uncle John made the great exodus for their seaside holiday to St Flannan's cottage – the old schoolhouse. It was only three fields away, but Grannie went in the carriage. The coachman shared the box with a commode; every inch of the carriage inside and out was draped with last-minute things, till it looked like a fairground stall. My brother and I raced across the meadows to be at the cottage to unload. Often heavy rain soaked everyone and everything, but the tenants were on their way, the show must go on. At the cottage the only form of heat or drying was the one fire and the little kitchen range, so I remember always the damp musty smell and the blue mould on our shoes.

This move saved the Manor from becoming so full of junk, letters, clothes and broken furniture, that in time no one would have been able to get in at the door. As it was, sheets and blankets were laid on the floors and everything not wanted was thrown into them for safe keeping up in the loft over the stables. I was faced with these same bundles two generations later when the place had to be cleared for sale. The carpets were laid on the grass; the blankets were draped over the fuchsia bushes, wet or dry; mattresses were put in front of the kitchen range and pande-monium reigned, but it was a godsend for the house. We were often dragging loads of goods out of the back door while Aunt Jane, crimson in the face, delayed the entrance of the tenants with pleasant welcomes and conversation in the porch.

We all liked being in the cottage, for various reasons. Grannie and the aunts liked the big whitewashed room with two windows facing the mountains and one overlooking two little lakes, the sea and sunsets. Also there were no stairs and their bedroom opened into the kitchen – so convenient for morning tea, that feast of thinly cut bread and butter and morning prayers. Uncle John liked it because he could sit on the wall and talk to everyone that passed; in fact the wall became a cheerful meeting-place. My brother and I liked it because of the little stream connecting the lake with the sea which ran at the bottom of the garden. It was very shallow and had a small bridge on which we could sit, where the stones and rushes made foaming channels down which we sailed home-made boats, sometimes as far as the next lake. I remember the pure joy of sitting on a stone with my feet in the water, watching dragon-flies and butterflies, tiny fish and water-beetles, the wild flowers and reeds making a tunnel above my head. Then there were the early morning outings when the cobwebs and grasses were sparkling with dew as we crept out to gather basketfuls of mushrooms. We were very near to Candoolan, our favourite bathing-place, with its long strip of yellow sand and rock pools full of shrimps. So altogether we enjoyed our change of scene.

It is from those early summers in the cottage that I have a fear of the tinkers; we were terrified of them and although they came to the Manor also, there was more room to hide from them there, and they did not force their way in as they did to the houses by the road. I remember a day at the cottage when my aunts must have been out, and the maid rushed round putting up the shutters and locking all the doors, telling Donald and me to hide and keep quiet. The wild-looking dirty men, women and children came and tried the doors and peered in through one unshuttered window. Then the woman with a baby on her back took down our clothes-line and the men took two buckets from the dairy and went out of the gate, spitting towards the house.

In later years I had the same trouble at the Gate Lodge and it was a great nuisance having to lock the door during the summer months. I never thought of them as human beings suffering from cold or hunger, until many years later in London I saw a beautifully produced little film called *No Resting Place*, which told the story of a tinker, his sick wife and boy, with no artificial trimmings; the characters looking exactly like the tinkers one sees about the roads today. I have often seen them crouching on the wet ground round a fire outside the beehive-shaped shelters made of old sacks, clothes or tarpaulin; the high shallow carts nearby and always several starved-looking horses, black or skewbald, and many donkeys feeding on the roadside verge. After seeing the film I looked at them differently and spared some sympathy, but I still fear their intrusions.

After begging pathetically all day for food or money, they spend the evenings in town drinking; then, very drunk, they pile on to the high carts and one hears the galloping horses passing by, being beaten with a heavy stick – the whacking never seems to stop. The carts have high wheels and the constantly galloping horses are traditional and stem from the time when speed would get the tinkers away from the police or farmers. Now with the telephone and police cars they have no chance of escape, but still they beat the skinny animals and appear to sail along the roads.

The flourishing tourist trade has changed the tinkers in the last few years. They have taken to brightly coloured circular vans, more like gypsies, and pose along the main roads, where tourists stop to photograph them and give them money. The pictures of ragged, starving people with their head-hanging horses round their caravans must be shown in all countries of the world. The tourists always give money, which they drink, instead of the milk or bread that in the past they would have extracted from farmers, with a sack of potatoes taken by the way. This means the women and children look extremely unhealthy.

While we were at the cottage I saw a funeral that I have never forgotten. There was no coffin, the woman's body being laid on a plank covered in a white cloth. The men carried her on their shoulders and a boy walked in front with a wooden cross. Others had dug the grave and they stood round saying the Rosary and prayers as there was no priest. Then they left her there by the lake: a lonely end with no one to mourn her. I painted this scene later on.

When I was ten, while we were in the cottage, one lot of tenants had a visitor, a young man called Charles Kennedy, who was to be of the greatest importance to me when I was grown up. He took my brother and me fishing from the rocks and I remember one special picnic we had on the back of the Look-out Hill in the ruined houses left over from the Famine. Charles carried heavy stones into the grass-grown kitchen for seats, and we lit a fire on the old hearthstone. Our roof was the sky and the leaves of the trees that had grown amidst the ruins. We pretended all that summer that it was our country house, but when Charles left it lost its magic. I did not see him again until he met me off the school train in London when I was sixteen.

Most of the tenants who came to the Manor were interesting and many had children with whom we made friends, but sometimes there was trouble. One family arrived on a dark misty day; everything was wet and dripping, nothing could be seen but the ground, and they would not believe that there were mountains and lovely country all round them. They glared at us disappointed and angry and said they would leave the next day. Aunt Jane was so upset when she heard this that she left the setting up of the cottage dairy and, exhausted as she was, walked across the wet haygrass meadows to the Manor to find every mattress in the house crowded round the kitchen range, even the ones we had slept on the night before. Mercifully the next day dawned sunny and bright; the blue of the lake and mountains delighted them, and they came to apologize and ask to stay.

Another tenant complained that the water in the tap smelt bad (not the drinking water, which came from the well) so Aunt Jane assured him, with pardonable pride, that we had a twenty-thousand-gallon dam up on the hill, where no pollution could possibly reach it. It was open to the four winds of heaven and only the purest rain-water could fall into it. They asked to see it, and poor puffy Aunt Jane staggered up the steep hill through the wood, talking brightly all the way, until they stood on the rim of the dam. Aunt Jane waved her hand over the shining water, but the tenant looked downwards and said in an ominous voice, 'What is that?' There was a decayed rabbit draped round the grid which had obviously acted as a sieve for some time.

All the water had to be allowed to cascade down the hill and, as it was a dry summer, barrels of water had to be carried in a donkey cart from the lake, and manhandled up to the tank. A few days later I was coming down through the wood and saw Micky Conneely sitting with his back to the tank. Stopping to talk I heard a faint trickling sound, and realized the boy had connected the pipe up again, so the tank was filling as before. He had to stay there to disconnect it if the tenant appeared.

'The auld *amadán*,' said Micky. 'If he knew what's in the lake, he'd prefer his rabbit soup.'

Some other tenants let their maids go bathing in the lake, although they had been warned that it was dangerous. They got into difficulties and the chauffeur was drowned trying to save one of them.

One other tenant was memorable. It must have been again when I was about ten years old that a couple came to Great-aunt Alice's cottage, called Glendowie, which is right on the edge of the sea. Phelan Gibb was a painter and brought enormous canvases which stretched thirty feet along the wall of the big room. Many years later I found one of his Paris exhibition catalogues and realized that he had been a Cubist and possibly a good painter, but of course at that time and in that place, his queer shapes and colours labelled him as mad, apart from what came later. Not many years ago I came across a reference to Gibb as 'one of Picasso's circle ... who disappeared into Ireland with a volume of Gertrude Stein under his arm'.

Mother liked him and he became very friendly with us all. He enjoyed sand-eeling by moonlight; and joined my uncle in dyeing two white ducks, that belonged to my brother and me, pink and green for a joke and then put them up outside our window with a light turned on them. We told him the ducks had died because of this treatment, dug two graves and put up tombstones labelled 'Green Duck' and 'Pink Duck'. We sat by the graves and howled when he passed by until he said that he would give us two more ducks. Then he saw them on the Manor lake, but took it in good part. He seemed a friendly, normal man.

Then trouble began when a Captain F. came to stay with the Gibbs and gave Phelan every cause for jealousy, so he ordered a boat and forced Captain F. into it on a very rough day. When the boat pulled away towards Clifden, Phelan went into the house and saw Captain F.'s sandshoes lying on the floor. He rushed out and threw them after the boat, but unfortunately the tide brought them up to the house again. This started him off and in a frenzy he started shouting at the Captain as though he were in the shoes. A few days later, Donald and I heard loud screams coming from Glendowie. We ran down with Swannie, our nurse, after us, to be met by the Red Devil (a local girl), waving her apron and shouting, 'God! oh God! the master's killing the missus and the dinner will be spoilt!' We found Mrs Gibb lying on the grass shrieking and Phelan walking up and down with his hands behind his back and a very queer expression on his face.

A mental specialist was sent for, and my father and uncles went down to meet him. Donald and I had found a good place on the lavatory hut roof, from where we could see and hear everything. I must explain that this was not without its penalty. The lavatory worked on the principle that a little stream ran down the hill under the lavatory seat, but the weather was hot and there was no stream. We buried our faces in the honeysuckle that grew all over the hut, but the smell and the flies nearly made us sick.

That evening Mrs Gibb disappeared. It got dark and the rain poured down while every available man was sent off to search the lakes. From the drawing-room window we watched the slouching figures, led by Uncle George, tramping round the lake. Many years later this suggested a painting to me. They went miles up Ballinaboy Hill to the Devil's Lake, where a girl had thrown herself in years before. Squelching through the bog in the rain and dark did not put the men in the best of tempers, particularly when they found that Mrs Gibb had been sitting in the Gate Lodge all the evening talking to Lizzie King.

Phelan went quite mad for a time, but a few weeks later he travelled up to Dublin with us and seemed quite his old self. Then we heard that he had been found kneeling in the gutter in Dublin praying for his wife and had been put in a home. We were all very sorry about this. His catalogue and the volume of Gertrude Stein remained in Errislannan and Uncle Deanie used to sit like a toad quoting long passages from it that he had learned by heart, which produced groans from all of us.

In later years it was found more profitable and less trouble to let the cottage instead of the Manor, and so our summers there came to an end.

CHAPTER 9

France, the Great War, and Back to Errislannan

In July 1914 my mother took me away from school to be her companion on a trip to France. A friend owned a ship which plied between London Bridge and Boulogne with cargoes of horses, and he offered us free passages. It was a great adventure, but I was nervous about going alone with Mother as she was so often ill. It did not help matters when she told me to ask for 'eau de vie' if she fainted while in France. It was a breath-taking experience to board the ship at midnight and sail down the Thames among a myriad lights and their reflections. The journey took fourteen hours and was very rough, but we went up on deck and would have enjoyed it had it not been for the thought of the horses down below.

We were waiting at Wimereux for my brother, sister and Swannie to join us when war was declared; a man read out a large poster at the street corner and then pinned it up for all to read. Pandemonium ensued, all the beach tents came down in a flash and the gay summer scene collapsed. The French began being rude to the English visitors as they thought we were not coming to their aid. Our cheques were refused and we had hardly any money. At last we reached Boulogne and were sitting hopelessly on the quay, when lo and behold the family came cheerfully towards us. My father had thought that they would enjoy the trip even if war did break out! I was still feeling shaken after seeing a girl step off an open-sided tram and go under the wheels; in the excitement I had lost sight of my mother, and I have never forgotten the misery of being momentarily lost with no money or address in a foreign land.

We were forced against the chains at the edge of the quay in the hysterical scramble to get on board, and once on we stood like vertical sardines on the deck. We arrived in England with half a crown between us, but a kind man in the train lent us enough money to get home, his stars telling him we were honest people. My father met us beaming and hoped that we had had a nice time! Soon we left for Ireland and were never to have a home in England again.

In the early summer of 1914 my father had sold mares and foals to the value of £30,000 to the Russians for their National Stud, but now the deal fell through and he was left with a lot of useless horses and nothing to feed them

– 49 –

on. All the foodstuffs were being taken up by the army and the situation became desperate. At first my father was employed going round the country commandeering everything in the way of horseflesh for remounts, and this involved stabling and exercising them in London. My mother was called upon to help and every day in Rotten Row she rode strange horses who were often frightened of the traffic. Once one bolted with her from Hyde Park Corner, down the Row and out into the park. At the last moment she managed to turn him and my father was able to head him off before he crashed into some iron railings.

Meanwhile in Warwickshire Jimmy McGuinness, the head groom, was struggling on as best he could to find food for the stud. He fell into devious ways of obtaining it and landed in trouble. My father had great difficulty in getting him off, and so decided to take the yearlings to America and give the mares and foals to his brother Deanie, who was living at Knockadoo, the farm which had been left to the four brothers in Co. Sligo. Miraculously, he managed to ship twelve yearlings to New York in the middle of the war. Almost at once racing stopped when America came into the war, and there was no hope of selling them. My father had no money and had to sleep out in the park, where he got pneumonia. He was befriended by a German waiter, who took him home and looked after him and wrote to my mother. Somehow money was raised and he came back, looking like a skeleton and silent about the terrible times he must have gone through. His natural optimism helped him and it was not long before he had established another stud at Knockadoo, with the five mares and foals saved from the financial wreck in England. This became very successful and he bred a number of winners, taking the yearlings over to Newmarket every year. He paid off some of the debts, but Errislannan had become a continual drain on everything he made; he had to cope with its mortgages and other debts, although Knockadoo could hardly support itself. There were also accidents to the yearlings it had taken so much money to produce. Two were killed one day being led by a groom past the hall door; a second groom had run noisily through the house and frightened them so that they dashed madly down the drive and crashed into the iron gates and stone pillars. At another time a yearling was being led down the gangway on to the boat by my father, when some idiot gave it a whack behind, causing it to jump on to the deck and break a leg.

It must have been very sad when my parents were separated for the first time. My mother's many illnesses eventually made it necessary for her to be near doctors and hospitals and so she went to live in her sister's flat in London; my father went over whenever he could, but he had no one responsible to leave in charge of the farm and stud.

This arrangement was to have been a temporary measure, but continued until she died three years later. She was always so bright and cheerful that no one knew how ill she was. She had remarkable courage and never complained at the loss of her own home, her friends, and her painting and music, which had meant so much to her. In Errislannan during the years before she left she was not allowed even to drive the horse, as no women drove in those days, though any boy who had driven a donkey was considered quite safe on the box. This is not to say we did not have very happy times, we did, and the aunts and Uncle John could not have been kinder, but it is strange how the kindest people can stifle an artist until the very desire to paint or play just fades away and is replaced by nothing but misery. I experienced this myself in Errislannan when growing up, so I know how my mother felt. It has taken me a lifetime to get over the assumption that the aunts were always right. I don't think I ever stood up to them about anything without feeling guilty.

Mother's paints and easel must have been sold with the furniture in England, but no one could have painted in the Manor, and the piano was flat and used only for hymns on Sunday evenings which always made me cry. My mother was far more intelligent and capable than the aunts, but they crushed her between them, although they really did their best to be kind.

I cannot think how money was found to send my brother and me to good schools, but Donald went to Rugby and on to Sandhurst, where he did very well, largely on account of his riding. He was six foot two inches and very good-looking, but he would not have considered joining the army in peace-time.

When our English home disintegrated I was sent to Upper Chine on the Isle of Wight, at the suggestion of a friend who lived in the island. Considering the expense of the fares to Connemara every holiday it seems a curious choice. It had been a finishing school for foreigners, but the war had swept them all away and there were only seventeen pupils when I arrived and forty when I left aged sixteen because my fees could not be paid. It was in a beautiful house with a ballroom opening into a conservatory, and a tapestry-lined dining-room; all set in a garden of eight acres with a stream running through it in a deep valley called the Chine. I was extremely happy there as the headmistress had not got used to the idea that we were not young ladies to be finished pleasantly, but should instead be taught common or garden lessons. There were no qualified teachers and no exams, but we rode a lot on the seven horses, looked after by a handsome groom – a friend of mine was expelled for dressing up in his clothes and going to the town to buy cigarettes.

The real horrors of the war were largely mitigated, but the terrible death roll entered our lives in the form of telegrams saying that fathers or brothers had been killed. Silence fell when a girl was called out to go to the headmis-tress's study; and how many there were. It was worse in some ways than in the

Second World War because of the slowness of communications and the difficulties of getting the wounded out. Two of my special friends lost their brothers and I was sent out with them for walks in the country. In one case this was the last thing she wanted, so we went to town and wandered on to the desolate winter pier. We put pennies in slots without looking at the results, and I have never forgotten that cold grey sea, the grey pier and the desolation that surrounded us.

Then a boy called Phillip that I had known for years was badly wounded at Loos and sent to Osborne House, the convalescent home for officers on the island. He brazenly came to meals with the girls, undaunted by twenty pairs of eyes fixed speechlessly upon him. I fell in love and was allowed to go out with him in his little car, often returning after lights were out having spent the evening dining at an hotel and been well kissed on the way home.

This was all very exciting, but the end of term came and we had to say goodbye. I dreaded the thought of being buried in Connemara away from Phillip for two whole months, but as it turned out I never went back to school. On the last day of term I received a letter from Charles Kennedy, who had been asked to meet me off the school train in London and take me to Euston in time for the Irish Mail. Someone always had to meet me. Once it was my father who had some horsy friends with him and we went to the Café de Paris in Coventry Street. I was given wine and my first cigarette and I remember thinking how vastly superior my father was to all the other men within sight.

As the school train drew in I looked eagerly for Charles's tall thin figure and saw him standing very still among the hurrying crowds. He got a bit of a shock, as he half expected a ragged child of ten to emerge from the train. We stared nervously at each other and then I remembered how nice he had been to us in Ireland and knew he would be nice now. He led me out to his car and we had a lovely day, spending some hours in St James's Park and then having tea in his flat. Before the train we had dinner in a restaurant and talked of Errislannan and that summer day six years before when we built a make-believe-house in the ruined cottage.

Time flew and we still had so much to talk about, or rather I talked and he listened and made me feel quite grown up. He was engaged on some project in Scotland to do with the navy and was wearing country tweeds. It was chance that he got the letter asking him to meet me, and both our lives were to be changed again in the future when we met in a strange place among strangers.

It was nice to arrive at Euston in a car and have porters rushing to serve you. Dark, impressive, smelly Euston and the Irish Mail, so secure and unchanging that it was almost like home, with the same friendly guards and ticket collectors. It had been an exciting and happy day, and if I had not considered myself in love with Phillip at this point, I might have fallen in love with

Charles, but people you have known as a child seem more like relations and I thought no more about him. As the train moved out we had a long look at each other and he told me years later that this must have been when it all began, although in the following years, when I was in Connemara, he married a French woman. They had no children and soon parted company.

When I got home I expected long letters from Phillip but they did not come and then I heard that he had married a nurse that he had known for only a fortnight. I thought I was heart-broken for months, much encouraged by romantic Aunt Jane. I even put black lines under my eyes to help the illusion of sleepless nights.

Errislannan became a more cheerful place with the arrival of young Captain Jack Bentley at the Marconi Station. We climbed mountains together and became soulful on the top; we walked miles over the hills and in the evenings he sang old-fashioned songs to my accompaniments – 'Where my caravan has rested', 'Believe me if all those endearing young charms' and 'Under the wide and starry sky'. He made a good impression on my grandmother by saying that he was going into the Church after the war. Everyone fell for him and I treasured his almost daily letters and a book of Browning's poems that he read to me on the rock above the house.

One day in a narrow path between gorse bushes, we met old Mrs Molloy; she was filthy and the smell was overpowering. The old devil pretended she thought the young man in khaki was my brother, and flung her arms round his neck with many blessings; only I saw her wink and put her tongue out over his shoulder. His reaction to this gave me quite a shock and made me doubt his charity, but still, he was a handsome young man. I must have been soaked in my aunt's Victorian manners and incredibly naïve, for I thought that kissing was equivalent to a proposal. Daily the family expected him to arrive with an engagement ring, but he left for England, and three days later his engagement to a girl he had never mentioned was announced in *The Times*.

I went up to our rock and after weeping a little made a bonfire of all his letters and the book of poems. This rock – according to the old diaries – had seen many a love-letter read or burned and many a tear shed by different generations. A steep path leads up to it through the wood past Great-aunt Rachael's moss-covered seat, from where she looked out over the lake and sea, past the rock with seats for two, shut in by bushes except for the side facing the view, like a theatre box. Great-aunts and the great-great-aunts they sat exactly on that spot, and I knew from their diaries that they had felt as lonely as I did and yearned to get away. Although I longed for young companions, however, the love of Errislannan bound me and was never to be broken; later on I was free to come and go as I pleased but I never left England without a return ticket in my pocket, even if I was 'of no fixed address' at the time.

One good thing came out of the Bentley affair. I let Jack see my drawings and he was so enthusiastic about them that the family tried to like them too, but they really wanted realism and more detail, whereas I was interested only in strong uncluttered shapes and movement. Jack spoke of my work in the Mess at the Marconi Station and an ex-schoolmaster came to visit me; he knew nothing of drawing but evidently deplored my idle, ignorant state and lent me a microscope, which absolutely enthralled me. I put every small thing, insect and flea, into it and drew the result. I made a slide of the crystal-clear water from our seventh-century well, and, delighted with all the moving things I saw, showed it to Aunt Jane. I was amazed at her reaction. Her face went red with fury and she tried to break the slide. Now I realize that if word had got about that our well had things in it, we could never let tenants or anyone drink from it, and there was no other.

If only I had filled those years by studying flowers, birds, shells or anything as I do now, life would have been happy, but I had no books, and, like all the country people, did not think the names and habits of such things of any interest. I let four years slip by, almost paralysed by loneliness. My brother was at Sandhurst and then in Germany; my sister was with my mother in London, and my father was back at Knockadoo trying to make enough money to pay hospital and doctors' fees.

Looking back, though, perhaps those years were not quite wasted, as it was then that I started walking or rowing my little boat into town on Saturday mornings with bits of paper and a pencil in my pocket. I drew the women in shawls and full-length skirts striding along carrying heavy loads, or making monumental shapes standing in the market or leaning forward against the wind; the men walking or sitting on carts or donkeys. The harbour provided the black currachs and the islanders landing, themes that run through my work even now when I make groups of figures and animals in pottery.

I did have one absorbing hobby: collecting butterflies and moths. I watched, I chased, I pounced, I dropped in the stinkpot; I pinned out and finally filled boxes with fascinating trophies. Later I took the ones I could not name to the Natural History Museum in London, where they stuck little labels under the specimens. Two were rare; the Camberwell Beauty and the Swallow-tail. I caught an Elephant Hawk Moth on the sail of our boat when miles from land., and trapped lovely moths with treacle on trees at night, or when they flew in through my uncurtained bedroom window. I shall always remember the smell of the hot bramble hedges and the bushes on the back drive where I watched the unexpected things that come near when one just sits; the rushy marshy ground, the open hillsides where the many blues and the red and blacks darted about; the wild flowers decorated with fluttering wings in that sheltered sunny place: Red Admirals, Tortoise-shells, Brimstones, Painted

Ladies and dozens of others. I also collected caterpillars, and chrysalides from the loose stone walls and holes. I should hate to kill a butterfly now, but thank God I did not think it cruel then as I should have missed many an hour of complete happiness.

*   *   *

The spot I liked best in Errislannan was the stable yard. The stables, the coach-house and the loft above made up one side; the stores and the cow-houses the second and third. It was a sheltered sunny place; untidy, smelling of cow dung and chickens, but beautiful, with a climbing yellow rose that spread over one wall and hung down over the coach-house doors. It was the centre of everything, where everyone had time to talk, sitting on the shafts of a cart or an old box. On the fourth side, by the large gates, was the barn yard and then the kitchen garden with its rows of vegetables and fruit, sweet peas and other flowers for cutting; next to it was the seventh-century graveyard, excellent for fertility.

To return to the yard, the coach-house had a long earthy table, which was a work-place for everyone: a place to sit all morning looking out at the rain, and smelling all things at double strength because of the penetrating damp. I watched the drops fall like a curtain from the yellow rose and listened to the musical trickles of rain from the broken guttering bring different notes from different things. One object on which the rain dripped was the rusty old plough – the first to be seen in Errislannan. It was tried out in the kitchen garden with a crowd lining the walls to see this wonder. A great cheer went up as the horse reached the far end. The great invention was to put an end to hand labour.

As I sat, Uncle John and some of the men would join me, their clothes wet and steaming, content to rest until the bell clanged down at the house for dinner.

After the death of the 'coach' when the loft floor fell down, we bought an elegant conveyance known as the 'Glass Case'. It was a four-wheeler with windows all round and looking-glasses in every corner. It held only two inside and two on the box. There was also the side-car, with a deep well between the seats, big enough to hold a calf or luggage. When this went to be repaired, the man could not resist the polished wood at the back and painted red geraniums on it. Lastly came the four-wheeled trap with two rows of seats facing front. Half of this was left draped round the gatepost of a house we were visiting while the front portion went on to the front door.

Once a year the coach-house had to be cleared for the threshing of the oats. One end was swept clean of dust and two men with flails got to work. These flails were two uneven lengths of stick joined together with a leather thong. The men had to be experienced and beat alternately or they would have hit each other.

I think some visitor must have organized the only dance I remember in the yard, as the aunts never did that kind of thing. A great fire was lit in the middle, and benches and carriages were used for seats. The fiddles made a gay sound that we could hear from the house and everything seemed very jolly until Aunt Edyth and Aunt Jane went up to view the fun and with pleasant smiles settled down to see how boys and girls enjoyed themselves. A dreadful silence fell, though one fiddler continued to play. Bottles of whiskey were slid out of sight, but not before my teetotal aunts had seen them, though they did not show any signs of disapproval.

A little tree-shaded lane leads down from the stable yard to the lake and the long shallow boats; ideal for fishing or lying in, hidden in the rushes, whiling away the sunny hours when the house hummed with domestic activity. I seemed to lead a charmed life, never being expected to join in these orgies of cleaning and polishing carried out with local help. The most I was asked to do was to gather baskets of flowers and buckets of fruit in the walled-in garden; a place that catches the sun and is sheltered by tall trees from the wind. The paths and herbaceous borders formed a cross in the centre which was arched over by rambler roses. The four squares were filled with lichen-covered old apple trees, glorious in the spring. There were red, black and white currant bushes, loganberries, and raspberry canes, which provided Aunt Jane with jars of jam for the whole year. Along the wall were the strawberry beds and a small glasshouse for peaches. In the shadow of this, during the winter, was a carpet of dark green, dotted with the lovely faces of Christmas roses which flourished year after year with no care. Picking flowers and fruit was wet work and like a pleasant shower on a hot day after rain.

Lily of the valley had spread in wild confusion underground and came up along the walls. In the borders were all the usual flowers, roses, lilies, phlox, gladioli and always a hedge of sweet peas. Tall white Japanese anemones stood behind the other flowers and shone in the moonlight like ghost flowers against the dark of the trees. There was the thick stump of a paeony tree, the flowers of which had been so much admired by Arthur Nicholls, Charlotte Brontë's widower, when he walked up and down that path with my grandmother or sat in the early morning enjoying the profusion of flowers and trees. He had returned to Banagher on the Shannon to marry his cousin Mary Anne Bell and had forty years with her before he died in 1906. I always felt sorry for the faithful Nicholls, who after Charlotte's death had to spend six years in Haworth with his uncongenial father-in-law, fulfilling a selfish promise extracted from him by Charlotte, to stay with her father until his death.

I had always thought my grandmother had got mixed up about the Bells, as Charlotte had used the name of 'Bell' as a *nom de plume*, but no, she had used Mr Nicholls's family name, as she admitted when she came over to Banagher on her honeymoon. My grandmother said Mary Anne had a wooden leg and this may have been true as she had had a bad hunting accident and was very lame.

When Charlotte was on her honeymoon she visited the west coast of Ireland and was amazed at the wildness of the sea and the cliffs. Her one worry was that her new husband might be in the way while she enjoyed the sight, but he was tactful and retired a little way, after wrapping her up. Poor Mr Nicholls! Charlotte must have been a self-centred person to live with – artists have to be. She was amazed to find that his family were aristocratic, well-educated people living in a lovely Palladian house near the Shannon; she had always thought her family superior to his. His second wife was pretty and kind and put up with all the souvenirs that Arthur brought from Haworth, including the dog Plato and Charlotte's dresses. She edited all Charlotte's letters for publication, and, when Arthur died, she even had the corpse laid out in the dining-room under Richmond's portrait of Charlotte.

CHAPTER 10

The 1916 Easter Rebellion

In spite of the tragic history of Ireland during the past seven hundred years, when people talk of the 'Bad Times' they refer to the period between the Easter Rebellion in 1916 and the mid-twenties when the Civil War came to an end. This chapter is about those times and the way they affected the family.

We were 'loyalists', which meant that the men of the family were often in the British army, we sang 'God Save the King' and had generally been to boarding school in England. We were totally ignorant of what was going on in Ireland. Two of my uncles were in the Gunners and Donald, my brother, was in the Loyal North Lancs, with whom, unfortunately, he was sent to Ireland in 1920. All Irishmen with the forces of occupation were on a special list to be killed as traitors; this list was found on a man killed when my brother's men were ambushed in Tipperary. Even my mother's London flat address was given, so that as he travelled backwards and forwards when my mother was dying, Donald never felt safe and always carried a loaded revolver. As a soldier he was not allowed to come back to Errislannan for five years, so the two of us met in England from time to time. We lived in dread of a telegram coming to say he had been killed, as had so many of his brother officers. The strain of never knowing who your enemy was, of continual ambushes on lonely roads, began to tell on all of them. Donald got a bullet in his foot, but he was lucky. He loved and understood the Irish country people, and the brutality of the Black-and-Tans towards them made him ashamed and furious.

During the Bad Times the boys' orphanage near us – founded by my great-grandmother and Mrs D'Arcy of Clifden Castle – started a Boy Scout troop, and when I stayed there with the Master's daughters I saw the boys saluting the Union Jack every morning. This – understandably – caused trouble and the Republicans burned the whole place down in 1922. The Scout movement was a piece of folly encouraged by the Viceroy, who founded Boys' Brigades and Scouts on the British model. Because of this, Countess Markievicz – formerly Constance Gore-Booth – now an officer in the Citizen Army, started her troop of Fianna boys, dedicated to fight for Ireland. She taught them to drill and how to use rifles, so that when the Easter Rising came they were of officer material and accustomed to arms.

I remember hearing of one strange incident in which Constance and her Fianna boys were involved. Thousands of the Volunteers and the Citizen Army had no weapons, though they drilled and marched about Dublin. Constance and her boys had orders to join a column of Volunteers with a trek cart and march to Howth. They took this to be one of the usual exercises and the cart to be full of provisions, but it proved to be full of staves for the Volunteers to defend themselves with while unloading a cargo of German arms from Sir Erskine Childers' yacht, the *Asgard*. De Valera was there, unloading. Half the arms proved to be useless and there was only one round of ammunition for each good rifle. The Germans had also sent Mausers, which were banned by international law. Knowing nothing of this, they soon loaded the cart and many cars, while the coastguards tried to rouse the military. The column marched back to Dublin to the cheers of the populace, a priest blessing them from the top of a bus. Meeting a company of Scottish Borderers, who charged with fixed bayonets, the exhausted Fianna swerved down a side-street, but they heard the firing and the blood-stained Volunteers dashed past shouting at them to save the arms at all costs. The boys wheeled their cart into a large garden and buried the contents temporarily, later taking them to the safety of Constance's cottage in the mountains. No arms were lost.

The soldiers, returning to Dublin, met with abuse and stone-throwing and raised their rifles. The officer gave the order to prepare to fire, but this was misunderstood and they fired, killing three and wounding thirty-two – the Bachelor's Walk incident. The Dublin people staged a great display of mourning, as occurred in Belfast in 1972 after Bloody Sunday. The Republican Brotherhood met to decide on armed insurrection; men and boys drilled all over Ireland. The fuse was lit for the 1916 Rebellion, which now became inevitable.

Despite all this, when 4th August 1914 came and the European war started, Redmond took nine-tenths of his 15,000 Volunteers to join the British army in France, and the two Irish divisions from the north and the south fought magnificently side by side before Ypres. According to the British Legion's records, thousands of them were killed.

So the time passed until Easter 1916, when there were six thousand British troops in Dublin. My cousin, wounded in France and attached to the Sherwood Foresters, was there, and two of my uncles were stationed in Athlone. Uncle Deanie was sent with his battery to Dublin, but trouble arose as many of his men had homes there and were not willing to fire on the city. Fire was concentrated on the General Post Office and it was their fire-bombs that set it alight. Now, knowing of the heroic fighters inside and on the roof – saying their Rosaries – when there was no more water, it is terrible to think of, but Uncle Deanie gloated over the fact that the outside walls of the building were not hit.

The British were so accustomed to the Volunteers drilling that they ignored the signs and went to the races that fateful Easter Monday. They ignored the fact that Sir Roger Casement had landed from a German submarine and been caught. That a German fishing boat, the Aud, *camouflaged and loaded with arms, had scuttled herself when caught the following day. So* they went to the races and an officer, by chance, put the key of the Dublin Armoury in his pocket instead of hanging it on its nail, thereby thwarting a plan to obtain more arms for the rebels.

Two of the leaders, Connolly and Pearse, knew they would meet defeat and death from the moment, two days before, that Professor Eoin MacNeill – who was opposed to violence – discovered their intentions and sent messages all over Ireland; he also put a notice in the paper that their plans had been cancelled.

Their Commander-in-Chief, James Connolly, said to a friend, 'We're going out to be slaughtered.' 'Is there no hope at all?' asked the friend. 'None whatever,' Connolly replied cheerfully. He and Pearse knew that their deaths would help the cause along, and how right they were! W.B. Yeats wrote later:

> 'But where can we draw water,'
> Said Pearse to Connolly,
> 'When all the wells are parched away?
> O plain as plain can be
> There's nothing but our own red blood
> Can make a right Rose Tree.'

The leaders were an extraordinary mixture of men. Patrick Pearse, towering above them all; a poet and writer, no soldier; a Gaelic revivalist, who founded a bilingual school; in his mid-thirties, with an English father and Irish mother; tall and full of dignity. James Connolly, forty-six; thick-set, tough socialist, born in Edinburgh, where he worked as a baker until his health gave way. In Dublin he was head of the General and Transport Workers' Union, and he helped Jim Larkin in the days of the terrible strike in 1913. He brooked no distinction of class or sex and made the Countess Markievicz an officer in the Citizen Army. Thomas Clarke, a small frail man, broken in health after sixteen years in English jails for his political opinions; now running a little shop in Dublin which was a meeting-place for the rebels. Sean MacDermott, dark-haired and handsome; although limping with sticks from polio, he tramped all over Ireland preaching rebellion. Joseph Plunkett, son of a Papal Count and from a well-known Irish family, had his neck still bandaged after an operation for glandular tuberculosis. He came down the steps leaning on the arm of his ADC, Michael Collins, a post-office worker, strong and efficient, a future commander and leader of Ireland. Thomas MacDonagh, a Professor of English and a minor poet; temperamental and flamboyant. De Valera, Professor of Mathematics, future President of the Republic of Ireland, survived the rebellion because, owing to lack of communications, he did not surrender when the General Post Office fell, and so came before the court martial last, when even the English were sickened by General Maxwell's killing of prisoners of war. Also de Valera had a Spanish-American father.

On the fateful Easter Monday their arms were contained in two drays and a cab, filled to the roof with every kind of junk – farm implements, axes, crowbars, spades. By twelve o'clock they were marching up O'Connell Street – then called Sackville Street. Turning sharp left, they charged up the steps of the General Post Office among the astonished customers. It was not until the Volunteers began breaking out the windows and barricading them that the customers and staff ran panic-stricken for the door and were hustled out. One British officer was taken prisoner and put in a telephone kiosk, where later a bullet missed him by an inch, fired from across the road by the rebels entrenched there, who were as ignorant of firearms as those in the Post Office. In fact all the early casualties came from home-made bombs going off or rifles fired by mistake.

Soon a flag was flying on each side of the British coat of arms on the pediment: the green ground with a golden harp and the words 'Irish Republic', and the tricolour of green, white and orange which is the Irish flag today.

Batches of Volunteers coming in were being detailed to strategic points in the city. De Valera was to hold Bolands Bakery and Mill and stop reinforcements coming from Britain to help the army. When they did come they marched in formation up the street and were shot down with terrible slaughter.

At the side-door of the General Post Office, pandemonium reigned when hundreds of women from the slums – called 'shawlies' – demanded their 'separation money'. This was the allowance the British offered to those with husbands or sons serving with the British army. As there were 150,000 Irishmen with the army in 1916, one can imagine the crowd that came to collect their money in Dublin.

Pearse now went out on to the steps and read aloud to an indifferent crowd a proclamation:

THE PROVISIONAL GOVERNMENT OF THE IRISH REPUBLIC
... We declare the right of the people of Ireland to the ownership of Ireland, and to the unfettered control of Irish destinies, to be sovereign and indefeasible ...

... The Republic guarantees religious and civil liberty, equal rights and
equal opportunities to all its citizens ...
Signed ... Thomas J. Clarke, Sean Mac Diarmada, Thomas MacDonagh,
P.H. Pearse, Eamonn Ceannt, James Connolly, Joseph Plunkett.

In spite of the broken windows, the guns and barricades, the people of Dublin
continued to crowd the streets, full of curiosity but not taking the Rising
seriously. Then a fantastic situation arose. A troop of Lancers in full regalia
cantered down O'Connell Street just as a group of Volunteers were trying to
scramble in through the GPO windows to escape the shawlies. I quote from
The Agony at Easter by T. Coffey:

> They came in columns as straight as their lofty ceremonial lances.
> Carbines still holstered, heads fixed high, they declined to acknowledge
> the scruffy volunteers. The street was their parade ground ... About a
> hundred yards north of the GPO the troop broke columns smartly,
> fanning out across the street, and came to a halt. As the jingle of their
> trappings ceased, a deep silence fell. A voice shouted a warning, but not
> a lancer turned his head. The colonel in charge glanced to the right and
> left at the Post Office and the sandbagged windows across the street and
> at the flags. He saw in the middle of the street a tram the insurgents had
> overturned for a barricade. The colonel stiffened, reached for his sword,
> raised it high and gave a command. The lancers, still in formation,
> charged forward.

Inside the building, forty riflemen, their barrels resting on the window-
ledges, waited, nervous at this, the first time they had had to fire at human
beings and horses.

They had orders to hold their fire. The Lancers were in full view of the men
on the roof. They must have known that the insurgents had them in their
sights, yet on they came. Though the moment might call for door-to-door
infantrymen, that was not the Lancers' style. They reached Nelson's Pillar ...
the insurgents' plan was to let them come even further until they were under
every gun in the building, but a rifleman lost patience. A shot rang out and a
volley followed.

Four Lancers toppled from their saddles, three of them dead and a fourth
wounded. The ranks broke. What had been a disciplined unit became a
milling mass of horses and men, bunched together at the mercy of the
insurgents.

Then the guns became merciful and fired over their heads, hitting the
buildings opposite. A horse fell dead and another rider was unseated, but he
was allowed to walk away safely and the others retreated at a gallop the way

they had come. An urchin retrieved one of the carbines and threw it into the GPO with 'Here yiz are!'

Another group of Lancers were in trouble in Bachelor's Walk. Unsuspecting, they rode along with a wagon of ammunition which they had just loaded up. The first party of insurgents let them pass but the next opened up, and the Lancers took cover after two of them had been killed, leaving the wagon of ammunition in the street.

The Castle was left undefended and the insurgents easily took the guard-room, then made their biggest mistake in retiring, unable to believe that there were only twenty-five men there to guard it. At the GPO Desmond and Mabel FitzGerald arrived offering to help. Mabel was asked to bring a flag to be hung over the Castle, but she was met there by a British soldier with a bayonet and had to turn back. An Irish flag was not to fly above the Castle until 1922.

Inside the GPO there was intense activity stowing bombs and ammunition, binding injuries from broken glass, stowing the food upstairs, placing men on the roof, who later had the task of fighting the incendiary shells which eventually burned the whole place inside. Flames spread down from floor to floor and down the lift shaft as the last of the wounded were carried out into other houses through holes in the walls, up ladders on to the roofs, and back into a small yard. Connolly with his smashed ankle was on a stretcher, a young boy leaning over him to guard him from bullets; his secretary, Winifred Carney, did the same on the other side. From the yard they tried to get into a cottage to shelter the wounded, but the door was locked. Someone fired at the lock but the shot went through the shoulder of a man inside and killed his young daughter. The mother behaved with extraordinary courage. Twelve wounded men, a wounded British soldier and her wounded husband, as well as her nine small children, were crowded into that tiny room, but she tore up sheets for bandages and helped. When Joseph Plunkett arrived he was horrified to see the dead girl and demanded angrily who had been responsible. The mother, Mrs McKane, looked at the men and said, 'It was only an accident; move now, I must go for a priest.' They tried to stop her, as bullets were flying, but she searched street after street until she found a priest. When he came in and saw the dead and wounded he burst into tears, but eventually went round administering the last sacraments.

Meanwhile in O'Connell Street, the crowd from the slums had begun looting and setting the big stores and hotels on fire. The whole street seemed to be alight and the looting filled Connolly with shame and bitterness. He had given his life to fighting for the poor of Dublin and now they disgraced the name of Irishmen with their behaviour. A drunken shawlie sat singing on the rump of a dead horse. The rebels were puritanical in their insistence on paying for everything they took or commandeered, and no drink was allowed. No bottles were taken from the bar of the Coliseum, where they had to halt with many of the wounded on their way to the hospital, which says a lot for the idealism of their leaders, as the fight was then over. There were about twenty women who stayed to the last nursing and helping, refusing to leave and showing the same courage as the men. It was a woman who finally carried the note of surrender up the street, after two other people carrying white flags had been shot down. A white handkerchief was all they had and it drew a hail of bullets when first put out, but after a pause Elizabeth O'Farrell tried again and bravely walked towards the guns and the barricade.

After the surrender the prisoners were marched to the green in front of the Rotunda Hospital – wounded and unwounded, but all completely exhausted; and there they stood or lay in the rain all night. Captain Lee-Wilson, who belonged to an English regiment, had many of them stripped in front of the watching crowds and the nurses at the hospital windows. Some of the leaders were subjected to this to humiliate them in front of their men but they behaved with great dignity. Captain Lee-Wilson taunted and mocked the naked men, especially the crippled ones, and took away MacDermott's sticks.

In the morning they were marched to Richmond Barracks for more serious trials, and on the way rubbish and slops were thrown over them by crowds on the pavement. Fifteen of the leaders were executed. Constance Markievicz was condemned to death but was reprieved against her will, and had to listen to her friends being shot in the yard below her cell. Connolly was carried out on a stretcher and propped up on a chair to be shot. Bernard Shaw spoke out strongly against this shooting of prisoners of war.

The night before his execution, Joseph Plunkett married Grace Gifford, who went out to buy the ring and had only ten minutes with her husband. Waiting his turn for the firing-squad, Pearse wrote a poem which is in striking contrast to that written by Constance Markievicz from her prison cell.

By Patrick Pearse, written in Kilmainham Jail on the night before his execution:

> The beauty of the world hath made me sad,
> This beauty that will pass;
> Sometimes my heart hath shaken with great joy
> To see a leaping squirrel in a tree,
> Or a red lady-bird upon a stalk,
> Or little rabbits in a field at evening,
> Lit by a slanting sun,
> Or some green hill where shadows drifted by,
> Some quiet hill where mountainy men hath sown
> And soon will reap, near to the gate of Heaven;

Or children with bare feet upon the sands
Of some ebbed sea, or playing on the streets
Of little towns in Connacht,
Things young and happy.
And then my heart hath told me:
These will pass,
Will pass and change, will die and be no more,
Things bright and green, things young and happy;
And I have gone upon my way
Sorrowful.

By Constance Markievicz – reprieved but also in prison, 1916:

On your murdered body I'll pledge my life
With its passionate love and hate,
To secret plotting and open strife
For vengeance early and late.
To Ireland and you I have pledged my life,
Revenge for your memory's sake.

Michael Collins happened to be in the wrong queue while waiting, and was sent to an internment camp in Wales.

Cathal Brugha and de Valera survived, to fight Collins at a later date, over the treaty which started the tragic Civil War. The night before de Valera was reprieved, while he still expected to be executed in the morning, he was an unwilling participant in a macabre game devised by his companions. Among them was Count Plunkett, whose son Joseph had been executed the previous Thursday and two other sons condemned to death the previous Saturday; the latter sentence had been changed to penal servitude for life. His wife had also been arrested. The other men were Sean O'Kelly, later President of Ireland; big John O'Mahony; Larry O'Neill, future Lord Mayor of Dublin. As they lay on the floor, they had a mock trial to pass the time: not a happy choice. The bearded Count was the Judge and de Valera the Prisoner, charged with being pretender to the throne of the Muglins, a rocky island. They continued until the black cap was to be put on, but no one had the stomach for this and they tried to sleep. O'Neill slid over to de Valera and pressed a crucifix into his hand.

After reading many eye-witness accounts of the Easter Rebellion and detailed records made by those who survived, I am overwhelmed with admiration for the rebels' courage against insuperable odds. The accounts of individual heroism are legion, and through them all runs the thread of the Roman Catholic religion. When the roof of the General Post Office was burning and no more water was available, groups knelt saying the Rosary. When the situation at the station was desperate, a priest came and they gathered to take the sacrament. De Valera, so deeply religious himself, was not pleased to find vitally needed sentries missing while they joined their companions to pray.

At home in Errislannan, I remember Uncle John being horrified and sad at the rebels' fate but Aunt Jane was a loyalist to the backbone, and, with most of Ireland, condemned the Rebellion and its leaders. Her mouth shut tightly, down at the corners, thus settling the question and making everyone else feel guilty, as usual. I used to get my information from the postman before he arrived at the house, and Uncle John talked to me about the fighting, sitting on the table in the coach-house – our usual place for conversations. He was a far-seeing, intelligent saint and realized that Ireland would have to be given her independence before long. He lived to see it happen.

As down the glen one Easter morn to a city fair rode I,
There armed lines of marching men in squadrons passed me by,
No pipes did hum, no battle drum did sound its dread tattoo,
But the Angelus bell o'er the Liffey swell, rang out in the foggy dew.

Right proudly high over Dublin Town they hung out the flag of war;
'Twas better to die 'neath an Irish sky than at Sulva or Dud-El-Bar.
And from the plains of Royal Meath strong men came hurrying through
While Britannia's sons, with their great big guns, smiled in the foggy dew.

But the bravest fell and the sullen bell rang mournfully and clear,
For those who died that Eastertide in the springtime of the year.
And the world did gaze in deep amaze at those fearless men and few;
Who bore the fight that Freedom's light might shine through the foggy dew.

'Twas England bade our 'Wild Geese' go that small nations might be free,
But their lonely graves are by Sulva's waves and the fringe of the grey North Sea.
Oh! had they died by Pearse's side or fought with Cathal Brugha,
Their place we'd keep where the Fenians sleep, 'neath the hills of the foggy dew.

CHAPTER 11

Picnics

The Rebellion was over but this was not the end of the fighting. People who had shown no interest in an independent Ireland now became idealists and Protestants began to wonder what would happen to them under a Roman Catholic government. In Errislannan everything went on as before for some years; we were in a backwater, our only excitement and entertainment being picnics.

Picnics in London, in the cloisters of Westminster Abbey, in St James's Park, or on a barge on the Thames; in a forest in Hungary; in a graveyard in Brittany; in the snow high up on the Alps; standing in a street on the Island of Dogs listening to the Salvation Army in the dark, whilst engaged on a crusade for Maud Royden; many a one in Bruges and on the Dutch Canals: happy ones and horrible ones, it depended on the company and the weather, but perhaps I enjoyed most those taken on the cliffs of Sark just behind my cottage – generally breakfast ones – or in a small boat drifting, with no time to keep and no one waiting for my return. Charles was a high-class picnicker who had a proper hamper and stove in the boot of his car, and generally a bottle of wine; more feasts than picnics, but such delights.

My mother had a passion for picnics, which I inherited. Many of the bright happy memories of my childhood have an outdoor background. I remember sitting on grass in most strange places, often in terrible weather, and always there was a horse or donkey involved. In Warwickshire we used to drive a long distance to a sheep farm my father had, where there was a ruined cottage; we took food for the day and let the horse run free. All was well until he had to be caught again, and sometimes it was dark before he allowed us to corner him, after running the sheep about until they were frantic, their pale blue shapes dashing round the dark fields and leaping through hedges. Then would come the long drive home, clopety clopety clop; often with no lights, but we sang loudly all the way.

In Errislannan it was generally a donkey with creels that carried my sister on one side and the food and stone for balance on the other. We always lit a fire, which boiled the kettle and warmed us up after icy bathes, but we spent most of our time exploring the shore. I have already written of the picnic in the ruined cottage on the back of the Look-out Hill when I was ten and first met Charles Kennedy. It must have been at about that time and near the same place that my brother and I wandered away from the picnic party along the shore. As we clambered over a large rock we suddenly found ourselves looking down at a nightmare face, greeny-white and dead with no eyes; the black-clothed body was wedged between two rocks. I screamed and ran back to the family, followed by Donald, and have always remembered the grown-ups sitting in a semicircle staring at us with food in their hands. Then a man got up and went to see what we had found.

Another place for picnics was the ruined castle across the bay, where the D'Arcys had lived in my great-grandmother's time. We went by boat from the bathing rock, from which Great-aunt Alice did her parachute jumps, and landed in a small sheltered bay under the castle where we tied the boat to rocks, hoping it would not be high and dry or far out to sea when we wanted to go home.

One day when there were about seventy people gathered, a man left his shoes and socks on the sand, where they were washed away by the tide. He walked barefooted, painfully up to the castle, stepping delicately like Agag and writhing in agony when he trod on sharp stones and thorns. My brother and I were little beasts and enjoyed his antics, but Charles took pity on him and lent him his socks lined with grass. When it was time to go home, we collected on the beach and looked at our boat, far out to sea. Charles volunteered to swim for it and a woman stood with her back to him and spread out her skirts to shield me from seeing.

The castle was very lovely then; the curved staircase was still in place, and the drawing-room had some beautiful moulding and panelling. There was one long room upstairs with an enormous table where we had our picnic meals, and a surprisingly handsome lead bath, meant for a giant, or for the whole family to bathe together.

Clifden Castle has always been my dream castle. It had two round towers and a great arched doorway, with the D'Arcy coat of arms above it. The roof was castellated and my brother spent many happy hours playing up there, round the ivy-festooned chimneys. The castle looked larger than it was, standing on the steep slope of the hill above the sea, backed by lovely woods. A swift little stream glittering with quartz came down through the trees from a fern and moss grotto, then divided, forming an island on which grew a vast blue hydrangea. It ran on under bridges which had had stone figures at each end, now fallen and broken.

It was a wild and beautiful place, but still haunted by the D'Arcys as we knew so much about them. I still love to wander through the woods, but now the trees are dead; broken white skeletons standing on the nearly bare hillside. The castle is a hollow shell since the Black-and-Tans threw bombs into the basement and blew out the inside. Now, looking up from the muddy, cattle-trodden basement, past the lovely Gothic arches of the windows and passages, one can see the hanging fireplaces, and shudder at the thought of the storm winds whistling through that great empty space on dark nights, through rooms where my great-grandmother and my great-aunts used to dance and sing before setting out for Errislannan in the roomy old coach I remember so well.

One of our picnics was very full dress, as Grannie came in the Glass Case – the successor to the coach, which seated only two people. Our destination was the derelict little harbour of Coronagh at the end of the famine road. Not a boat or soul in sight as usual. The carriage had to make a long round over Ballinaboy and back on the low road, about three miles. Uncle John drove from the box, which was piled high with baskets of food, a frying pan and kettle. Grannie sat in state, the image of Queen Victoria in her short black cloak and widow's bonnet, a nosegay of heliotrope and pink geranium on her chest; crimson in the face with the excitement and exertion. Aunt Jane sat beside her, also crimson from baking in the hot kitchen all morning. On their knees were piled rugs and mackintoshes, as by this time the sky had clouded over and it looked like rain. One visitor referred to our picnics as 'Moontide' picnics, because we started late and returned in the dark.

Aunt Edyth and I walked across the meadows and took the short cut by Candoolan beach, which was grey and bitterly cold; the 'picture of desolation' was how a friend had described it, shocking us all at the thought of our beach not being admired.

We arrived quite half an hour before the carriage, but could not light a fire because the oil-soaked sods of turf were with the food. We collected wood and gorse and put them in the shelter of a rock. Greyness everywhere and black mud in the empty harbour, grey rocks, grey sea, grey sky and the odd drop of rain: what morasses we wallow in while trying not to douse the jollity of family entertainments.

At last the carriage arrived and we arranged the sods of turf by the rock, hung the kettle on three sticks and made a place for the frying pan. Kneeling on the damp ground, Aunt Edyth proceeded to make relays of delicious hot flapjacks, handing them round to us on a fish-slice. A hot greasy flapjack is not easy to hold and several dropped to the ground. Grannie sat in the carriage, so we had to gather round it away from the shelter of the rock. We had unhitched the horse and left him free to graze as it was obvious that this picnic was going to be a lengthy affair. Then at long last came the tea. Oh! for the thermos flask of modern man, but one could not have lived through the afternoon without the fire.

Then, miraculously, the mackerel came in and the black muddy water was alive with silver fish. Uncle John manufactured a hook out of a safety-pin which, attached to the carriage whip and baited with winkle, soon caught one fish, providing silver streaks of skin to catch some more. While all eyes were turned on the fishing, the horse, bored and cold, wandered off towards home. Then the rain began in earnest, and the aunts packed while I went after him. When he saw me he quickened his pace and I had to scramble over a bramble-covered stone wall and squelch through some bog in order to cut him off. He stopped for me only because his reins were twisted round his legs.

Grannie sat dozing in the Glass Case surrounded by her daughters, frantic at the thought of the cold she would catch, but it was Uncle John I was sorry for. His cheerful face as he tucked the rug round his mother belied the fact that he could hardly stand or haul himself up onto the box. The fishing had saved the day for me as I became oblivious to cold and wet when engaged in the chase. I ought to have been a seal.

Our most exciting picnics were in the sailing boat to the islands. There were four within our range. The two nearest, Turbot and Inishturk, were inhabited, with a little school on the former but no chapel. Then, farther out, uninhabited Cruagh with its high hill and terrifying gulf between fearsome rock at the north end and strange strip of white marble to the west. High Island, the most difficult to land on, had the remains of an oratory and beehive huts from the sixth or seventh century. St Brendan and his monks are said to have been there, but his letters have been lost and his journeys were not written about until the eighth century. Many of these beehive huts up and down the west coast were built by monks who spread out from the Aran Islands in the sixth century. It was the age of learning and marvellous works of art, such as the Book of Kells and the Cross of Cong.

High Island was known as the island of birds and is still a remarkable place for them. Hundreds of Mother Carey's Chickens or storm petrels sweep in just after sunset to their nests, hidden under rocks with the one egg. The nests smell as they are oily birds; in the Hebrides they made candles from them with a rush passed through as a wick.

After dark, clouds of Manx Shearwaters would come in, making a tremendous noise, but of course we were always gone by then. We had to keep one eye on the weather because the landing was so difficult that two men had to stay in the boat, mooring being impossible. We were in the *Dreadnaught*, built in our barn yard at the beginning of the century by a man called Gorham, assisted by Patrick Clogherty. The *Dreadnaught* was twenty feet long with mainsail and jib and did very well with plenty of wind, but many a night we had to row home with an oar and a half, as one oar could take only half a stroke before hitting the mast.

On one dreadful day, we caught some mackerel and Aunt Edyth set about cooking them in a tin on the boat. It caught fire, the stove was thrown overboard and the whole day had to be lived through without even a cup of tea.

The island people were very shy of strangers, so as we approached, nothing could be seen but a few men well back from the shore and a few children's faces peering from behind rocks, boys and girls dressed alike in long grey tweed dresses. Later a few men would show up and even help with the mooring of the boat. They were paradisial days bathing on the white sand and wandering over the islands, beautiful in themselves with the black currachs turned up like black beetles along the shore, from which one got the most magnificent view of the cloud-shadowed mountains across the sea, alternately vivid turquoise, inky or pale blue To the north were other islands, backed by the towering cliffs of Clare Island, and on a clear day one could see Achill.

One year we had changed the colour of our boat and sails, and, on nearing Turbot Island, were greeted by a shower of stones from slings. Aunt Edyth stood up in her scarlet cloak, was recognized and all was well: the islanders explained later to our boatmen that they thought it was a trick of the police, who were after the bit of drink they were making, which came in to town under the potatoes on Saturdays.

We seldom went to High Island as the weather had to be very good but supply enough wind to take our heavy boat along. The men would have preferred to fish, but we always wanted to land and explore the misty islands that we looked at so often from Errislannan: the 'Islands of the Blest' or 'Hy Brasil' of ancient legend. It was as though one were landing on another world.

The journeys home from High Island were often alarming. Sometimes the wind rose suddenly and we were collected to stand on the slippery rock, waiting for a wave to lift the boat near enough for us to jump in; the frightened boatmen treating Aunt Edyth like a sack of potatoes, since she could not help herself for laughing. Donald and I were as scared as the boatmen as the heavy clumsy boat leaned over, relying on the rocks below the floorboards to weigh her up again, while Aunt Edyth would lie full length blocking any deck-space, sublimely ignorant of sailing or the sea, enjoying the spray and the rocking.

Coming in among the rocks and seaweed at Glendowie with no lights of any kind was a slow business, and transferring ourselves and mountains of picnic gear and fish to the dinghy or on to the loose stone, seaweed-covered quay could be equally dangerous. One night we hit a rock as we made for the light we thought was in Glendowie window, but Great-aunt Alice, having walked along the shore with a lantern, was sitting on a rock like a lighthouse or a Cornish wrecker, and we heard her voice floating over the water after the bang: 'Are you safe, my precious?' and Phedora's high sad voice answering: 'Yes, mother dear, but we'd be safer if the light were in the window.'

The men were furious, but expressed their feelings in Irish.

CHAPTER 12

Alcock and Brown; Sundays at Home

On Sunday, 15 June 1919, we were on our unwilling way to church in Errislannan when the Rector came hurrying up on a motor bicycle shouting, 'No service today. Alcock and Brown are above.' He pointed to the sky and we heard an aeroplane, then saw it above Clifden Castle across the bay, possibly hoping to land on the steep sloping field. Then it made for the Marconi Station. Alcock later wrote, 'We fired Very signals and circled and to our dismay, what we took to be a green field turned out to be a bog.' Alcock bumped his head as they came down in some soft bog, missing rocks by a few feet. The nose of the plane went in, smashing the lower wings and leaving the tail standing in the air.

It must have been a depressing view that met their eyes, the first land since leaving Newfoundland, sixteen hours and twenty-seven minutes earlier; the first men to cross the Atlantic by air. Nothing but bog all round them without an habitation in sight. They were cold and exhausted – Brown had been scraping ice off the wings on the way over – but it was not long before the soldiers from the Marconi Station came to their aid and took them back to their huts. We could see all this as we beat up the horse, hurrying over Ballinaboy Hill. In that dark land of heather and inky blue of Errisbeg, the white plane stood out distinctly. We were joined by a few others as we trudged across the bog, but most people were at Mass and in their Sunday clothes, and gumboots were needed. Without newspapers or radio we did not realize the special importance of this plane. It appeared to be made of canvas tied together with string, an impression that was not much altered by seeing it later in the Aeronautical Museum in London as a milestone in the history of aviation.

As the wings were broken we began pulling the plane apart, taking pieces of canvas and wood. Squares of this tough canvas crowned little haycocks for many years to come. Then we went home for our cameras, bringing all our souvenirs, some of which I have still. We took photographs from different angles with the family posed in front of the plane. In the afternoon a reporter's small plane came from Galway and nosedived into the bog also, so the two planes stood side by side, tails up. After a gap of fifty years I was asked to describe all this on television and the old photographs came out very well on screen.

According to Alcock, the soldiers did not believe they had flown from America, but the Marconi men must have been expecting the plane at least to pass over, as it was supposed to land in England. Later that evening they were taken down the track behind the petrol engine, which had taken the place of the old steam loco. Some iron rails were laid out over the bog to the plane, and eventually it was brought to London and new lower wings put on.

Nothing marked the spot for forty years. At times Americans came and looked for a memorial; one offered to contribute £10 but Aunt Jane looked at him coldly, saying it was not her responsibility. Now a large stone tail fin has been put up on top of Ballinaboy, two miles from where the plane landed. Coachloads of litter-dropping tourists come and the bins overflow with their food and paper on our lovely hill. A white stone beacon has also been erected nearby.

That bit of bogland has made history before. At the beginning of the century, Senator Marconi thought it would be the best place to experiment with wireless telegraphy as there was nothing between the bog and America. The railway from Galway to Clifden was working then. He stayed with my grandmother at Errislannan Manor while he was planning it, as she and his mother, an Irish girl, had been friends when they were young.

The first wires went up on kites until some wooden masts were brought in on Darby Green's hooker just in front of my house. They were dragged up the rocks to the road and then up the newly made track. These were the first wireless masts ever and it is curious to think of them arriving on the ancient sailing boat.

One day before the track was made, some Marconi men were struggling up the grassy path when they met Mrs Conneely coming down with her ass and creels full of turf. They asked to borrow her ass to carry their heavy equipment, unloaded the turf, and the precious instruments arrived by ass and creels. They gave her a golden sovereign, the station's first payment to a local.

In 1921 a man from the area with some friends in the IRA who had a grievance about work, went across the bog and set fire to the station, and so it closed and 300 men, who cut turf for the fuelling of the station, were left unemployed.

Now there is nothing to show that it was ever there except a few slabs of concrete. The bog has crept up and covered the beginnings of what has become the most powerful influence in the world. As one stands on that lonely moorland, there is no sign of human habitation, only black turf cuttings in the heather, many lakes with white water-lilies and the dark blue side of Errisbeg.

In September 1978 a BBC television crew of six arrived at the quay and took me up that rocky, worn-out track to show them where the plane had actually landed. I stood on a heather-covered hillock in my Connemara jersey, jeans and gumboots, and told them about that day sixty-odd years before. They filmed the lonely ruins of the Marconi Station, the empty bogland and the mountains, and broadcast it to the world. How little my brother and I had imagined this as we ran barefoot across the bog to the plane all those years ago.

*   *   *

Sundays: for us the most hated day of the week; best clothes; no expeditions to the shore; everyone tired and cross after cooking a huge Sunday lunch, which took until four or five to clear up, while the sun shone invitingly out of doors.

When I was young I thought out many schemes for evading church, such as last-minute pain or sickness, or soaking my feet in puddles on the way. There seemed no connection between church and God, whereas wandering about on the hill or on the shore I was very conscious of him. The family were the only congregation except in August, when our tenants helped to fill a few pews. A senile old Rector of eighty-six came seven miles to take the service, and sometimes brought with him his much younger wife, who had been a school-teacher but who then thought she was the Virgin Mary, and was so alarming that even our formidable Great-aunt Alice went down on her knees in the drawing-room to her.

The Rector took the service standing at the east end, and we sat in one of the three square pews at the west end with a fire behind us, two comfortable armchairs, and plenty of cushions and musty footstools. When a storm was rattling every slate and creaking every beam, we could see his mouth opening and shutting, but could not hear a word. Between him and us stretched a vast sea of empty pews that had once seated two hundred people.

The pew next to ours was occupied by an old wheezy harmonium on which Aunt Jane accompanied her solos, pedalling furiously to make the music drown the wind and the belching of the instrument.

Because there was no one to sing, our advertisements in *The Irish Times* for a cook always ran:

'Wanted: singing Protestant cook ...'

We got one called Mrs Keegan, who could not cook but had a voice like a corncrake, and who sang every word of every hymn in Aunt Jane's ear as she pedalled on. One Sunday on our return from church, we were greeted by a smell of burning. Mrs Keegan rushed to the kitchen, flung open the oven door and tipped a trayful of burnt potatoes over the kitchen floor. A harsh shout met us: 'To hell with the bloody roasters! why can't ye have thim boiled?' From then on, the hot potatoes given to departing guests to keep their hands warm were offered as 'bloody roasters!'

The third square pew beyond the harmonium was occupied by Great-aunt Alice when she was in Errislannan. As there was generally a feud going on, she did not greet us, but glared across the intervening space with her huge eyes surrounded by grease-paint. It was very uncomfortable, especially as later on, when I was in my teens, I came to like her. Torn between the two factions, I left the church with my grandmother, to be followed by a hiss of 'Judas' from Great-aunt Alice.

Saturday afternoon was given up most unwillingly to cleaning the church, and choosing the hymns which had to be practised. No cross was allowed inside the church, so a vase of flowers adorned the table. At Eastertime we decorated the window-sills of the pairs of beautiful tall lancet windows, which were filled with plain glass, so one could see the heather and gorse or the bare winter trees outside. One Easter I made a cross of arum lilies and hung it on the pulpit. The next morning it was thrown outside the church, so I hurled it over the churchyard wall and refused to go to church for some time, making it an excuse because I disliked going so much. This caused great trouble and I was very unpopular. The grieved silence was quite awful and I felt guilty, but persisted. Eventually a new parson came and a picnic was arranged on the coral strand where he was to convert me. The aunts wandered tactfully away and he tried, but failed. However, he did persuade me to go to church for the sake of the aunts. Later, when I went to London, I was thankful to find that the other girls in the Cecilia Club thought of nothing on Sunday mornings but washing, ironing and mending for the week.

Considering the vast chasm that yawns between Protestants and Catholics in Ireland, I think our local Catholics were very good to us. Occasionally the boys broke the church windows, or let cattle into the churchyard, but only once was there serious trouble, and this was caused by the mission that came every year to Clifden, with the intention of inflaming the people against the Protestants. After one of these meetings, boys dug up my grandfather's grave and scattered his bones. Aunt Jane wrote to the priest and he denounced the perpetrators from the altar and sent them to apologize. They arrived at the hall door and stood very sheepishly in front of Aunt Jane, who took the opportunity to preach them a sermon on morals and manners. I listened from an upstairs window with much enjoyment, but it had upset the aunts very much. The boys tidied up the grave and nothing like that ever happened again.

When I was about seventeen, the church in Clifden decided to have a fête in the field near the harbour, and my mother was roped in to do the fancy-work stall. A heavy burden this was to all of us. I was forced into making a tea-cosy, and every stitch went in with fury. Mother and Swannie worked away and at last boxes of unwantable goods were ready.

We were staying in Glendowie at the time, the cottage whose walls are washed by the sea; in fact sometimes the floors were carpeted with seaweed, so it was natural that we should go to town by boat. We loaded up and set off in our best clothes, quite forgetting that there was a spring tide. We arrived in the harbour and grounded about thirty feet from the steps. Thirty feet of black mud! Time went on while the boat settled down even more comfortably for her long wait. At last I got out, tucked my skirt into my bloomers and, carrying my shoes and stockings and a box of goods, waded ashore. The others followed, staggering under boxes and baskets, and forgetting the mooring rope. Back I went, and as the rope was exceedingly long it trailed in the mud and messed up the hands and dresses of all who went near it.

Things were so bad that we sat on the steps and laughed and I thought hopefully that would be the end of the fête for us, but alas, no! A cheery voice hailed us from above: 'Oh there you are, welcome travellers. We were so afraid you were not coming. We will all lend a hand and have your stall ready in no time.' Looking up I saw the Rector's large black paunch and then his crimson face and black hat. My heart sank as I was made to put on my stockings over the mud, which showed through.

At last the horrible procession, led by the Rector, started for the festive field. Mother was giggling but I felt sulky, and stood behind the stall aching with boredom. There was no one under forty or fifty, and all were beaming. At last I saw a shooting competition surrounded by town boys, so I went over and spent all my money on targets. At the end of the day I had won, but the prize was suitable only for a boy, so the Rector dashed away to the fancy-work stall and came back waving my tea-cosy. I was speechless with rage, but there was nothing to be done but to give it a watery grave on the way home. I dangled my muddy legs over the stern, and watched it floating away, wondering whether a mermaid would use it in her coral cave. Years later, when painting the Mermaid of Zennor, I was tempted to put it in, but finally turned it into a large sea-urchin.

The only winter entertainment was an occasional home-made concert in aid of church funds. One I remember had as performers two elderly sisters who looked like twins. They were dressed in brown and had the name of Mothersill. One played the piano and her sister whistled the tune, with only her head showing over the top of the piano. Whistling is unbecoming, and very dry work, so she stopped in the middle and, in a secretive way with much use of her eyes, said 'I must get a drink,' and crept away off the stage.

I heard a snort behind me and turned to find two young soldiers doubled up, and in the hand of one a long strand of my hair, which he politely asked if he might keep. I felt better after that.

The drive home in the dark I enjoyed. I sat on the box with the man who had spent the evening happily in a pub being a Roman Catholic, and who had not been expected to come to the concert. He obviously hoped the horse knew the way home, so I took the reins and loved watching the walls and bushes lit by the carriage lamps, and the moon's path on the sea, and rocks turned into quite different shapes by the shadows. As we went over Ballinaboy Hill, the moon changed sides, but still made a path from the islands to the shore. Errislannan lay a black silhouette surrounded by a pale sea as we followed the white road down the hill and finally through the dark tunnel of trees to the front door.

CHAPTER 13

The Galley, *and the Lake*

I annexed a small green boat for myself called *The Galley*: nine feet long, broad in the beam and safe for one. It was my pride and joy for forty years and gave me the tremendous pleasure of independence, in that I could row myself to town instead of having to walk. The intense happiness I felt when on the sea in the only visible boat owed something to a touch of fear that the sea might be too strong for me, the sight of the mountains and sky changing at sunset, the continued vigilance required to cope with the fishing-line, and, as I had no engine or sails, the silence. There was also the realization of the sea-bed below the dark green water, the forest of rhythmically waving seaweeds, the patches of light sand, all teeming with life. Fish of all sizes and shapes, and once a shark, longer than my boat, glided along beside me, its fin cutting the water like a sail, which quite spoilt my fun for that evening. Sometimes a seal with its round brown eyes and its 'faithful dog' look, followed me, but this meant no more mackerel that night.

If the weather were fine, I went to town in the boat on Saturday mornings to do the shopping. In those days there was enough water at Clifden Quay for hookers and large boats to come in, but later a boat with a cargo of cement sank and blocked the main channel, and mud accumulated. I remember the wrecks of large fishing boats rotting by the quay. This fine quay and the great warehouses for storing grain were built in 1822, and later Clifden, almost unbelievably, became the biggest corn market in Ireland. Everything was carried by sea as there were no roads, so the quay where my great-grandparents remembered the warehouses full and big coal boats coming in must have been the centre of activity.

I was often the only person on the quay and used to sit in a high window of one of the old warehouses and draw the harbour and town. On Saturday mornings it was very different, as about six currachs would come in from the islands and the men used to pretend to race me to the quay. The currachs were black, round-bottomed, canvas-covered boats made by the men themselves. They took very high seas if you knew how to ride them, as they floated on the surface like a bubble, instead of cutting through the water. There were generally two men and two or three women to each boat, and creels of fish and potatoes. The women sat on the wet bottom as there were no thwarts for them, the boats being used for gathering seaweed or bringing turf to the islands. After helping the men to turn the boat over on the grass to dry out, they slung the creels on to their backs, the rope across their chests being run through a piece of wood. The men sometimes carried creels, but often walked away freely up the hill to spend their day in the pubs or sitting on window-sills.

In town the women sat on the creels, stooping forward, draped in their big black shawls, talking with their heads together like the witches of Endor. The fish lay on the sacks on the ground, dusty and fly-ridden. Everyone in the market would stand in groups hardly moving, smoking pipes or chewing seaweed, which required a lot of spitting. Their immobility was a great help to me, as I used to sit and draw them from the windows of the Railway Hotel – now the Bay Hotel. This market-place was a small lake with fish in it before the D'Arcys built the town of about three hundred houses between 1815 and 1835.

Nearly every shop in Clifden had a bar; even the drapery stores had one hidden away behind hanging lines of clothes. I felt greatly daring when one hot day I went in and asked for a glass of beer. The woman hastily hung a protective curtain across, and turned another customer away. Her behaviour showed more clearly than any words how I had let the side down. I am sure she whispered sympathy for my aunts into every ear that came in afterwards. On other occasions I tried several shops and at last found a welcoming publican, but I was firmly taken upstairs and put in the parlour, where my drink was served. This unused but spotless room was lush with rugs and antimacassars, little mats on tables, holy pictures and statuettes and spotless frilly lace curtains over the windows. I enjoyed the polite conversation of my hostess, which was carried on against the thumps and shouts of the waiting customers below. I also enjoyed the rest on days when I had walked into town and was hot and tired.

The open space where the island women sat had as a centre-piece a square, whitewashed, castellated building which was the men's lavatory; round the walls of this was an iron bar to which many donkeys were tied, head to the wall, in hot sun or rain, without food or drink all day. The island women and the donkeys are no longer there now and the open space is filled with visitors' cars.

For the return journey, when the tide was right, the islanders came down to the quay; generally the women arrived first and got the boats into the water. The men were often too drunk to row, so the women took to the oars, the men lying in the bottom with the sacks of flour and groceries on top of them. It was often a much harder pull home against the west wind, and one hoped that the men would have recovered sufficiently to carry the boat up the shore. The competence of the island women in their boats contrasted with local women, very few of whom could row and who did not go out fishing.

If for any reason the islanders could not go home, either because it was too rough or because there was fishing to do, they turned a currach over on its side and used it for a tent, lighting a fire in front of it.

*   *   *

The lake: all our lives we were influenced by the lake, for our first glance out of the window in the morning rested on its changeable waters and we knew the weather for the day. When grey and misty, inspiration was lacking and my spirits sank; bright blue water meant cheerfulness and quick dressing; a dead calm, with every reed and cloud reflected in the water, was so strange and beautiful I could not leave the window, but when rain lashed down and the lake was grey and rough, a deep depression settled upon me at the thought of the household chores that would be gently suggested; best of all was a sunny stormy day, its dark blue water dotted with white horses and spray flying, which carried me downstairs with a rush to eat breakfast and be off to the most westerly point of Errislannan, where I could see the breakers rising near the islands a hundred feet into the air and the great waves come surging towards the land. I watched for a time to see exactly how near it would be safe to go and then, wedged into a rock crevice, deafened by the noise and oblivious to the whole world, I stayed splashed and happy all morning.

On a good fishing morning, very early, I would try to get my rod and leave the house without being heard, but Aunt Edyth's ears were sharp and she did so much like being rowed round the lake while she sat happily in the stern with her rod tucked under her arm, dragging the line behind her, an old fly on the end that some visitor had left behind. One was always told to carry her rod with the tail fly stuck in the cork handle and prop it up in the porch ready for her next sortie. This meant that the rod had a permanent bend, but she seemed to have an understanding with the trout and often brought in one for each person. She could not take them off the hook or row the boat, so needed a compliant companion like Uncle John, who seemed quite content to do all that was necessary, whereas I was itching to fish myself.

I liked to drift down the lake alone when fishing, especially in the late evening. There used to be plenty of white trout – or salmon trout, as we called them – so long as we kept the stream open to the sea, but a storm would hurl great boulders over the entrance and it was such a struggle to open it up again that we finally gave up and now there are only brown trout to be had.

The lake was like heaven; another world was entered by stepping into the boat. I loved to set out on a windless day when the house and the trees stood trembling upside-down in the water and the blue hydrangeas on the shore preened themselves in the glassy depths; on a stormy day they turned their heavy dollopy heads away and looked at the house instead.

In spring the trees stood in a mist of bluebells and in autumn among rusty red leaves, while more golden showers fell through the air. From the boat I liked to look at the house, so warm and bright in sunshine, so dark and grey in the rain, but best of all I liked to watch it when the lamps were lit, and know that the family were sitting round the blazing turf fire in the soft glow.

Sometimes I would row to the far end of the lake and force the boat through the white water-lilies and I can remember nothing more beautiful than the lilies lying on the brown water with their yellow hearts open to the sun. I would hang over the side of the boat mesmerized by their loveliness, then row into the reeds until I was invisible. Dragon-flies whirred about, often alighting on the boat, little damsel-flies red and blue flitted by or clung to the reeds. Birds chirped and white clouds passed over the top of my shivering green enclosure. I would hear the cattle squelching into the shallows below the old graveyard to stand sleepily musing, immobile, except for the flip of the tail at some offending insect, and the clockwork moorhens would dart about, surprised to see me. I would hear the ducks waddling down the lane from the yard and splashing into the lake, and the rattle of the pails as someone came down to the well for drinking water. This well in the wood, by the lake, was a thing of beauty. A dome of large rough stones sheltered it from falling leaves and there was a flat stone in front of it on which one stood while dipping the bucket into the clear water, where often a frog swam in the green shady depths. The walls, inside and out, were covered in mosses, differing in colour and texture, with little hart's tongue and maidenhair ferns growing out of the spaces between the stones. The tall trees of the wood, uncluttered by undergrowth, stood behind it and the well-water overflowed into the lake.

From this far end of the lake I could see the old round graveyard, almost in the lake, so overcrowded it rose to a mound in the centre round the seventh-century chapel. The nettles and brambles now climb above the walls and the Stations of the Cross can no longer be followed.

The outlet stream from the lake to the sea long ago turned the only path to the graveyard into a swamp of bog and rushes, and the coffin-bearers performed feats of agility, as they felt for a stone or plank of wood to step on, the mourners balancing and hopping precariously after them. I'm afraid this used to amuse us when young, as it looked like a ballet of dark figures in shawls jumping forward, with hands linked. And the keening that went on! Only a few old women could do it, but the lake acted as a sounding-board and the weird unearthly wails carried for miles across the land as they rocked themselves and cried to the spirit world.

From one angle or another, most of Errislannan can be seen reflected in the lake. The distant mountains, the Look-out Hill, the house and woods, the meadows, and the glorious pageantry of sunrises and sunsets; Venus makes a pathway over the water to the house, and the famous comet of the eighties stretched its flaming tail across it. Aunt Jane and Aunt Edyth as children were brought from their beds to see this, and Aunt Jane wrote in her diary when she was an old woman that she 'had never seen such magnificence' in her life: 'The star part was over the croquet lawn and the tail stretched right across the lake, the calm water giving us two of this wonder.' I am glad that when I gazed at the romantic face of the moon from the Lake Room window, I did not know that men would walk upon it and leave all their untidy bits and pieces.

Still in my boat I would be recalled to the present by the beating of the church bell on the tree in front of the house, which meant dinner. If something had to be eaten at once, Aunt Jane would come out and give the bell a proper rattling, but if there were no hurry a boy or maid would come and pick up the stone, giving a few half-hearted bangs. Then I would row home with suitable speed and with no qualms of conscience that I had been in heaven while others sweated in the kitchen.

CHAPTER 14

Johnnie Dan, Val Conneely,
Anne Gorham, and Mrs Molloy

The western face of the Look-out Hill is composed of enormous bare grey rocks; from the sea one can see nothing else and yet cattle graze on the sweet salty grass in the hollows. All the earth has been stripped by the fury of the Atlantic gales and on the shore the sea has eaten away all but the hardest rock. On one of these is a white beacon, a valuable landmark for any boat finding its way among the reefs and islands into Clifden Bay. From the top of the hill there is a magnificent view in all directions. To the east across the bay are the Twelve Bens, the mountain range that forms a backcloth to everything in Errislannan; to the west the Atlantic and the islands. The highest point is marked by a pile of stones, the remains of the coastguard's hut, which I built into a shelter so that I could sit there for hours and see everything that went on in Errislannan. The climb up the heather-covered hill, ablaze with low gorse, is pure enchantment; there is a feeling of space and cleanliness that I have never known in any other place.

I sometimes had the company of Johnnie Dan Conneely, the shepherd, who knew the history of every house and person and could tell tales of everyone who had been in Errislannan during the last seventy years. Johnnie was amusing, very loyal, and a good cattle and sheep man. From the hill he could see the whole of his domain, so he sat with his dog and his pipe for hours on end in complete contentment: 'We are what suns and winds and waters make us.'

As a young man he had gone to America in desperation owing rent, leaving his wife and family entirely dependent on the farm of a few small rocky fields. I found a letter he wrote to Great-uncle Walter imploring him not to turn his wife out. First he enquires politely about the health of our family, and then explains that he is working for a company which employs 18,000 men, the largest in America.

> ... I intend to go home next July if I am living at that time. I may have money saved. Dont think I came away to deprive you of your rent, it was the dull times. I expect to be as clear a tenant as any on your estate. I will give you up the two holdings near Coronagh, my wife is not able to manage them times is so bad. Wait till July for the rent as my wife will

have cattle to sell and I will have money saved. I expect you will see me justified and I pledge my hand word. I hope you wont disturb my wife and my children out of my home, it cost me a good deal to build. I hope you wont give the pleasure to any man living as to let them have my house. So I depend on you. You have known me since I left the cradle and I have good confidence in you. You will show my wife justice by making a good slash wall between the holdings. There is plenty of stone on the spot. You can show my wife how it is done. With three men on it, it should take about a week. Do you see it done and show it to my father. I send the money, you to give me third seaweed, me to pay third rates and county, less me to be allowed half poor rates in the rent.

I remain your sincere friend
John Conneely Dan

He came back and had two more wives before he died in 1940. When he proposed to his last wife, our cook, Bridget, he was still wearing deepest mourning for wife number two, which meant black shirt and collar. Aunt Jane wrote: 'After a time he picked up his heart again and courted our cook. While she hesitated a woman came into the manor kitchen and said, "Take him Astore, take him, he treats them well and he buries them decent." ... He was a very ardent lover and it was most inconvenient. So that is where Norah Christine came from.'

Johnnie would stay sober for months if he did not go to town, but when he went to a fair or on other business, he was sometimes lost to the world for several days. Our aim was to load him on to the side-car in town, and keep going at such a pace that he could not get off. However, when we reached Ballinaboy Hill and slowed to a walk, he would often roll off roaring and make for town again. One day I followed him staggering down the drive under a pitchfork of hay. He stopped to sing and then fell gently on to the hay and settled for a sleep. I covered him with some of the hay and left him to recover.

He was buried in the round graveyard by the lake in the snow, and waiting for the priest the boys played snowballing to keep warm. I painted this funeral as though from a boat on the lake, with Johnnie's hill and his cattle in the background. I missed him very much; he had helped me over hours of loneliness on the Look-out Hill in my youth, when companionship was sorely needed.

Johnnie's second family were the ones we knew best and they have been our lifelong friends. The two girls, Mollie and Annie, were both deaf and dumb. The boy, Tommie, grew up to be a tall strong man, very good at shooting and fishing. He was responsible for locking one of our family into the pantry and throwing the key into the lake. Following this episode, Tommie, with strong encouragement from my grandfather, went to Australia, where one night when he was drunk he fell out of a boat and was drowned.

Mollie was a tall strong girl, with rosy cheeks, large grey eyes and a mass of dark curly hair which stood out round her head. She was always laughing and playing practical jokes, and was a very hard worker, digging the turf and potatoes and making the hay. The heavy work mostly fell to her, as Annie was thin and delicate; her mother died when she was born. Their grandmother brought them up and their Uncle Tom always lived with them as Johnnie had now married Bridget and lived nearby. The 'Grannie' was a wonderful woman; very intelligent and industrious, always dressed in neat black with a pretty apron. When we were coming to tea or to a picnic near their house the apron was shining white with frills. As well as the usual spinning-wheel, they had a loom for weaving coarse tweed; most people took their wool to the local weaver. There was also a rather frightening great-aunt of one hundred and eight, who sat by the fire but never spoke.

After one of Johnnie's longer bouts he was persuaded to take 'the pledge', which helped until the next time. One day Aunt Jane had arrived on a visit very wet and cold. The grannie offered her whiskey, which my aunt refused, saying she had taken the pledge when twelve years old. Grannie replied, 'Aha Miss Janey, thanks be to Almighty God,when I go out I can always command myself.'

Mollie, Annie and Tom always made us very welcome and it was the first house we went to when we came home from England. They gave us a lovely tea in the room, exactly as diaries record two generations of my family had been entertained as children. Mollie and Annie never sat down with visitors but entertained us in all sorts of ways. We soon learned to speak on our fingers, but their miming was so expressive it was easy to carry on conversations.

As children, Mollie and Annie had been sent to Dublin by the nuns, and taught to read and write. This was the greatest help to them and they generally carried a bit of pencil, writing on a stone or wood or anything that came to hand. One cold wet evening I met Annie by the shore when the tide was out and she wrote with a stick on the sand a lot of unpleasant things about a neighbour – which were true but best not left for the world to see. I delayed and delayed as the tide came up to wash it out and walked over the rest. It had been a relief to Annie and her tears dried up, but I have never forgotten her bent grey figure on the grey sand in the misty evening light.

In later years Mollie got arthritis in her hip and suffered agonies of pain. This was when reading books and the neighbours' calls were such a help. The sisters always knew more about what was going on than anyone else and several times a year they wrote all the news to me in England, giving dates and remembering anniversaries of their own and our family.

Their house had the usual loose stone walls whitewashed inside and out, with a heavily thatched roof which kept it warm and dry. The roof was made of branches – gone black as ebony with the smoke – which supported the heather scraws, which in turn supported the thatch. There were two rooms and one end of the kitchen was boarded off for the cow, which also helped to keep it warm. There was always a good turf fire with the pot and kettle hanging from the crane, and two pigs used to lie like cats with their noses resting on the hearthstone. All their bread was made in the pot oven on the hearth. Hens were everywhere and flew round one's head like seagulls when they were shooed out for us to sit down.

There was a dog tied up in a corner which we were very sorry for, but I think they relied on him to let them know if anyone were outside. One moonlit night Mollie had gone in to bed and Annie was raking the fire when the dog began pulling at her skirt. She hit out at him, but he persisted and she went into the room to find Mollie, who had been kneeling at her prayers, lying on the floor. The moonlight was on her face and Annie knew that she was dead.

Annie ran half a mile across bog, heather and rocks, to her half-sister's house but when they heard the banging they were afraid to come out. Then they recognized Annie's cries and came running back with her. It was arranged that she should sleep with them and go home for the days, but eventually she lived with her half-sister altogether and the dear old house fell to ruin.

I could not bear to go near the place for some years, but when I did I felt as sad as if I had lost my home. The roof had gone but the dresser was too big to come through the door and remained there, with much of Mollie's painting on it: she decorated it with flowers and animals, constantly changing the colours. The mantelpiece was still there, which had held a statue of Our Lady in the middle with a photograph of their granny on one side and of our granny on the other. There had always been big pictures of saints and the Sacred Heart, Holy Water on the wall and a red light burning. I remembered the two big tent beds along the wall, a table in the window and two small wooden chairs. The deep little window was hidden by a geranium which allowed only a green light to come through. The high shelf in the kitchen had as a centre-piece a tin shaped like the trunk of a tree but with very little paint left on it. My brother and I had given it to them when we were children, full of biscuits, and it had been used for generations as a tea-caddy.

Along the wall had stood the remains of the spinning-wheel and the red bench, which always held the bucket of spring water. Behind the fireplace was a loft over the room, where ladders and the old loom had been stored. Some of the roof-branches and scraws were still in place and I remembered the day I had come to find Uncle Tom thatching the roof. I spoke of the quality of the thatch he was using and he replied in his deep booming voice, 'Aha Alannah,

Burmount Manor on the river Slaney, Wexford: the Heather family home before Errislannan.

Errislannan Manor, Connemara (water-colour *c*.1855). Allanah Heather's great grandmother planted the trees; St Flannan's seventh-century church is to the left of the painting.

AH's mother, Florence Harrison,
in Warwickshire, England.

AH's father, Walter, equipped for a fancy-
dress ball at Lissadell, Co. Sligo.

Florence Heather in the Errislannan garden.

Walter Heather at Knockadoo, Co. Sligo.

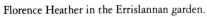

AH's sister, Kathleen.

AH's brother, Donald, in the Loyal North Lancashire Regiment uniform.

Alannah Heather in riding-habit.

Val Conneely, 'the old man of the sea'.

The islanders in Clifden market-place during the 1930s.

The ruins of Clifden Castle, once home of the D'Arcys.

The first aeroplane to cross the Atlantic, a twin-engined Vickers Vimy, landed in the Marconi bog near Errislannan on Sunday morning 15 June 1919. AH's Uncle George, Aunt Minnie and the MacPhersons (foreground) were photographed that afternoon before the lower wings were dismembered for souvenirs. The Marconi Radio Station (below), Clifden, 1890–1921, the first erected, used kites not masts to support the wires; Marconi stayed at Errislannan when it was built. It was burned by the IRA. Pilot John Alcock and navigator Arthur Brown took the 'Marconi Express' in the evening, travelling via narrow-gauge railway to Galway and London.

The cottage at La Fregondée, Sark, in May 1934, which was used as a studio and retreat by AH from 1929 to 1960, with a gap of ten years during her marriage.

The interior of the cottage-studio at Sark.

AH outside Errislannan Manor with son Donald and husband Roger in the donkey-chair drawn by Belinda.

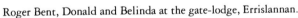
Roger Bent, Donald and Belinda at the gate-lodge, Errislannan.

Donald in the green nine-foot *Galley*, which he learned to row from the age of three.

Derrygimlagh Quay, Ballyconneely, and AH's currach, built by Patrick Clogherty.

'tis sedge that I found on a faraway mountain, but the way was long, and for that reason I have little, very little but 'twill serve; thanks be to God!' The faraway mountain was a small hill half a mile away, but I could see Tom in his light-coloured homespun and old black pointed hat, following the ass and creels with his slow stride over rocks and bogland, as it chose its own way to the hill. Returning, the yellow sedge would be piled high across the ass's back as it came down from the 'faraway mountain'. The next day Tom would recline at his ease on the rounded ridge of the thatch, settling the ropes that Mollie and Annie would be throwing over it; fastening them down with stones against the winter storms which sweep in from the Atlantic on to the gable end. The little house is mentioned in our diaries for a hundred years.

Tom was a great story-teller of real adventures but he excelled in ghost stories, which he told in such a way one was forced to believe them. I still feel the grey woman at Ballinaboy Bridge and the white pony that attacked everyone at night as it galloped along the road. It was hard on such a superb talker to live always with two deaf and dumb nieces, but they made a contented household and the handicap could be ignored.

I was too shy to call on many of the Errislannan families uninvited unless I had a message to give, but there were a few old people left alone for their last years who were my friends and always made me feel welcome. Despite their isolation they never complained. I suppose they filled their days remembering when their homes were crowded with children; their stories peopled Errislannan for me with those who had lived generations before in the same houses. They worked as long as they were able, after which a neighbour did their turf and hay for a few years. Then they retired into their houses and a neighbour would bring their pension and food from town, until eventually they died, often alone. Everyone for miles around would go to their funerals, then the house would fall to ruin and the neighbours graze the land until it went back into bog. I can recall looking round Errislannan from a hill with Joe King, who remembered when there had been twenty-five more families and every inch of the land was cultivated.

One of these old men, called Val Conneely, lived alone at the extreme end of the peninsula in a thatched house, sheltered from the sea by a rock. His eyes and nose showed through a mass of hair crowned by a cap; his clothes were in tatters, his knees showed through, but he did not seem to mind the cold. He sat by the shore, sheltered by the sea wall, day after day so I always knew where to find him and spent many hours sharing his patch of grass. He liked reading so I took him papers and books and we always found plenty to talk about.

His family had been described to me as 'tall and beautiful, the daughters, with red curly hair, who danced along the roads singing'. His eldest son, Val, had gone to America and left no address, so that he was as though dead, but if old Val made no will the land would belong to him. One daughter was determined that this should not happen and came over from Scotland when she heard that her father was very ill, intending to take him to a solicitor and have a will made. They got a side-car to the door, but as they were hoisting old Val on to it he died. He was buried in a habit with the Sacred Heart, a pair of white gloves and some visitor's tennis shoes.

He called himself the old man of the sea, because as he was about to be born, his mother embarked for the eight miles into town in a boat. When in Clifden Bay she knew the baby was coming and was landed on a rock, where she produced Val. Bundling him up in her shawl she carried him to Mollie and Annie's house, where the old grannie looked after them. He had little comfort coming into the world and none going out of it.

Dear old Val, he was very kind to me and a good friend. One day he went into his house, which latterly was in such a bad state that he could not invite anyone inside, and brought out a pound note. 'If I could go to town,' he said, 'I would buy you a present, but as I am situated, you will have to buy it yourself.' I bought some scarlet flannel and made a long wide skirt which lasted for years. I missed him so much that Ardmore was never a favourite walk again, and now only a few stones of his house remain and the skeleton of his boat.

Another of these old people left alone after bringing up a family was Anne Gorham, who lived in a little house between the church and the sea. It was very dark and the thatch was like a field with the grass growing on it. She slept on a bed of straw and her ashes were left in the hearth until they formed a pile right up the chimney. Her husband, Paddy, was an unforgettable character; an Errislannan man, but a deserter from the American navy. Old, grizzly, very dirty and dressed in clothes so ragged that they fluttered like pennons round him. He had a wickedly amusing tongue and a digestion that coped with cormorants and conger eels. As he and his wife were the last Protestants, he was the sexton at the church.

Their eldest son had been a sergeant-major, decorated for swallowing his dispatches before being killed in France. The pension his mother got helped her to keep alive. The three daughters all left home and Marcus, a handsome curly-haired boy with a beautiful voice, stayed to look after his mother. He spent most of his time in a rotten old boat with the holes plugged up with sods of turf. Several times it went down, but Marcus was the only one in Errislannan who could swim. My mother and I were lent this boat on one rough day when our boat was too small. The seat gave way and we were carried down the bay before making a landing.

Alas! the day came when two single ladies rented one of our cottages. Aunt

Jane's description of them was '"Holy Romans"' playing cards and drinking porter!' They got Marcus to row them about and sing to them and then carried him off to marry one of them. The next year the previous husband of the bride turned up enquiring for his wife. Marcus later went to Australia; poor Anne had beaten him out of the house with a broom when she heard he was to marry a Roman Catholic, so now she was left alone and bitterly bewailed that harsh act.

She lived a solitary life for many years in her small dark house. There were no neighbours, all the houses nearby being in ruins, and as a Protestant she did not meet people at Mass on Sundays. One Christmas afternoon I was sitting with her, when my chair went over backwards. I had not noticed that a calf was tied to it until it decided to get up. Anne was the only person I have heard of who could spin bog cotton; with the yarn, she knitted gloves for my great-grandfather and stockings for my great-grandmother. I painted her portrait by the light from the open door on a sunny afternoon, her faded blue eyes looking out at the sea; I have it still.

When she died my aunts went to the house and settled her up with true Protestant decorum. Bravely they set about the task of cleaning her and tidying up and then left, doubtless shedding tears for the sake of old times and putting Annie, the deaf mute, in charge. As they went up the boreen heads popped up all round, and when the coast was clear the Roman Catholics gathered from far afield, whiskey bottles in pockets, to give Anne the kind of wake they would like for themselves. It was kind, because they knew there would be no drop to be had except what they brought with them. They soon had the fire going and began an hilarious evening with talk and laughter, the wake games and racing round the house. Anne was laid in the kitchen and they -gathered round at midnight for the Rosary before starting on more wake games. Our garden boy, Mickey, was there and suddenly he pointed at the corpse and shouted, 'She sturred! she sturred!' and fell down in one of his epileptic fits. It was a bad one and they had to send for the priest and the doctor, which put an end to the wake that had been so well intentioned.

I am sure the old obscene wake games were not played at Anne's wake, but when I asked Annie what had happened, she raised her arms above her head and her eyes to heaven, expressing horror without words. Wake games have been forbidden all over Europe, but they still go on in lonely places as an excuse for a party when the corpse is old and alone with no relatives to mourn. Sometimes the men – probably full of whiskey – played very violent games, but women and children went only during the day.

The funeral was not the end of Anne, as some visitors took a photograph of her grave to send to her daughter in Australia. They were showing this to us in the dining-room and said, 'Look, doesn't that look like Anne standing up by those trees?' The dining-room hatch did its usual mischief and by evening word had gone round that Anne was not resting in her grave, because she had really been a Roman Catholic but had not dared to tell my aunts so. She must be dug up and buried in the other graveyard. Unfortunately a reporter in Clifden heard of it and built it up into a story. One of our workmen from the south road said he saw her coming up her boreen and he fled across the bog, falling into a turf cutting and arriving home black and shaking. He never came to us again. Several others said they saw her, but now I hope she rests in peace.

Sometimes, when walking to town, I had as my companion old Mrs Molloy, who had offended Captain Bentley so much by flinging her arms round his neck. I made so many drawings of her walking or riding on her ass, that her shape became almost a symbol for me of a peasant woman and crept on to many a canvas. She was a solitary, a squatter on the bog on the far side of the lake from the Manor. She and her husband had come in from the islands, and in the course of time had taken in a little land, but their cattle fed on the roadside or on other people's land, mostly ours. She was very handsome and very dirty, and liked to defend her husband with, 'Why what's on my Mathias but his nose?': this was the one feature missing and it was difficult to look him in the face.

Mathias died and the daughter went to America; so Mrs Molloy lived on alone. On Saturdays she rode to town on the tail of her big grey ass with creels; dressed in a scarlet petticoat, a pale blue jersey coat from America, and a yellow head-shawl, looking really magnificent. When I walked with her she told me stories, glad of an audience, because she was reputed to have the evil eye and had no friends. Once she went to her neighbour's house to give her the seven curses and knelt down in the doorway to begin, but the neighbour had a bucket of water handy and fired it over her, which put an end to the ancient rite and made way for some modern curses. In some places the ancient cursing stones – the *clocha-breaca* – still exist, though they are mostly in overgrown graveyards and hard to find. One not far from Errislannan had a flat stone slab with cup-shaped hollows in the surface, into which fit rounded pebbles. The curse is made while turning the stone anti-sunwise in the hollow. An unjust curse could return to the curser.

Whenever my grandmother saw Mrs Molloy approaching the Manor, she went upstairs and locked herself in the lavatory, this being the only room with a lock. Mrs Molloy would follow her up and loudly weep that she was fainting; her realistic act always melted my grandmother's heart and the whiskey would be produced.

Mrs Molloy used to wash our blankets at the spring-cleaning by trampling them in a barrel by the lakeside; there was a fire under a big black pot to heat the water. She climbed into the barrel and pranced up and down singing. Afterwards we dragged the blankets after the boat in the lake to rinse them and laid them on the grass to dry. They finished up fluffy and as good as new. The carpets got the same treatment.

The Molloys had a small stone shelter for the cows, but this now had no roof, so Mrs Molloy brought them into the house in winter for warmth and shelter and slept between them on the rushes. One evening the door did not open to receive them and they were seen sheltering by the house. The next morning they wandered off to feed on our back drive. No one noticed that Mrs Molloy's door remained shut and no one will ever know how long she lay on the bed of rushes, happy at last to go to her Mathias.

CHAPTER 15

Civil War, and Leavetaking

Between the Rebellion in 1916 and the Treaty in 1922, the British army and the Black-and-Tans fought the invisible men. It came to be known as guerrilla warfare, a new phenomenon. Hundreds of rebels were on the run, hiding and living off the countryside, waiting to snipe at a soldier or arrange an ambush. My brother was in some of the most dangerous places in Tipperary and Limerick and was wounded, but worse was the uncertainty as to who your enemy was: any bush or rock could hide a gunman, any man in the street could turn a gun on you as you passed. However, tennis parties and dances still went on, where the officers were in great demand.

In Clifden, an eighteen-year-old boy who worked for my uncle on the far side of the bay had his name drawn to go up to Dublin and assist at the killing of fourteen soldiers. These plain-clothes officers had been sent from Egypt and assigned to separate lodgings to act as spies; but information had leaked out. The killings were undertaken with the utmost cruelty, some men being killed in front of their wives. The boy from Clifden was given a bicycle which he could not ride, so he was caught and hanged. In retaliation for the killings that 'Bloody Sunday', 21 November 1920, the Black-and-Tans went to a Gaelic football match in Dublin in the afternoon, shut the gates and fired on the crowd, killing twelve and wounding sixty. In Clifden, reprisals for the hanging of the boy Whalan took the form of killing two policemen in the street, which brought the Black-and-Tans in an uncontrollable mob into the town. They raided shops and put on women's underwear while they burned down houses. They threw an ex-soldier into the street, tearing him to pieces: he had not been involved in any way. Mrs Whalan was regarded as the mother of a martyr and the anniversary was kept up for some years, when she came into town and people paid her respects as she sat in a window. Now, very late in the day, a large stone memorial has been erected with wording in Irish that few can read it. In 1969 the Roman Catholic Bishop of Tuam ceremoniously laid a wreath upon it before a great crowd.

When the general election was held in 1918 in England, there were 105 Irish members. Of these, 73 were Sinn Féin, who instead of taking their seats in Westminster, set up an Irish Parliament in the Dublin Mansion House and formally declared Ireland a Republic. De Valera was in Lincoln Jail but was declared Prime Minister and President of the Irish Volunteers. After his comic escape in 1919, he was greeted in America as 'President of the Irish Republic', a title that had to wait until 1948 to become real. The new government functioned as though British rule did not exist. One object was to drive the hated Royal Irish Constabulary out of their barracks and many were killed.

Then came the terrible mistake of separating the six counties, forcibly held by Edward Carson with his armed volunteers in 1921. By 1922 Dominion status was being offered, but with many strings attached, and Lloyd George threatened Michael Collins and Arthur Griffith that if they did not sign the Treaty, more troops would be sent and even worse times would ensue. Collins, Griffith and the other delegates signed, but on their return met with violent opposition from Rory O'Connor, de Valera and the rest of the leaders, who took to arms. And so the Civil War started.

British troops left Ireland for the first time for seven hundred years. My brother, Donald, was in the garrison when Dublin Castle was surrendered to Michael Collins in 1922, and they had to march out between jeering crowds, not sure of reaching the boat safely. When they finally sailed away, all the hooters and sirens followed them and they felt an overwhelming bitterness at the thought of the fiasco of the Irish war and the useless loss of so many of their men. Michael Collins wrote of that day: 'The Castle is now ours. It has been a place of terror in the past, symbolizing – because of its contents, the English – all that oppression could offer.'

The Treaty split the country into pro-Treaty Free Staters, under Michael Collins and Griffith, and anti-Treaty Republicans, under de Valera, Cathal Brugha and others. Brothers and friends were fighting against each other, and were almost indistinguishable in dress, usually wearing raincoats, so no one was certain who was a Republican and who a Free Stater. Unbelievably barbarous things were done all over the country by both sides. Prisoners were executed and worse: some were tied, back to back, in a circle, an explosive was put in the middle and they were blown to pieces. One man was blown into a tree and lived to tell the tale. Many bodies were found in the mountains and 2000 were on the run by the time the Republicans surrendered, but de Valera, before he was jailed, told his men to keep their arms and not to leave Ireland.

On our Ballinaboy Hill in Errislannan two snipers were killed and a stone cross marks the spot, with the inscription: 'In memory of Patrick Morrison and Thomas James, Co. Mayo, who were killed in action defending the Republic on this spot, October 28th, 1922 RIP. Erected by Connemara IRA.' It overlooks the Marconi Station, which was burned out in 1921 by the Republicans.

This was the time when the Ballyconree orphanage across the bay was burned, also by the Republicans. While Cathleen Purkis was in Clifden shopping, old Mr Purkis, half paralysed, was carried out and the boys driven out and locked into the gate lodge. Then the whole building was gutted and Cathleen returned to find forty terrified little boys, whose only home it was. She got her father into the trap (her mother and sister were in England at a wedding) and marched the boys seven miles by the Sky road into town.

My aunts, when they heard of it, made up bundles of clothes and blankets, but they were too late; the boys had been carried through the sea, by the sailors and Cathleen, to small boats which took them out to a gunboat waiting in the bay. This brought them across rough seas all the way to Plymouth; and from there they were taken to London and housed that hot summer in a laundry in Shepherd's Bush. I visited them in that empty house, sitting on the floor and playing in a tiny asphalt yard. The neighbours had given some furniture, but it was tragic to see them like birds in a cage. Eventually they were sent to Fagan's Homes in Australia.

I had been in England with my mother when hunger really began knocking on the door at Errislannan. The Galway road had been destroyed and little food had got through. They had been drinking a beverage made with cocoa husks meant for the pigs, and living on potatoes upsets the strongest digestion. A little ship called the *Dun Aengus* came round from Galway occasionally with food and mail, but it was six months before my letter arrived telling of Mother's death.

My father was at Knockadoo in Co. Sligo and when lorry-loads of Republicans or Free Staters sought accommodation, he told them to light a fire in the drawing-room and sleep round it. The men often came out into the yard and offered to help with the stable work, and in haytime they were invaluable. My father enjoyed their company and the noisy evenings. They sat on, and played the Bechstein grand piano, a relic of Aunt Etta's days, and it seemed very unwarlike. My father did not ask which side they were on and this lack of curiosity was dangerous; as one day, while he had the company of the Republicans, he went down to the shop, where he found more men very cold and wet. He said to them, 'We've got some of your chaps up at the house, why not join them?' They came back with him and walking up the drive were met by a hail of bullets from the house. A bad misunderstanding. Some were wounded and a regular battle raged from behind trees and round the stables. The men did not seem to aim to kill if their opponents were in full view at close quarters; and with my father to arbitrate they cooled down and the Free Staters left, their wounded being taken later in the lorry with the Republicans.

Another time my father was woken up by two men standing by his bed pointing guns at him. A court was being held on the hill, they said, and he was needed to identify his men. He told them he would come when he was dressed and they retired from the room. It was typical of my father that he dressed properly with a collar and tie. He was taken over the river and on the hill he found his workers guarded by men with guns.

Then a dreadful situation arose. He could not remember the surname of a small pale boy he had taken on because he was so good with the horses; in fact the other men said he had the 'horseman's whisper', an inherited power to calm the wildest, most vicious horse. He was the only one who could go near the stallion when it was in a bad mood. The boy would just walk up to the frenzied animal, which would be pawing the air on its hind legs, eyes blazing, teeth bared, and after a whispered word or a touch, down would come the feet and, in a miraculous calm, the boy would lead the horse like a lamb to his box. Matty had just arrived with no history or references, and his hands were not the hands of a farm worker so my father was not believed when he said Matty had been with him for some months. The boy was being dragged away when one of the other men called out 'Gorham, I will write to your mother!'

It was not too late, as my father could be very persuasive, and they let the boy go. Some were roughly treated, but at least they were safe in the end. Others were not so lucky, and the survivors heard the shots as they returned to the house.

*   *   *

After leaving school at sixteen I spent four years in Errislannan getting more and more desperate and determined to go to England. I had hardly spoken to a young person except Captain Bentley, and he was thirteen years older than me. I had not even got a bicycle, so Clifden by rowing boat or walking was the limit of my horizon. Terrible things were happening all over Ireland as the resistance fighters faced the British army and the Black-and-Tans. Michael Collins was on the run and the surviving leaders in and out of prison. After Sandhurst my brother had gone to Germany; then he was sent to Ireland with his regiment, but was not allowed to come home. I missed him dreadfully.

Errislannan depended on my father in Knockadoo to pay its mortgages and debts; Mother depended on him to keep her in London and pay medical bills, so there was no hope of my leaving unless I could earn my own living. I had not a single qualification for this, only a lot of drawings. I could ride, fish, shoot, and row a boat, but I had never cooked anything or done any housework. I think this must have been subconscious self-preservation as I should certainly have been forced to take some kind of domestic work, the refuge of the uneducated, and once in that treadmill I might never have struggled free to be a painter. With aunts and maids there was nothing for me to do in the house, so I wandered aimlessly about the hill or the shore, getting to know it so well that it has been a background to my life ever since. A background to call up at will, of grey rocks, heather and gorse, mountains and bright or stormy skies, and the sea with its wild white breakers on the west coast, or creeping up the yellow sand at Rossmenla in the bay.

At last I thought of writing to the new headmistress of my old school, asking if she would take me back in any capacity; she agreed, seeing a way of retrieving some of my unpaid school fees. So I started off into the world full of blind faith that somehow, sometime, I would be a painter.

The evening before I left quite excelled itself in beauty, making me wonder if I were making a mistake. I sat in my shelter on the top of the Look-out Hill, and saw the sun set in a blaze of flame crossed by purple. Overhead the pale green sky was lit by pink clouds reaching back to the mountains, which were themselves bathed in a pink glow. I recorded all this in my journal when I came down from the hill and settled in the Lake Room window. Venus was reflected in the lake in incredible beauty, and beyond was a gleam of yellow sea and the beams of Slyne Head lighthouse. I got up several times in the night to sit by the window and watch the lake and the trees, and morning brought a dead calm in which the lake mirrored every reed and the pink dawn clouds.

Uncle John was the hardest to part from and I knew he would miss me the most. It was sad to know that he would never be the one to go, but was always saying goodbye to others, having cut their sandwiches and filled their thermos flasks. At last it was over and the horse moved off. I stopped on the top of the hill for one last look, and forgot all the times I had come up there to look out on the world, desperately hoping I might go, or meet someone to speak to.

This was the first day I had put up my hair, and as it was very long and thick it was most uncomfortable. When it came down on the boat, I could not get it up again. I enlisted the help of a cleaner in the ladies' room at a station and she coped with hairpins efficiently, but I must have looked a dreadful sight when I arrived at the school in a home-made tweed costume and tam-o'-shanter to match. I was given various chores to do but soon found myself teaching art and helping with the dancing; all for thirty pounds a year, so I took a job in the New Forest teaching a boy to ride. His mother was master of a pack of harriers and mounted me well.

I left when my mother was ill and went to stay with her in London where I found work teaching a charming boy of ten, acting as painting companion, courier and chauffeuse to his mother. She earned my lasting gratitude by having me taught to drive a car. We went to Saint-Jacut-De-La-Mer in Brittany for three months, accompanied by Mrs Stephenson's brother, Colonel Lewis, and his friend, Major Randall. They were a delightful lively pair, who made a four for tennis and dancing. A very happy time it was with some harebrained escapades. St Jacut then was a small fishing village with a graveyard that became my favourite retreat when solitude was required. I have always had a taste for graveyards, fancy or plain. This was a mixture of a best parlour and a museum. Photographs of the departed, done in some medium that withstood the weather, brought each tombstone to life, and seemed to me an excellent way of remembering the dead, Sunday clothes and all. Marble, waxed or cloth flowers vied with each other; wild flowers and weeds covered the ground in rich profusion and climbed up the angels and gracious figures that looked down at me. Baby-like cupids perched on tombs and flew about amid the crosses and monuments. The whole place was seething with life and I sat entranced with it all, comparing it favourably with the tidy English cemetery.

Mrs Stephenson was very good for me: she was the first educated Roman Catholic I had met, and, greatly daring, I went to Mass with her. I could hardly breathe as the horror of what I was doing, and what the aunts would say, flooded over me. I was still in chrysalis form with a tight shell of Irish Protestantism enveloping me. As I disliked the Protestants too, I was in a no-man's land.

From Brittany we went to Switzerland for another four months, of which I will retail only one day's adventure. We set out for the monastery on the top of the St Bernard Pass, where there was thirty feet of snow. Only the tops of the telegraph poles could be seen and it was hard going. One of our party, Colonel de Mauduit, had some kind of heart attack as we neared the top. I was alone with him just then with the others out of sight. Bad moment! But the monks had seen him from inside and were soon at hand with dogs and a sledge.

When we entered the monastery it was as though we were blind; we had to grope our way about. There was no hostel there in those days and the monks entertained us to bread and wine. At the chapel down below I was given a Rosary and a cross which had been blessed. Then I set off to put my feet on Italian soil over the border. There was nothing to be seen at first but snow and a large statue, but then I spotted the border guards and, sure they would stop me, climbed up the hillside. We played hide-and-seek for a while until I slid down to their feet on my seat. They laughed, but it was very wet and cold for me, and I could not say I had been to Italy.

My sister's term at her school in Vevey ended and as she was travelling home with the school I arranged to follow her the next week. The night before I left a telegram came to say that my mother was dead. Mrs Stephenson gave it to me as I was standing on a balcony watching falling stars over the lake of Geneva. A kind houseboy and maid offered to wheel my luggage some miles down the mountain in the early hours of the next morning. It was a rough wet walk but I caught the train to Paris. There I wandered about for some unhappy hours, bitterly regretting that I had not come home before. Although we had expected Mother's death for six years, it was a shock in the end.

When I arrived in London my father, brother and sister were there to meet me, my father calm and kind as usual, the others heartbroken as without Mother they had no English home.

My brother had had so many compassionate leaves from Ireland because of these alarms that his Colonel had ceased to believe in the necessity, but he did let him come over for the funeral. He had to travel on the engine as a form of protection, and arrived tired and miserable. The funeral was at Golders Green and how we wished it could have been in Ireland with friends around us, but it was touching to see strangers taking off their hats as the coffin went by. We had a few miserable days in London together and then my father and sister went back to Knockadoo, my father doubly sorrowful because he had been kept apart from my mother in these last years by lack of money. My brother rejoined his regiment in Limerick.

It was at this time that I found the Cecilia Club near Hyde Park and Marble Arch – 'A club for the daughters of professional men' – where a few students aroused my envy by being at the Slade. With the eighty pounds from my mother's will, I wisely took a three-month course in secretarial work which was to make me independent for life. It cost twenty-six shillings a week at the club for a bedroom with gas ring, breakfast and dinner and all meals on Sunday. There was a nice drawing-room with chintz-covered chairs and a good fire. After training I had a job which finished at five, so I went to the Regent Street Polytechnic for evening classes in sculpture; but later I worked for a doctor and had the afternoons off, so I went to the Central School of Arts and Crafts and took courses in drawing, pottery and stained glass.

My brother, back from Ireland, was stationed at Tidworth and I was able to entertain him at my club, where he was in great demand to sing with the Welsh girls. I was glad we had this time together, as he felt very lost without my mother or a home in England. His girl had married someone else, so now he took two years off to join the Iraq Levies, where wages were so good he hoped to pay off all his debts, but he was killed within a year.

CHAPTER 16

London, Bruges; a Grandmother's Funeral, and Brother's Death

It was now that Charles Kennedy came into my life again. A friend had invited me to spend Easter with her parents in the country and I went down by train on Friday evening. At the little country station there was only one person on the platform and it was Charles. I was surprised and delighted, and all the happy times I had had with him came rushing back. He looked just the same; very tall and thin with hair a little grey at the sides and amused brown eyes. When he heard that a girl from Connemara by the name of Alannah Heather was arriving he suggested that he should meet me. Before returning to the house, he took me for a drive and we talked about old times. By the time we reached the house I think we were in love with each other, but we kept up the pretence of friendship for some time.

One day we went to Cambridge, and it was in King's College Chapel that we looked at one another and the pretence fell to the ground: from then on we knew that we were in love. The beauty of the Backs and Colleges were not appreciated that day and we soon drove away into the country.

After that Charles was in London a good deal; on Sunday mornings he called for me in his car and we explored London, or on sunny days went off into the country. Now it was that we came to love the Sussex Downs and many other beautiful places, making Rottingdean our centre. We were utterly happy together, so life became rich in spite of the idiotic jobs I had to do to keep myself alive. Charles wanted to change this, but pride made me refuse – pride causes so much unnecessary suffering when one is young. I would not have married him, as even then domesticity did not appeal to me. I could see that running any kind of a home would have been the end of any real painting, and I was thankful that I had been firm when eventually I got a studio of my own and began to work.

I lived a double life of luxury and poverty. When Charles was in town he took me to expensive places and we feasted; but mostly it was life in a cheap studio, cheap food, walking instead of driving and working for other people until five o'clock. Then a rush home to paint or mess about with clay and spend hours in galleries.

I continued to go backwards and forwards from London to Connemara between jobs or for holidays. Once we were turned out of the train at Athenry by
soldiers with fixed bayonets. However, side-cars were provided with ex-
hausted-looking horses, and on to one of these crowded four people and the
driver. My enormous trunk was placed on top, making it impossible for
anyone to lean back. We arrived in Galway and found the place so crowded
that to get food and pass the time I followed some men into an ordinary-
looking house. We were shown up to a bedroom with an iron bedstead on
which we all sat. The men went down for plates of food and brought one up for
me along with a cup of tea. They had flasks of whiskey and I was offered several
swigs, which choked me but cheered me up so much that I joined in the
singing and the time flew by until my train. One of the men carried my
suitcase to the station. Irishmen are the best at such times. On a similar
occasion I arrived in Galway just before Christmas and wandered in the snow
down to the market. I sat on a stall among Christmas trees and piles of turkeys
and a man brought a bottle of whiskey out of his pocket and passed it to me
after wiping it on his coat: a kindly act. Others gathered round and it became
a party and was as good as having a fire to sit by.

There was such a contrast between life in law-abiding, mundane England
and life just across the Irish Sea, where the idealists, the young and the best,
were being executed or shot by one side or the other. My life also was full of
contrast: an anonymous office worker, moving about among millions of
similar nonentities, feeding at marble-top tables in dirty cafés; and then over
the sea to Connemara where I was known by everyone, spoilt and fussed over,
lived in a manor house and walked on my family's land with beautiful scenery
all around.

From the beginning of the century, in spite of the fighting, there had been
a renaissance of writers, painters and poets in Ireland. Lady Gregory and the
Abbey Theatre, W.B. Yeats, AE (George Russell), Oliver St John Gogarty,
O'Casey and many more, all working on Irish subjects and producing first-
class work. I saw and enjoyed some of the latter's plays in London, such as *Juno
and the Paycock*.

In Dublin, Constance Markievicz and Maud Gonne, now elderly and worn
with their work for prisoners and their own prison sentences, were campaign-
ing desperately for the release of those held without trial after the Public Safety
Act had been rushed through. There were 11,316 in all, 250 of them women,
crowded into an old workhouse with iron beds and thin grey blankets. Many
went on hunger-strike and two men died as a result.

When Michael Collins ordered the bombardment of the Four Courts held
by the Irregulars, irremediable harm was done to Ireland, as the country's

archives, records, land deeds and wills were lost when it caught fire. The Irregulars retired to Hamman's Hotel, where Constance Markievicz fought from a dangerous position on the roof, sniping, until Cathal Brugha commanded them all to lay down their arms.

In September 1922 the government gave the Free State Army the right to set up military courts and inflict fines, imprisonment and death. They executed four political prisoners, among them Liam Mellows, one of Constance's Fianna boys, Rory O'Connor, and Erskine Childers, who wrote, 'I die full of love for Ireland ... I die loving England and passionately praying that she may change finally towards Ireland.'

On 27 December 1922 George Russell wrote an open letter to the Republicans in *The Irish Times* which could so well be written now:

> I do not like to think of you that the only service you can render Ireland is to shed blood on its behalf ... can you name those, who, if you were all killed, would have left behind, as Pearse or Connolly, MacDonagh or Childers did, evidence of thought or imagination?

We took an interest in old Tim Healy (the Land Leaguer of long ago who had been at Errislannan) when he was made the first Governor General of Ireland. He had been one of those condemned to die in de Valera's prison cell the night they played games. On 24 May 1923 the Civil War ended. It had cost the Free State government £17,000,000. The Republicans surrendered physically but nothing altered their feelings or prevented the hiding of arms for future use.

De Valera was arrested and imprisoned without trial, spending a year in solitary confinement, but lived to hold the office of head of state for longer than anyone else in Europe.

On Errislannan life went on peacefully except for money worries, but in other places people lived in fear of reprisals from their neighbours, as many had used the political turmoil to pay off old grudges. Having burned down their landlords' houses, they then found themselves out of work, with a day of reckoning approaching when the insurance companies set about proving the cause of the fires. Looted valuables still turn up in farmhouses, to the benefit of antique dealers who scour the country for bargains. The Purkises' silver from the burned orphan-age at Ballyconree was found in the house of a neighbour and so-called friend.

A common sight in those days were crosses or bits of wood along the roadsides, inscribed with RIP and the name of the person killed on that spot, or just 'Murdered by the foreigner.' The road from Sligo through Mayo to Connemara was littered with such signs when we drove down from Knockadoo for my grandmother's funeral in 1924. It was a hair-raising journey as little bridges had been blown up and the car crawled across planks while we jumped from rock to rock. My father's funeral top hat had already telescoped when it met the roof of the car over a humpback bridge, and I had a good laugh at the sight of us all dressed up in black – my covering a long black mackintosh, my father's tall figure punctuated by the hat – poised over stepping-stones like dancers. After this tiring journey to Errislannan the last straw came when my grandmother's coffin fell head first into the grave and a man swore loudly. I disgraced myself by letting a hoot of laughter escape and cowered back inside my mackintosh although the sun was shining warmly. My father had put on his squashed hat at an angle to free both hands to help in the extraction of the up-ended coffin. My grandmother was eighty-six when she died, and was buried where she was wed in the same church sixty years before.

Poor Uncle John, Aunt Jane and Aunt Edyth were utterly miserable. Unmarried, elderly, they had given their lives to the care and love of their mother; everything had been arranged for the comfort and pleasure of 'The Mistress'. The light of their lives had literally gone out, and they had to face a frightening future smothered in debts and mortgages, with no one on whom they could lavish their affection, who would sit smiling while they told her all the doings of the day. They were brave and cheerful as they looked after the numerous mourners, who, following custom, came back to the house. Their greatest comfort was from an old woman who raved at length with many prayers and 'Glory be to Gods' about the beauty of the corpse, and how she remembered the Mistress in a white satin gown cooking in the kitchen.

Late one night, some time before my grandmother died, they were all sitting round the fire when there was a frightening soft knocking on the window. Uncle John found a naval officer outside who had come to tell them that a gunboat was waiting in the bay, which might be their last chance to leave. There was no thought of accepting this offer as my grandmother could not have boarded a boat, and even if they had all gone to England, they would have nowhere to go and nothing to live on. So they thanked him, fed him and led him up to the stables to show him the shortest way over the hill, with a sinking feeling in their hearts; there was no means of communication with the outer world at that time.

Reports began coming in of friends in the south of Ireland being killed and their homes burned. The son of a friend of Aunt Edyth had been buried in the sand and drowned as the tide came in. Two other soldiers we knew were shot in a friend's drive near Galway, and so it went on. We thought it must end when the Treaty was signed, but no: it was out of the frying pan into the fire. Protestants and loyalists were naturally looked on with disfavour by both

sides, but we were lucky and our neighbours rema.

During the year 1922–3 the homes of thirty-seven
the Republicans. These included the old Blake home
mara, then belonging to Senator Oliver Gogarty, and fa
the family home of George Moore, whose brother Mau.
Everything was burned except a church vestment, which
considered unlucky to destroy and was instead laid out on
suspected that some of the burnings were not directly political
by local people to obtain land or free grazing for their cattle.

One great loss for Ireland was Kilteragh in County Dublin, the h
Horace Plunkett, who had a collection of fine paintings which were
His life had been spent in work for the good of the people and it was a
return. Many who tried to supply Ireland with art either paid dearly for
left the country.

*   *   *

Charles's work as an architect took him all over England. One day, when I
knew he was going to be away for some time, I heard of a job in Bruges with Sir
Henry Lunn's Tourist Agency. This attracted me because I knew of the
galleries there, so I dashed off to the London office and was interviewed by an
enormous, bearded man like a gorilla. He asked me what I knew of Belgium,
and when I replied 'Nothing,' he threw a guidebook at me, saying, 'Stew that
up, you're going to Bruges.' He told me to be at Victoria Station at a certain
time, where I would find a good lady with twelve Girl Guides attached. His
orders were: 'Take them over with you, show them round and keep them
happy for a week. God help you!'

Rather daunted, I collected my flock and all went well, even if it was a little
embarrassing coping with earnest girls in uniform who thought I knew my
way about. We were tempted into the town at Ostend and missed the train.
We waited for the next, as I writhed in shame at my failure as a courier. That
night was bad enough as all our luggage had gone on to Brussels and I was
expected to telephone in French to get it back. A kind man standing near the
telephone did it for me.

Feeling shaky the next morning I approached the office in the Belfry and
was given a German typewriter. I had learned touch-typing on an English
typewriter, and all the keys were in different places. Disaster seemed to follow
me that day as my dictionary and typewriting rubber were with my luggage
and I could not write a letter without them. The manager sighed, but soon
discovered I knew something about pictures and with great relief on both sides
I was made into a gallery guide.

thing could have been better than the hours in those marvellous galleries
emlings and Van Eycks. I had an absorbing time learning the history of
pictures and their painters, and planning what I should say to the gaping
rists. My greatest help was the curator of one of the museums who became
friend and taught me a lot. He had been a great authority on art in
msterdam, but had almost lost his sight. I used my eyes for him in many
ays and we rehearsed the number of steps he had to take to be in front of
newly hung pictures. Then he gave a lively interesting talk and I never came
across a tourist who realized he had this great affliction.

I came to love Bruges, a perfect little city with its old cobbled streets and
canals and bridges, its galleries and churches. I painted many of my favourite
places just for the joy of sitting looking at them and to have something to show
Charles on my return; it was all good for my drawing. The office provided
plenty of comic relief and some disgust that English people could behave so
badly abroad, especially in the Roman Catholic churches.

The agency staff were an interesting mixture, as it was only a four-month
summer job: an English colonel, his wife and family; an ex-Trappist monk; a
woman medical student; two lively young men; and the manager and his wife.
We used to pack into the firm's cars at ten o'clock at night and go off to the
coast towns dancing until five o'clock, as we did not open the office until ten
in the morning. The office was on the ground floor of the Belfry so we did not
get the full blast of the bells, for which we were thankful. My school French
was rusty, so I found a friendly housewife who walked about with me in the
evenings and took me on visits to her family, who gabbled away over endless
coffee. I became fluent, if with Flemish overtones.

The route between the office and my pension was exceptionally beautiful. I
had to walk beside the canal with its bridges and ancient buildings, under
shady trees and past the church of Notre Dame. This solitary walk became
extremely precious to me; it was an oasis in the desert of babbling tongues and
the staring eyes of the gallery groups. Mostly the tourists were dumb and
passive, but sometimes a sensitive, intelligent face would stand out and spur
me on to greater efforts to make them see those wonderful pictures. I became
so familiar with the Flemish School of the fifteenth century that I felt at home
in that long-ago world and full of admiration for their techniques. Nearly
every day I sat in the cool darkness of Notre Dame, mesmerized by the dozens
of flickering candles, statues and kneeling figures with rosaries; but it was
many years later that I lit a candle for my husband, as I knew he would have lit
one for me. I tried to like Michelangelo's white marble 'Madonna and Child',
but could not, and felt it would have been better sited in a museum. It was not
helped by the large dirty bit of cardboard propped up against it saying 'Do not
touch'.

At the Pension St Christoph I had a room in the garden looking out on flower-beds and trees, and was very content. One day a middle-aged clergyman sat next to me, and so began one of the nicest friendships I have ever had. Later I came to know his sister and brother-in-law, the Borrough-Johnsons, both very good painters, who did four portraits of me in London. One was in the Royal Academy. My friend's name was Reginald George, but I always called him the Padre.

It was fortunate that he arrived just then, because I needed a friend when I received a telegram to say that my brother had been killed in an aeroplane accident in Iraq. Troops were being flown up to the front line when the plane hit a mountain. On the wireless they were said to be dead, but the bodies were not found until three days later. In his last letter Donald told me that at last he was in the clear and had paid all his debts. The Colonel wrote that he had been mentioned in dispatches for bravery.

The Padre took me for walks and sat with me in silence and the office people were extremely kind. I have forgotten the name of the medical student, but shall never forget the tears of sympathy running down her face.

Charles came over, but we were not really happy; he was too worried about leaving me there and I wanted to stay. Then a girl-friend visited and I made the mistake of rushing about and dancing every night until I was well on the way to a nervous breakdown. The office closed in September and I went to Knockadoo to be with my father, my sister and Swannie. They faced Donald's death with tremendous courage as it must have been overwhelming so soon after that of my mother. Now there was no one to continue at Knockadoo and Errislannan, but my father went on as usual and never let us see his grief.

CHAPTER 17

The Journey Home

The next winter I went down to people I knew in Devonshire to help with their little boy and hunt. I was given a seventeen-hand chestnut hunter called Taffy, who had a head like a fiddle but could jump anything. He carried me along like a flea on an elephant, often ahead of the main body of the hunt, was very intelligent and often guided me home when I was lost. One day he plunged down a thickly wooded gorge hundreds of feet deep, sliding on his tail through the autumn leaves, which was rather like skiing down a mountainside dodging the trees. I could hear hounds running on the far side and the excitement made me blind to everything else. Taffy scrambled up with me clinging to the saddle and nearly falling off over his tail when he took the final leap over the edge. There were the hounds, but no Master or huntsman in sight, and I had a bad time holding Taffy back; he was pulling my arms out before the hunt appeared. I think he must have been a Master's horse at some time, since he always wanted to be in front. I got that brush, and another day two scuts when out with harriers, due entirely to Taffy, as over many a jump I shut my eyes and held on to the saddle.

One day we finished up sixteen miles from home and darkness was falling. We were very tired, so I walked sometimes, but my boots hurt and we had to keep moving because of the cold. There is nothing so satisfying as a long ride over hills, through woods and along country lanes after a whole day's hunting, when the horse takes you home at his own speed and the lights begin to shine from the houses.

Christmas was a wonderful time in that lonely farmhouse. A party went on until the early hours, but we were up for the Boxing Day meet. Another dance that night and another hunt the following day, by the end of which I had begun to wilt, and after bedding down Taffy, made for my own and slept all night in my riding clothes.

The hunt ball, held five miles away, was memorable because whilst my employers travelled in a two-seater car, I went with Bill — a nice Canadian helping on the farm — in a four-wheeler brake with a canvas hood. With my hunter in the shafts, we bounded unevenly along over hill and dale. It was a black night and raining so we were dressed in gumboots and mackintoshes. We swayed and pitched along, singing and cheerful, but I felt less happy when

I had to face the well-dressed crowd in the hall and pass through them dripping, carrying my dress in a suitcase to the ladies' room. Nonetheless it was a good ball and I had plenty of partners, apart from the faithful Bill, among the men I had met out hunting. Some enquired after Taffy, and when I said that he had brought me to the ball, they thought it a great joke.

When the winter was over I returned to London and took a job with the Friends of Armenia, my pay £2 a week as assistant secretary. As the secretary was away at least six months of the year, speaking, to gather funds, I quite enjoyed myself with the pleasant staff. The missionaries, who were sometimes uneducated, and who in their own country would have been waitresses or shop-girls, wanted first-class accommodation, servants to wait on them and the best of everything. 'Widow's mites' kept coming in to pay for this.

Sometimes I hated London with its drab clothes and sick, sad, ugly faces and sometimes I loved it, the parks, especially St James's, the river, and the wide open places at Westminster, in sunshine or in mist; the sky pink at sunset and the spires and domes, trees and chimney-pots blue, the hurrying crowd of ants silhouettes. The lamps wore haloes in the evening fogs, and rain brought stars and shivering lines of light on dark roads.

I loved Whitehall on 11 November, when the great guns boomed out and the two-minute silence fell on that vast concourse of people. Only the seagulls moved, gliding against the bright sky crying like spirits. Nearly everyone in those days had lost someone and the sharing of grief was a tangible thing. All the killed young men seemed to be in the air around us.

*　　*　　*

Two years before reaching the Slade School, while still an amateur, I painted the portrait of a friend. Her mother came to see the result and, to my joy, liked it so much that she offered to buy it. While still wondering what to ask for it she gave me a cheque for twenty pounds. This was untold wealth to me and I realized that I could go home for Christmas. The following morning I cashed the cheque, packed a haversack and waited impatiently for the day to pass until I could go to Euston and board my lifelong haven, the Irish Mail. I slept peacefully as we roared across England and Wales and woke to the rumble of the iron bridge on to Anglesey. It was a cold and stormy night at sea, and, as it was before the invention of stabilizers, a steward and I slid along the floor together, ending up at a pillar: his tray went sliding on.

I was starving by the time I reached the Galway train, and treated myself to an extravagant breakfast while I watched the old canal, then green, still, overgrown and useless, that appears and disappears beside the railway right across Ireland.

It was dark when the train steamed into Clifden Station, where I left my haversack and set out shivering and stiff with cold to walk the five miles to Errislannan. Fortunately, by the mill an ass cart caught up with me and I was offered a lift to the foot of Ballinaboy. Some sacks sheltered me from the worst of the wind, but it was very shaky and uncomfortable. The conversation helped to calm my excitement, which was mounting as I pictured walking into the house and taking the family by surprise. At Ballinaboy I got down and thanked the kind man who had walked that I might ride. I got many blessings as I faced the hill.

The darkness and coldness frightened me as I knew there would be no house or human being to see until I was down on the other side. How black it was; the road showed only as a faint white glimmer and was stony and rough to my thin shoes. I had no overcoat, and when I reached the top of the hill and the cold wind from America whistled round and pushed me about, I would have given up had there been any alternative other than lying down on the wet ground knowing I should be dead by morning. In such a situation – as I found later during the war – it is curious how one wants someone to know where you are, even if you are dead. I remember the light in the sky was a yellow line behind the Look-out Hill where the dark purple clouds were broken, and where we had once seen an amazing aurora borealis letting off fireworks.

My feet hurt and my legs were becoming paralysed with the cold. The church-yard wall gave a little respite from the wind, and, nearly there, I thought of the fire and the hot tea laced with Aunt Jane's trifle-whiskey, lavishly poured in. I could now see Joe King's light on the hill behind the lodge and pictured that red-faced, sandy-haired, jovial man sitting over his fire, always alone unless he bicycled precariously down his bumpy field and along a rough bog track to reach the post office and friendship for an evening. I was glad of his light then, as I came to be many times when we were living in the Gate Lodge. I had got that far safely. In England I should have been afraid in such a lonely place, but no humans, no murders, and I now reached the silver gates and the light in the Lodge.

I did not stop to call on Lizzie and Michael, as I knew that although they would look out when they heard the click of the gate, it was too dark for them to recognize me. I hurried squelching down the drive and into the dark tunnel of trees, and saw the drawing-room light. Even then I hung on to the pleasure of making an entrance, so I crept round to the kitchen and stayed just long enough in front of the hot range to make the maid keep quiet. Then I tiptoed along the dark hall and opened the creaking door of the drawing-room.

No one could have asked for a better welcome. When it was over I cowered on the floor by the fire, still shivering, and Aunt Edyth put the red cloak round me like a tent. Uncle John, still muttering 'Be Jabers' and 'Oh Moi!', went up to light a fire in the Lake Room for me, hobbling up the stairs with his one good leg, carrying turf and paraffin. Bottles were put in the bed and the sheets brought down for an extra boost over the range. Aunt Jane wished to prepare a meal, but I could not eat anything for shivering and feeling sick. Soon the hot fire and the whiskey-laced tea made me feel better. Smoke from the Lake Room fire permeated the house in the good old way as I went up to bed. The next day it began to snow.

Because ice and snow are very rare in Errislannan, I always found them beautiful and exciting. The lawn and the land beyond the lake being white, the lake became an inky blue, and the dark angels sweeping across it almost black.

One morning I woke to see the ceiling of my room lit by the cold blue light that snow brings. There was absolute calm and a silence that could be felt. I dressed and crept down the stairs to the porch, where I put on my gumboots and one of the scarlet cloaks, fastening the large hood tightly round my face. I went out of the back door and up the steep hill through the wood and it was so utterly still I kept stopping to listen. No sound came from the trees or the lake, nor even the slightest hum from the sea. The crisp air was hard to breathe as I climbed higher and higher through the white-furred branches which made the wood so magical.

My feet crunched the snow where I knew that even then there would be the beginnings of snowdrops in their mosses, to be followed by primroses and violets, and that later the whole ground would be misty with bluebells. Only my breath moved as it rose like steam. Above the stables I found some rowan and holly trees, solitary and leaning away from the west wind, with clusters of shining red berries, and dark green leaves that looked black in the whiteness. I shook the silver trunks and brought down a shower of snow and the red berries blazed out all around; it was a glorious sight against that crystalline background of reddish-coloured moor and blue mountain.

One memorable day that winter holiday I went up to the top of the Look-out Hill and all the tiny pools in the bog and the rocks were frozen, and the long grasses were stiff and white as though feathered. From the top of the hill, the sea all round was the darkest blue and the mountains were many shades of white. The grass crackled under my feet and here and there a patch of yellow gorse showed through the snow. A hare went leaping down towards the sea. It was exciting to make the only footmarks and know that no more would follow. Up on the highest rock I felt like a god standing among the clouds with a vast panorama of mountains, lakes, bays and the islanded ocean rising to eye-level.

When I came down, the Wren Boys were at the hall door, so it must have been Boxing Day, when staid farmers and boys blacked their faces and put straws and leaves in their hats and, with one playing the fiddle and one carrying a wren in a jar, went round to all the houses, where they were given drinks and food. In my grandmother's time a dead wren or robin was brought around on a small, highly decorated tray with a handle. Aunt Jane had said that if they brought a wren near her she would shut the door in their faces, so they left it in a jam-jar near the gate, where I found it. I was just going to let it go when I thought it would be better to let them do it. When this proposition was put to them, they laughed and released it, saying, 'What the divil good did it do us anyway?' This was foolish of me, as the wren away from its territory would have died in the snow, whereas the jam-jar might have taken it back to its home. I think my teetotal Aunt Jane had offered them oranges, probably with a cold look, knowing full well that they had a wren hidden somewhere.

Midsummer's eve on Look-out Hill provided a complete contrast. Everyone lit their own bonfires and we all carried as much wood, turf and paraffin as we could manage up to the highest point. There was always some bog oak that had been found when the turf was cut, preserved from forests long ago. (Once a barrel of butter was found in fairly good condition, but it was eventually used for greasing the cart-wheels.) When the fire was lit there was music of a sort; Michael Angelo played a mouth-organ when he was a boy, and later brought his fiddle, but mostly we were too busy eating and keeping the fire going to sing. Mollie and Annie Dan always had a fire on their hill and there were several others on Errislannan and a big one on the castle hill across the bay. All the dark land was dotted with light and there was a fellow feeling between the groups of people gathered round their fires. In England this happens on Guy Fawkes's night, but of course in Ireland he is a martyr. When the fire began to burn low, we stuck pitchforks into sods of blazing turf and ran zigzag down the hill setting fire to gorse and dry grass wherever we went, so saving Johnnie Dan from having to do it himself.

My brother and I had spent a great deal of time on the hill and in the woods long ago, shooting rabbits which were wanted for the pot. After he went away I continued to do this until one day I was up above the house in my favourite glade – a rich sunny spot, carpeted with moss, with a pale green ceiling of leaves – where I often sat on a tree-stump and watched insects and birds. A cock pheasant came walking in with his colours glowing and his head going this way and that, and he looked so beautiful I could not shoot him. The glade seemed full of light and in the silence I seemed to feel, rather than see, everything as though it occupied a translucent, disembodied world. Every small detail shone out in a way I had never before experienced .

After this I took a dislike to shooting anything and gave up taking my gun out in the evenings, but if a rabbit were wanted for the pot, I would still go out in the morning and get it. Later we had to cast both guns on strings into the lake to save them from being taken in the Bad Times when men were scouring the country for arms, so no question of shooting anything arose. A tame little fish in a pool, black with blue eyes, nearly stopped me fishing, as he came and ate out of my hand for months, and although the sea battered the rock face every tide, he was there whenever I looked for him. However, the lure of fishing was always too strong to resist.

CHAPTER 18

My Father's Death, and
Departure from Knockadoo

Charles had now finished his work on a house in Yorkshire, and was in London for a long spell. He had a new car which he let me drive, so we explored some beautiful places in Sussex at the weekends. We loved the downs behind Rottingdean and spent long days walking on hill-tops; another favourite retreat was Alfriston with its downs and farmland. One Sunday in September, we had walked all day over the hills and felt the beauty of it with an unusual intensity. The turf was eaten smooth by sheep, whose bells we could hear tinkling through the sunny air, but there were many wild flowers such as thyme and heart's-ease. The distances were a misty blue that closed in behind us as we walked along. Charles was tireless with his long stride, but I was beginning to feel I had had enough, so we came down and found a little lane where the hedge on one side was full of colour. There were blackberries with some deep red leaves, purple sloes; drooping clusters of elderberry, red spindle with yellow leaves, and over it all climbed the honeysuckle. Below were rusted fronds of bracken, some late loosestrife, poppies, blue scabious and other flowers. I took home some of each and painted them in an old blue saucepan; I have the painting still.

As we passed the lovely little church of Wilmington, the bell was ringing for the evening service and we decided to go in. In those days ladies wore hats in church and I had not got one, so I apologized to the Vicar, who was in the porch. To my horror he said, 'Come along with me, my dear, my wife will willingly lend you a hat.' His wife tried on one after another; she was about seventy and all her hats were like Queen Mary's. At last she decided on a black one, which with my blue cloak and bare feet in red sandals was so funny that I dared not look at Charles, who was shaking all over. How thankful I was to hand it back to its kind owner as we went out into the late evening light.

I did a number of paintings in Alfriston, as sometimes if I were not working Charles left me there when he went back on Monday mornings. A short walk across the fields was a huge barn as big as a church. I made many detailed drawings of it, and one day a woman asked me if I would like to come to the shepherd's cottage nearby and have a cup of tea. The first time I saw the shepherd, he was sowing barley in his own field behind the cottage. He was tall and bearded and seemed to express immense dignity as he strode along at an even pace, scattering the grain out of a wide bag hung over one shoulder. He greeted me kindly and we sat down to the table in that perfectly unspoilt old-fashioned cottage, with its rag mats on the floor, photographs of his dead wife and son, and nothing modern or out of place. The woman who looked after him poured out the tea and gave me huge slices of bread with home-made butter and blackberry jam. They asked me to come again whenever I should be that way, and I went occasionally for several years. I loved that little house under its tree beside the great barn, with the cornfields reaching away to the blue hills. It became a kind of haven of goodness; when journeying there I looked forward to walking in and the welcome I should get. Then one day I found the cottage shut and empty. I searched out the shepherd's grave in the churchyard and gathered wild flowers for it.

I was back at the Cecilia Club when my father came over to Newmarket with the yearlings. On his way back to Ireland we had dinner together at the club and I went to Euston to see him off. I thought he looked ill but he would not admit that there was anything wrong. I hated to see him go, and was not really surprised to hear that he was in Dublin for an operation. When I arrived he had had the operation and thought he was cured, but the surgeon told me that it was cancer and that he could not live more than about eighteen months. He went back to Knockadoo and tried to carry on as usual, but was in great pain. I took a job as secretary in a school so that I could go over for long holidays and also help with medical fees. With no health service, no money, the nearest doctor fifteen miles away, and no telephone or car, we were in a fearful state. The next autumn he again took the yearlings to Newmarket, which required supreme courage. He sold the last to Solly Joel for £1700 and returned home to bed, which he never left again.

When my father died it was the end of Knockadoo for our family, and I was glad to see it go. It had always been an unlucky house, not only for us but for the two previous owners, who had both died of cancer, and bankrupt. I sometimes have a feeling that houses which face north are unhappy ones, and it had certainly proved so for us.

Uncle George's wife had thought that she would make it pay with fisher-men paying guests, but after spending a lot of money, she did not have a single one. She was a huge jolly woman with hair dyed flaming red. She died at Knockadoo of angina in great agony, as the Roman Catholic doctor would not give her drugs. At the end she drank a lot of water and became quite blue. They got a coffin as quickly as possible but had great difficulty in fitting her into it. That evening a drip was heard in the drawing-room and a large patch spread over the ceiling; the coffin leaked. This was horrible, but it was worse for the men who had to carry the heavy coffin the long way round to the church, every man taking his turn out of respect. A short cut was never taken.

Then there was Uncle Deanie's funeral, a year before my father's. He was a fat lazy man who had never been known to do any work, or help in any way at all, but he was very witty and well liked because he always had time to prop himself up on something and talk. He drank to excess only when he had been in to see the bank manager in Tobercurry, but the horse brought him home and he was maudlin, not violent; even this frightened my sister and she barricaded her door. His funeral was a whiskey one and added to the debts at the local shop, so my father, when he knew he was going to die, told us to let people know in advance that his funeral was to be a dry one. We did, but it made no difference; everyone turned up as he was so much loved by the local people. Uncle George could not bear the thought of a funeral with no drink and sent out for two bottles of whiskey. I cruelly hid these in my trunk, for whiskey could not be given to some and not to all.

The Land Commission divided the estate, giving the house and some land to our faithful maid, Rebecca, and her husband, the spoilt priest, Johnnie. This very intelligent man had worked for my father and was a fine builder of stables. He married Rebecca, but she would not leave my father while he was ill. Later they lived in one room in Knockadoo and let the rest of the house go to ruin.*

When all was over, we got the men to pack the ducks, hens and turkeys into crates, as presents to our neighbours. The carts trundled away and we went to bed. Then from the early morning on, we heard the quacking and gobbling as they returned to their old haunts. The neighbours came to collect them, which meant hours of conversation and cups of tea, the last straw for us.

The dogs were the worst problem. One had to be put down, but a kind young farmer who lived fourteen miles away said he would take Jack, the sheep-dog. Jack had known that my father was dying and had dug himself a deep hole under the drawing-room window. Here he lay perfectly quiet, except for a long howling session when my father died. He kept returning to the house and so had to be killed.

My sister and I watched from the wood as the chain of mares and foals were led away for the last time. All the local men were enlisted in to bring them the eight miles to the station, a nightmare walk as the foals were running loose and had never been on a road before. Even the local fiddler had offered to help and did his best, but his mare broke away and they nearly missed the train while it was being caught.

Then we left for Errislannan, going by hired car the eighty miles along the coast road. As we passed Achill Island, a dim blue shape on the horizon, I

*Knockadoo was burned down in 1980 when empty during the night, watched from the hill by Rebecca, who wrote to us.

remembered that my father had been born there, and wished we had been able to bring him to Errislannan. I did not like leaving him in Sligo because I think the dead do linger for a while. The day after my father died I uncovered a mirror that Rebecca had covered up, as is the custom, and I saw my father looking out at me, but the image soon faded away.

We stayed in Errislannan until my godmother, Ethel Deakin, asked us to go to her in Surrey so that my sister could train as a nurse and I could look for work in London. The Deakins had been extremely kind to us all our lives, ever since my parents settled in their village in Warwickshire after their marriage.

Two days after my father's death my friend the Padre died. Another dear friend, John Trevor, died a month later, and Great-aunt Louie had died the previous spring, thus closing the house I loved best in England and where I had spent so many Christmases and Easters. So altogether it had been a bad year, but perhaps it is better for all the blows to fall at once and help to blot each other out.

In Surrey my sister started training at Guildford Hospital and I looked unsuccessfully for work until I became ill. At this point my godmother's brother died. He had been in a mental home, and Ethel gave me the money that had been helping to keep him, £500, to support me at the Slade for three years. I went to the Slade for an interview, taking some drawings and paintings with me. Professor Schwabe looked them over and said it was a pity I had no exam results, but that my drawings would get me in. So it was arranged that I should start in October 1930 and do the three-year diploma course. The secretary, Mrs Green, and Connel, the Beadle, were friendly and made me feel I should be happy in that great big stony place.

I travelled back to Surrey dazed with thoughts of the future, but I suffered from a very bad back pain. My godmother insisted on my going to an osteopath, and he made it worse. Then she sent me to a doctor who I think must have been a beauty specialist or quack to judge by the fat horrible women lying round his waiting-room. He had me X-rayed and told me that I had osteo-arthritis of the spine but that I should be able to get around for some years. This nearly finished me off just when I was preparing for the best time of my life. I was in despair when I met an old club friend who was a welfare officer and somehow arranged for me to see a Mr Bankheart at the Orthopaedic Hospital. He cheered me up and said I had something that would yield to treatment. He also dealt with the pain in my neck that I had had for years after a fall from a horse.

Slowly I improved, no doubt helped by the thought of three years at the Slade with enough money to live on. I decided to fill in the time until October with paints and canvases, away in some unknown spot. My guardian angel flapped his wings violently and led me to Sark.

CHAPTER 19

Sark and the Slade

It was now July 1930, and for the first time in my life I had a little money and a definite future, so I felt like being extravagant. I had seen a picture of Sark in a friend's house and it looked the kind of place I should like, so I asked her where I could stay. She gave me the address of a couple with a farm on the west coast of the island.

I set off by night from Southampton and arrived in time to see the dawn over Sark. I was utterly enchanted by the sight of that whale-backed island and have been so ever since, going back nearly every year until the war stopped me.

The sea was rough as I embarked in a small open boat. We passed the lovely islands of Herm and Jethou, and the long blue line of Sark became clearer and clearer, with its bare cliffs and no signs of habitation. The sea got very rough as we rounded the northern tip of the island, but it was a glorious journey and I felt that I had found just what I was looking for. There seemed to be no way in, but then I saw the little enclosed harbour and the tunnel through the cliff which led on to the island.

Elie de Carteret greeted me and drove me to his farm in a victoria with a big black hood and a heavy farm horse in the shafts. Here, I was greeted by Hannah, his Irish wife. They have been my friends through all the years since, sometimes coming to stay with me in England.

A week later I climbed down the cliff in front of their farm and spent the morning painting. I had a haversack on my back and, with my head down, started the upward climb on what turned out to be only a sheep track. Looking round I saw a deep gully on my left and held on to a piece of rock, but this came away in my hand and I fell seventy feet into the crevasse. I remember shouting, 'I'm being killed,' and then no more. My haversack must have caught on something as the strap was broken, and I must have slithered part of the way as I had no skin left on my right side from my heels to my head.

I know exactly what happened after that, as my rescuers visited me in the nursing home in Guernsey and told me all about it. Two ladies picnicking on a rock had seen my body falling through the air, and shouted to the Dean of Guernsey and his family, who were on the shore. They knew I could not be reached along the shore because of the gully, and so the Dean and his son ran up three hundred feet of cliff and down the other side. They could see me apparently sitting in a small pool of water, but I slid down and when they reached me my head was under water.

It was impossible to get a stretcher up the cliff, and too rough for the fishing boats, so there was a delay of seven hours. Then a Miss Mallet, who had a boat of her own, came round and, with the help of two men, ran her boat up on to the rocks. I was put on and the next big wave carried us off. We had to go by Little Sark, with a curious incident on the way. There was a young woman in the boat who had been looking after me on the rocks. I saw her pour some brandy into a silver kidney-shaped cup, which dropped into the sea but floated, and she put out her hand and caught it. Now I was lying in such a position that I could not possibly have seen her or the cup, but this was exactly how it had happened.

They brought the boat round to the east coast, and on to the shingle beach at the harbour, so that a cart could be backed down to it and the stretcher put on. They took me right across the island to the farm, where I was put in through a window. I remained there for three days, as it was too rough for the big boat to get into the harbour. Mrs de Carteret and her aunt nursed me night and day. I was unconscious most of the time, but the poor watchers could not relax. I had two fractures of the pelvis, a damaged kidney which was bleeding, a damaged left knee and broken right wrist. My skull had a gash in it and of course the lack of skin made nursing difficult. In fact, it was, as the newspapers put it, 'A Miraculous Escape of Lady Artist'.

The third day the stretcher was put back out through the window and on to the farm cart and taken down to the harbour. I do remember this and also being put on the deck, where the boatmen tiptoed past to have a look. In Guernsey I had to be moved on to another stretcher as mine would not fit into the ambulance; then at the nursing home to a soft stretcher, as the stiff one would not go up the stairs. I had been sent there to have my kidney removed, but fortunately I managed to keep it.

My godmother, Ethel Deakin, happened to sail round Sark the next day in a friend's yacht, and the boatman said, 'A lady fell down there yesterday.' It never occurred to her that it might be me, and so she sailed away and I was left on that strange island, where I had known nobody until the accident. As it turned out, I had only two days without visitors all the weeks that I was there. The Dean and his wife and family brought friends to see me and my room was always decorated with fruit and flowers. I could see a little garden and a wood from my bed, and I came to love this very much, especially in the evening light, which I waited for all day.

The de Carterets wrote that I must be having unexpected expenses and not to bother about their bill. When I considered all the blankets and the mattress covered in blood, and the nursing and work they had done for me, I thought I had never met with such kindness.

When I was well enough to walk, but not well enough to cope with London, my sister came over and we went back to Sark. It was then that I saw the little one-roomed cottage, the last house before the common, by Brechou Island, that was to become my home for so many winter and spring holidays. It belonged to the de Carterets and was built of stone, whitewashed inside, but the chief thing about it was the large skylight, which made it ideal for painting.

I arrived back in London in October, just in time to start the new year at the Slade. My godmother had found digs for me nearby. My first day was not the unmixed joy I had expected. It was the longest walk I had attempted since my accident and I found it difficult to climb those high stone stairs or to carry anything in my right hand. I reached the famous antique room and at the sight of those ghastly plaster casts of the Elgin Marbles, my courage nearly failed me. I could not hold a pencil properly and sitting astride on the donkeys for hours on end was torture. I weakly excused myself by saying I had had an accident, but the sardonic young staff replied, 'More mental than physical I think.' I had to go to the orthopaedic hospital twice a week, where history of art books helped to pass the hours of waiting. My right wrist had to be broken down again and set properly, and the next term I could use it.

I was extremely happy at the Slade. The History of Art lectures opened up new worlds for me, and Professor Borenius took a few of us for extra lectures in galleries and museums. During my first year I had only one frame good enough to submit to an exhibition, so had to paint to fit it. One of these paintings called 'The Fair', a fussy composition and not in my line at all, I rather brazenly sent in to the New English Art Club at the New Burlington Galleries. It was hung very well in the middle of the wall in room one, fortunately in front of a comfortable couch, as my godmother and her sister came and sat there nearly all day, preening themselves on sending me to the Slade and listening to people's criticisms. They were so sweet and proud, as I was myself, being in the good company of Augustus John, Orpen, two of the Proctors, Nevinson and our Professor Schwabe. What a different world that was in the thirties.

I was painting on old canvases as a new one was quite beyond my means. Then, while staying with my godmother, a Miss Downing, who had been a well-known sculptress and painter, suddenly died. My godmother bought up all her art materials at the auction, and a few weeks later a huge box arrived containing everything a student could want. This saved me and kept me going for years. Among the rolls of drawing paper I found an illuminated address to

'Errislannan Manor from Look-Out Hill' (water-colour: 16 x 20).

'Tinkers in the Wind' (oil: 16 x 14).

'Evening in Connemara – Returning Home' (oil: 48 x 36).

'The Island' with the King family in centre (oil: 28 x 36).

'Johnnie Dan Conneely's Funeral, Errislannan 1940' (oil: 36 x 26). He was the family shepherd.

'Anne Gorham, Errislannan' (oil: 16 x 13).

'Mary Stephen King, Errislannan' (oil: 24 x 16).

'Darby Green, Errislannan' (oil: 16 x 13).

'Sean Mailley, Errislannan' (oil: 17 x 11).

'Cleggan, Connemara – the Morning After' (oil: 24 x 20). In 1927 the fishing fleet went down and twenty-seven men from this small village were drowned.

'War: "I was called for and I came"' (oil 36 x 48).

'Dante Baia Adriano, Charlotte Street Café' (charcoal: 14 x 11).

'Gaston' (charcoal: 15 x 12).

'Elie de Carteret, Sark' (chalk on grey ground: 17 x 11).

'Roger Bent, St Ives 1940' (red chalk).

'Woman on Boat' going down the Danube to
Doonafoldvar, eighty miles from Budapest.

'The Cherry-Eater' (right, oil: 24 x 40).

'Les Alpes Maritimes, Grasse', near Nice (oil: 12 x 16).

'My Lobster Boat, Connemara' (oil:14 x 18).

'Errislannan Manor' (water-colour: 16 x 20).

Miss Downing, thanking her for her courage in the suffragette cause. She had been a friend of Miss Pankhurst and had gone to prison and on hunger-strike. I managed to find the address of her sister and sent it to her.

When the first May after my accident came round, I arrived back in Sark on a very rough but bright day and Hannah and Elie de Carteret were on the quay waving, with the big black horse and carriage waiting in the background. This was to be the first time that I had lived in a cottage alone and I was almost overwhelmed with joyosity – to use Edith Sitwell's expressive word. Hannah had put in a narrow bed, a table, and a washstand that acted as my kitchen for years with a primus stove and a basin on it. The alcoves on each side of the fire held everything else required for living. The skylight filled one-third of the plain wooden roof, and the white walls made a good background for paintings. She had put a vase of wild flowers on the table and home-made butter and jam; I found eggs, tea, bread and all I needed for the first night. There was a pile of gorse and driftwood outside the door for the fire, which always gave me more pleasure than just warmth. The brilliant-coloured sparks and flames reminded me that the wood had been washed in by the sea; gathering it was always a joy in the years to come.

Although I was far from any other house, I never felt nervous and never locked my door. The rats were rather frightening, however. Their pattering feet on the roof-boards sounded as though they were on the floor and liable to run over the bed. The shaking brought down showers of wood-lice and an odd earwig, sometimes on my pillow. Elie trapped the rats in the end and then men and boys assembled in the field to see whose dog would kill them as they were let out of the trap.

I had come to Sark to paint in solitude, but through the years I made many lasting friends among the painters and visitors who stayed at the de Carterets' farm and came down to my cottage in the evenings if the weather were cold or wet; otherwise I would be out on the Guliot cliffs. I spent two summers there, but found it too distracting and afterwards confined my stays to the winter and spring. I have done much of my best work in that cottage trying to forget all the correct drawing and painting I had learned at the Slade and to develop in peace along my own lines.

An art gallery built on the island by a rich ex-Slade American was a great encouragement, with good artists sending their work over. It was run in connection with the Redfern Gallery, but soon it became a social centre for pseudos and art students until it closed down; later it was used as the German officers' mess.

I missed Charles very much and used to dream of him arriving without notice on the island. Perhaps I was not so much of a hermit as I hoped and solitude was not enough. I became involved with a painter and we saw a lot of each other, but it disrupted my work and only when he left the island could I really concentrate again.

I had a period of doing portraits in flat colours and black outlines, and had three strange-looking children for my constant models. I also did a large chalk drawing of Elie de Carteret's grandmother, aged ninety-two, who walked down in her Sark cloak and scoop with a book to read while sitting. She made four generations of the family to sit for me. I also had a phase of using animals as models: the white Seignorie horses, doves, sheep, the back side of a white goat, which was like a graceful vase; rabbits, a frog and many others; but my main occupation was figures in landscapes and Irish compositions, which I seemed to do better in Sark or London, being more detached.

My journal is one long paean of praise of all the beautiful things I saw on the island, and the times spent there: sitting up at the farm on the winter evenings; fishing in the summer evenings from Elie's boat.

One day some of us went down to the Guliot caves, where the walls were entirely covered with bright anemones like chrysanthemums when open; other strange shapes and colours were everywhere. There was a dark narrow passage where one had to swim to reach the large cave; it was said to contain an octopus and so we halted. At last Elizabeth Cummins and I plunged in chanting 'O jelly fish where is thy sting, where crab thy victory', and so we passed over and all the trumpets sounded for us on the other side. The trumpets were the admiring shouts of the men, who had waited for us to show them it was safe to follow. The next cave was brilliant green, lit by a shaft of light coming from far over our heads; the walls glistening crimson, pink, cerise and pale and dark green anemones. Eventually we came out into the open sea. Elizabeth wrote a poem about the seaweeds underneath us catching the sunshine. In spite of all this, I see one diary entry says, 'Every time I come to Sark I make good friends, and I have never made one in Errislannan except Da Barnett, but still I long to be there.'

Nearly every day that first summer I swam in the deep green sea, often alone, looking up at the coloured cliffs hanging over me, and then I would climb the valette carrying as much firewood as I could manage up that steep 300-foot path. Selling some pictures and a portrait more than paid my expenses so I could afford to go down to the pub with Elie and Hannah and join in the darts and other competitions, and go to the entertainments in the parish room and the dances. The best part of the dances were Hannah's commentaries about everyone in the room; she knew the financial and moral state of all the people on the island, and her rosy face smiled and her eyes never missed a thing. We came home arm in arm across the fields by the light of a small torch.

One spring I took an interest in my clothes for the first time as a man called

Tony, who was painting me, admired and criticized them. At that time I was very slim with long legs so I could wear narrow slacks and jerseys, but I often wore oatmeal-coloured overalls with balloon sleeves, long and full. I also had a tight-fitting, short sleeved coat of purple and scarlet woven Connemara tweed. I wore scarlet Basque peasant sandals and my legs were dark brown with sunburn. My hair was always very thick and cut to my shoulders with a fringe. One day I was making Tony a cup of tea on the primus stove when it caught fire. He dashed in and hurled it down the valette. The gorse caught fire and spread and we had a terrifying time raising the alarm and trying to keep it from reaching the cottage. Men ran to help and the fire was confined to the valette but I felt a bit nervous of the primus when it was brought back to me.

I had the ideal studio for any painter. One room only, so that when waking in the morning one's eyes fall on the picture worked on the day before and all the faults jump to the eye. One can rise and start painting at once and dress and feed later. Walking about the island was not an interruption, peace and beauty everywhere and no conversation or radios to mask the little sounds of animals, wind in the bushes, the sea far below, the birds. It was not always like this: sometimes the storms howled and roared, thumping on the cliffs, and I knew that Hannah would be cowering in her kitchen, while Elie had to stay upstairs to show that he knew his handiwork in building the house would withstand any storm. At these times no boats ran to Guernsey and we were cut off from the world. It was hit and miss as to whether I should arrive back in England in time to start the term.

One journey I remember in a small open boat clasping the neck of a calf which Elie wanted brought to Guernsey. His brother came with us to the harbour and they put it on board. I was the only other passenger so it sat by me as we bounced and swooped up and down the white-tipped waves. In Guernsey there was no one to meet it, and the boatman foisted the care of it on to me. A boy helped and we pulled it as far as the tiny Sark office, where I had the presence of mind not to announce its arrival but open the door, push it in and run.

Wild stormy seas, or a dead calm, those journeys were a source of delight and still are, though now there is a big comfortable boat with a cabin. I generally arrive too late for the tourist boat and am taken across in an open boat not unlike that of thirty years ago.

And so my life for the next three years followed the pattern of going to my godmother for Christmas, then two days later setting off for Sark, whatever the weather, until the end of January. Winter in my little cottage produced a lot of work and the solitude I enjoyed almost to the point of not wanting to leave when the time came, but the term soon passed and with the spring I was back again.

I often spent my evenings with Elie and Hannah de Carteret, and went for many a Sunday walk and picnic with them. One memorable night was spent sand-eeling by moonlight on the Grand Greve beach, where one is shut in by such towering cliffs that one looks like an ant from above. Hannah had a frying pan and cooked bacon and eggs for about ten of us. Then Elie handed round neat brandy in large china cups. After this we hopefully set out to climb the precipitous cliffs, two hundred and fifty feet high. We were merry and unsteady by this time and each became a different animal as we wended our way home, quacking, barking and crowing at four o'clock in the morning.

Another evening was spent at the hall, being entertained by a conjurer. We were all very unsophisticated in those days before wireless and television had come to put an end to the social side of island life. The conjurer laid a woman in a box and proceeded to cut her in half. This was too much for the Sark men and they made a rush for the door. Hannah could not get out, so she took off her hat and buried her face in it. Then on the way home across the fields by torchlight, a rabbit crossed our path. In a flash Elie was after it and caught it by falling on it. He, his father and his son were death to any animal they wanted, never missing a shot with a gun or a stone.

My cottage skylight made it possible for me to get up when the dawn chorus woke me. One night I was rudely awoken by the thunder of a horse's hoof on my tin roof as he noisily cropped the grass of the hillside, into which the cottage was built to stop it falling down into the valley.

Once I worked all night by the light of an oil lamp to paint an impression I had had of the green and grey winter island the day before. My oil lasted until the early morning, when it did not seem worth while going to bed. I went out in a thick mist and met ghostly sheep face to face, who silently vanished into that unreal world; boughs of blackthorn blossom materialized for a moment like a Chinese painting as I passed along the close-cropped grassy paths. I stood on the seagulls' rock and listened to the muffled surging of the sea three hundred feet below, feeling the draught of the gulls' wings as they turned away in surprise at finding me there.

I used to sit for hours in a cleft at the top of the cliff watching the storms, and the sea rushing through the narrow channel between Brechou Island and the Guliot caves below me. It was like listening to an orchestra playing a tremendous symphony, the sea roaring through the rocks and breaking, the wind singing as it brushed past holes and crevices, and the telephone wires humming different notes as they spanned the gap between the high cliffs and the island. The birds drew infinite lines between me and the dark sea, and hovered facing into the wind; one always seemed to look down on birds in Sark instead of seeing them against the light. I wore my Connemara tweed cloak, which was greeny-grey, flecked with colours that exactly matched the lichen on the rocks. It was very wide and long, so that I could sit for hours on the rocks without feeling cold and be quite invisible.

I remember the time a thirty-foot whale, cream-coloured, was washed into the Port du Moulin. It stank to high heaven, but I had to paint it because of its impressive shape backed by sea and blue islands under a purple sky, and in the foreground groups of people in dark clothes making a Sunday afternoon pilgrimage to it. Some wit in the Mermaid Tavern had said that whales' teeth were more valuable than pearls, so two avaricious men went down with pliers, but could not find its mouth as it was underneath. After nauseating work, green and vomiting, they relinquished the 'pearls'. Then the fisherman dragged the beast out to sea and sent it on the current to Alderney with their love.

One year some large barrels of wine were washed in and the men combined to get them up the cliff near my cottage. The Dame de Sark claimed one bottle from each barrel, so the men, amid much mirth, saw to it that she got the dregs, which almost had to be spooned into the bottle. Then the insurance men had the temerity to make enquiries, so I helped to paint one green and before nightfall it was outside my cottage as a rainwater butt. What matter that there was a piece of piping leading only down on to its lid. Another job I had was drawing the white patches on the blueprints of cows for stud-book purposes when a calf was born.

In spring the cliffs and common behind my cottage were carpeted with primroses, bluebells, wild thyme, violets, and ablaze with gorse and blackthorn in blossom. There were always lambs, sometimes black and white, which grouped themselves on ledges of rock or under blackthorn trees: the sheep would break off the lower branches, leaving an umbrella of white blossom over the lambs curled up around the slender trunk. I never tired of drawing and painting them – they became so used to me that I could sit just yards away – and I have never known such unadulterated happiness as on that common year after year in the spring.

CHAPTER 20

The Gate Lodge, and the Road to Clifden

When the first year at the Slade was over in 1931, I took the Irish Mail once more for Errislannan for the long vacation, laden with canvases and an easel. Fortunately by this time the lodge-keepers, Michael and Lizzie King, had been given a farm by the Land Commission and the Gate Lodge was empty.

After a few days' feeding up and cosseting at the Manor, I asked if I could live in the Lodge in order to get on with my painting. My aunts were very under-standing and helped to furnish it with pots and pans, a table and a bed. It nearly broke their hearts not to be allowed to fill it with carpets, chairs and junk. I kept the kitchen absolutely empty except for my easel and one chair. Everything else was crammed into the tiny bedroom. In the thatched shed outside, I kept a wooden box with the sprung seat of the old carriage, which could be brought in for visitors. Perhaps the most useful thing was the three-legged iron pot-oven, which cooked soda bread, chickens or heated up any dish. With the lid turned upside-down and a cushion, it made a seat by the fire. This fire never went out from the day I arrived until the day I left in October. It just needed covering with ashes at night to have a heart of red coals that would boil the kettle quickly in the morning. There was a chain from the chimney for the kettle or hot-pot to hang on, so cooking was easy and the house was always warm.

For the first time in Errislannan I was free to come and go at any time of the day or night, to eat or not to eat, to sleep or not to sleep, and I had solitude with work to do. This was heaven. The thought of my kind of cooking was pain and grief to my aunts, so they sent up a hot-pot dinner every day which also did for my supper. Dear aunts! how good they were to me.

On Sundays I cleaned myself up and went to spend a civilized day at the Manor. Once, when two cousins were staying there, I counted the number of things that went on to the dining-room table for midday dinner. One hundred and five objects were laid upon it by one little maid, and nearly everything had to be washed afterwards. This meant that her half-day off did not start until nearly five o'clock and she had to be back at ten, just when all the parties and fun would begin. What cages men make for themselves out of their furniture and belongings, and how thankful I was that I had escaped.

I got to know the local people better than ever before, as they would drop in to the Lodge on their way home from town or in the evenings. Uncle John was always a welcome visitor, and he was glad of a port of call at the end of the long walk up the drive.

I now realized how our boundary wall had cut me off mentally and physically from all the fun and friendships I might have had when I was young and lonely. I had never known that there were dances going on in houses where I would have been welcome. When people came to the Manor, they sat in the kitchen drinking cups of tea and we stood for a few minutes talking to them. Now in the Lodge, they sat by my fire and we became real friends. This friendship was later extended to my husband and son, as thank heaven, we lived most of our time in the Lodge without the 'wall', though we were on excellent terms with the inhabitants of the interior.

The Lodge was tiny, having only two small rooms with the fireplace between them. It was built of stone, whitewashed inside and out, and had a slate roof which leaked, so at the first sign of rain I put mackintoshes on the bed and basins round the floor. Michael and Lizzie King had brought up three boys and a girl in those small rooms, and my husband and son subsequently fitted in very happily. When the door was shut it was almost pitch-dark, as the windows faced into the trees and the silver gates so that Lizzie could run out to open them for the carriage. I managed to paint small canvases there with the door open, and even did some portraits, chiefly of a girl called Mary King, aged about twelve with Mongolian features, yellow eyes and black hair, but the big canvases required for the Slade summer competition, 48 x 36 inches, had to be done in the loft over the coach-house. The Slade apparently judged by size not quality. The Professor picked one a bit smaller as my best work, but it could not be entered. These large canvases were very awkward to travel with from Ireland, but at least they did not float away on the sea, as did my Sark ones at the Eperquerie, while I was being thrown into a hole in the ship's side from a small boat in a rough sea.

Throughout these long summers in Errislannan, I nearly always went to town on Saturday mornings; either in my boat, or on foot over five miles across Ballinaboy. One could hardly imagine a more beautiful walk, facing the mountains most of the way: climbing steadily until reaching the top of the hill, where I always stopped and lay on a special rock, surrounded by bays, lakes and the vivid changing blue of the Bens, with the Maumturks misty blue behind. I looked up into the vast dome of sky, which could include at the same time dark storm clouds over the islands, pale blue behind with small white clouds to the east, and all the variations in between. I thought of Charlotte Brontë on her honeymoon, viewing the west coast of Ireland and hoping her new husband would not intrude upon her thoughts. I hoped no one going to town would intrude on mine, so that I would have to walk along with them instead of stopping to look.

Just below my rock was the Devil's Lake, a long narrow strip of dark water enclosed by cliffs, with white water-lilies that seemed to float on a black mirror. A most sinister place, far from all habitations except one, belonged to Darby Green, who was our boatman. To a stranger the grey stone and grey thatch house would be invisible under a high towering rock of the same colour which almost overhangs it. Only smoke and a small patch of viridian-green potatoes showed where it was.

I went up one day to make a drawing of the house and Darby came out and took me in to see his father, 'Old Darby', who had been a very good fisherman in his day, and had had the only big boat – a Galway hooker – which could go up the coast as far as Sligo Bay. He it was who brought the first Marconi wireless masts ever into the rocks by my house on his hooker, as the big ship could not get in. He had also won a prize for story-telling in the Feis, in Irish of course. Young Darby, middle-aged by now and very weather-beaten, spoke little, but when he did, he spoke pure poetry in the deep soft way of the men around Errislannan.

Inside the house it was very dark with none of the usual whitewash on the walls, and only one small recessed window. They worked the bellows and the fire leapt up, revealing how little comfort there was in that womanless house. Although there was the most magnificent view in Connemara within a few yards, the house was so sited that none of it could be seen. From the garden the hill dropped down cliffs of rock, to Mannin Bay and the Marconi Bog, where Alcock and Brown landed. To the east were the mountains and two more bays, and to the west the islands to which Darby often sailed our boat for picnics.

One day I had been out with him having a sailing lesson, when we were becalmed and it became unnaturally dark. Under the purple clouds to the west a long white line appeared, which looked ominous to me. I expected Darby to do something about it but he knelt down and took out his Rosary; I got the mainsail down but there was no time for anything else before the sea struck us. Miraculously we ran before it (thanks to Darby's prayers) and came to a shingle beach where we were able to leave the boat. We could not get home to our moorings that day.

Leaving their house I looked to see if there were a short cut over the hill, and Darby pointed up the inhospitable slope, saying, 'God bless ye now; the path will lead ye.'

I could see nothing ahead to follow except a yard of faint track at my feet. I often think of those words '... the path will lead ye'. On another occasion, when I asked if we were sailing the next day, he replied, 'We will not then for the stars are sunk in the sky.' Perhaps one treasured his words because of his silence.

I never managed to sail the boat myself: partly because it was Aunt Edyth's boat and two men always had to go with her; partly because I found the gear too heavy for me at the mooring. So Darby Green sat for hours on end without passing any remarks; even when I had decided to take a short cut between Rush Island and the shore, and landed us high up on a rock, in imminent danger of falling sideways as the sea left us high and dry. Not a sound or movement came from Darby; even when a wave washed us backwards, still no comment.

I took three afternoons to paint his portrait, for which he sat immobile in his blue jersey, staring straight ahead. When he came to look at the finished painting he said, 'Wouldn't ye be taking the soul out of a person with thim things?' I had heard other old people refuse to have themselves photographed for this reason and I think Darby meant just that. Now he is dead and the painting remains; really his only memorial.

I must return to my rock, as I am still on my way to town after this digression, down the steep twisty road and along the valley to the beautiful little bridge where a salmon river meets the sea and dark pine trees crown a rusty-red bank. Here, where three roads meet, there used to be a small village and a monthly cattle fair until Clifden was built. The road to the right stretches for miles across moorland dotted with lakes and facing the whole range of blue mountains. One lake has an island, which is reached by stepping-stones. Here lived a man who attacked farmers returning from the fair with money, killed them and threw them into the lake. Their bodies were found during a drought when the lake dried out.

The road to the left follows the shore with its bright yellow seaweed, rocks and little islands on one side, and on the other hedges of fuchsia and honeysuckle, until one comes to the bridge where a roaring white torrent flows in and out of the Monk's Lake. Men and boys poach the salmon here by day and night, and it has been said that one of the Civic Guards sent out to catch the poachers could not resist the lure of a dropped rod, seized it and was dragged in, uniform and all; but he got the salmon and divided it with the owner of the rod. The next part of the road is a welcome relief on a hot summer day: a tunnel of beech trees which gives a green shade and coolness as one follows the shore of the Monk's Lake with the monastery beside the water.

As one nears the town there is the roar of a huge waterfall up which the salmon leap. Now that it has its old name restored to it – Clochan – the crossing of the waters, this is a beautiful town set on little hills with a background of mountains. It is formed by two extremely wide streets joined together by a smaller one, making a triangle at the apex of which is the market-place. All the two-storey houses are painted different colours, as in a foreign town, and the effect is quite lovely. On a height at each end of the town sit the opposing churches, glaring at each other, and one looks down the dirty street to the mountains and the river. Three names appear over nearly all the shops even to the present day, which must have inspired me to write this poem while waiting to see the Corpus Christi procession:

Corpus Christi in a Connemara Town

Ringed by blue mountains, the little town lives in the roar of the falls,
Up which salmon leap coming in from the sea.

Kings and Connollys, Joyces and Kings;
Two very wide streets of bright painted houses and fine Bay Hotel
    with no bay in view.
Two churches on hills, both claim to be highest, tho' one has so
    many and one has so few.
Tourists are charmed by old women on creels, black shawls in the
    dust, with fish from the ocean now lying in the sun.
Neat Civic Guards, no guns on their hips, and pretty young girls out
    for loving and fun.
Women like pyramids, sitting and talking, sitting and talking and
    watching it all.
Kings and Connollys, Joyces and Kings; a cattle market and Medical
    Hall.

Old men on sticks, spitting and talking; young men on window-sills
    talking of whether to go or to stay,
While foreigners' cars park high on the roadway, horses and asses
    doze through the day.
Shell Esso and Castrol are now the town's lifeblood; the street acts
    as cemetery for the wrecked cars.
Ropes teapots and fishhooks, blouses and beer, mix with clothing
    and plastics in some of the bars.
Whiskey and porter smells, musty and fusty, blow round the new
    lavatory and the great square.
Tweeds of all colours, piled high on the path, are for elderly
    sportsmen, the young ones don't care.
Kings and Connollys, Joyces and Kings: your family names have a
    pleasant sound,

And your beautiful children suck lollies and chocolate: bright-eyed
    and bonny they play on the ground.
With a hairy cow's leg and an old sheep's head, that someone has
    found.
    But! come Sunday
All will be clean; flowers lining the streets, for Corpus Christi
    is coming this way.
Priest under his canopy, incense and music; girls in white dresses
    throwing flowers away.
Children of Mary, women and nuns: men in dark blue, Rosaries in
    hand,
Will say a Hail Mary and slowly follow the little boys' band.

Kings and Connollys, Joyces and Kings, the fine Bay Hotel and the
    Medical Hall,
Have blocked up their doors with altars and flowers as God passes by,
    and all of us fall
On our knees, full of wonder, wonder, wonder.

Finding a convenient window-sill or box to sit on as much out of sight as possible, I started drawing, absorbing the wonderful shapes made by the people or groups clustered together. The women then wore lovely shawls with patterns in a border; plum, grey, but mostly black, with black skirts over red petticoats. They walked slowly but gracefully, even when bent forward under a heavy sack of flour or groceries, or a creel of fish or potatoes.

On the return journey I was glad of a lift on an ass cart or side-car as far as the turn to Errislannan. If it were raining they put half their shawls round me to make a warm waterproof tent. All they wanted in return was conversation giving them any kind of news to take home. Then they would talk about my family, going back to my grandparents long ago, or about my aunts and their virtues, but never giving anything away about themselves.

CHAPTER 21

Return to Errislannan

During my third year at the Slade I was living in a basement room with the window under a grid in the pavement, so that it had to be kept shut. In the cavern-like hole ferns and mosses grew, which looked strange and beautiful when lit at night by the lights in the shop above. It was cheap but money was running out and I felt so tired it was an effort to do anything at all. I had a horror of debt after all the misery it had caused my family, but I owed rent now and became more and more depressed. I was getting free treatment for rheumatism at the Peto Place Clinic, but this took time and energy.

Among the many friendly Slade students, only a few stand out, and those not for painting. One, called Meriel, attracted me because she was quite impervious to any teaching, whereas I was inclined to believe everything I was told until I began to think it over. I used to go to her bare comfortless studio where I learned the useful lesson that an individual cup or plate is quite unnecessary. We all sat round the saucepan on the floor and used a spoon or piece of wood to convey the food to our mouths, and a jam-jar did for a cup. This was a great help later on. She also showed me where the cheapest food could be had, in little workmen's cafés in back-streets where everyone was friendly. In her basement lived a huge Negro who used to go out into the area to shake himself and his clothes free of lice.

We always had interesting discussions and I came away feeling that London was the only place to live. I laughed as I walked along thinking of the cage-like atmosphere of Errislannan and the hour-long meals at the flower-laden table, eating off numerous plates, with solid silver spoons and forks, the silver teapot on a silver tray and all the creditors grinding their teeth at the hopelessness of being paid. One day I met Meriel in the street when the rain was pouring down. She was bare-footed and had a shawl round her; on her head was a shabby padded armchair turned upside-down, acting as an umbrella and also getting itself from shop to home. Meriel was extremely intelligent and worked in museums, sorting them out for a few months at a time, earning enough to keep her for a while doing nothing. She married the potter Michael Cardew and lived in Cornwall with a large brood of children.

Another friend was Frances Lane, niece of Sir Hugh Lane of the Lane Collection of pictures that adorn the walls of the National Gallery and the Tate, who by going down in the *Lusitania** caused years of official argument between England and Ireland. A compromise was arrived at whereby half the Lane pictures remain in England and half in Ireland, to be changed over at stated intervals. Frances was a very good painter, but was forced to teach for a living and so had no chance to do serious work before marriage, and then three children filled her time. If only her uncle had left her even one Van Gogh or Cézanne a good painter would have been saved, but I am sure such a thought never entered her head. Her mother and sister were like relations to me; putting hot-water bottles in my bed and getting food in before my return from Sark or Ireland.

Frances's great-aunt was Lady Gregory of Coole, near Galway, a centre for famous writers and painters during the early century, including G.B. Shaw, George Moore, W.B. Yeats, AE and earlier Synge and Casey. Their names are carved on the great tree at Coole though the house has now gone. Not far away is the little cathedral of Loughrea, which contains 'the finest stained glass north of the Alps'. Sarah Purser's workshop, 'The Tower of Glass', in Dublin turned out most of it and Michael Healy was the chief artist. It was largely due to Sarah Purser that Dublin eventually got its Municipal Gallery of Modern Art, which houses at least half of Sir Hugh Lane's collection, its principal glory.

When the gallery was opened and a bronze bust of Sir Hugh Lane was in place, but hidden by a sheet, Frances was asked to go over to Ireland to represent the Lane family. De Valera made a speech and the *Daily Telegraph* got a photograph of him standing by the bust with Frances on the other side suppressing a large smile, as Uncle Hugh's drapery fell off too soon and he listened to the President's speech in person.

**The Irish Times,* 18 June 1915: 'Bodies washed ashore at Aran from the *Lusitania*' – Several bodies have been picked up off the Aran Islands, Co. Galway, which are supposed to be those of victims of the *Lusitania* outrage. One was that of a lady clothed in expensive garments and with a wristlet watch. Three of the bodies were conveyed to Kilronan and buried, as the Coroner, on being communicated with, did not deem it necessary to hold inquests.

At the Galway Board of Guardians meeting on Wednesday, Mr O'Flaherty RO wrote stating that he had the bodies interred at Killeany Graveyard, as far from the other burial ground as space would permit. The RO, in his report, added: – 'Father Farragher PP says I had no right to bury the bodies in consecrated ground, that he would have to write to the Bishop and that probably the bodies would have to be exhumed. I wrote to Father Farragher that I did not know to what denomination they belonged, that I had no other place to bury them in, and that I saw Protestants buried in Inishene Graveyard, and at the new cemetery in Galway.'

Mr Cooke said these unfortunate victims of the *Lusitania* were human beings and why should they not be interred as such? (Hear, Hear).

The Board expressed concurrence with this action of the RO.

At the Slade I made several temporary friends and went to many parties, but few students were dedicated to paint; most of them would settle quite happily for some side-line. I felt impatient when they encroached on my Sundays, and still felt so tied to Charles that I was not interested in the young men. I worked hard and became more fluent in drawing, and stored masses of facts about the history of art and anatomy, but the painting seemed to be an exercise that was bad for me. I fell in with the curriculum and painted – I even won a prize – but was marking time until I could return to my own ground, which was Connemara; to that spit of land enclosed by bright sea where all my ideas and inspiration came from; to the brightly coloured town and the winding narrow roads that run along the shore or through the mountains. To the figures that expressed so much in their old clothes, moulded to them by the wind and the rain; figures that were as expressive back view as front. *En masse* they were people led by the spirit, moving unconsciously towards the goal of a good death and heaven. To me they typified more than people going to town or returning home, working at essential things like digging turf or potatoes, or rowing home in the long black currachs to those dim blue islands faintly seen on the horizon.

Later the Hungarian peasant meant the same to me, seen on those vast empty plains, transformed by the hot climate and gay clothes, but the long full skirts had the same statuesque shape and they moved with slow dignity, heavy baskets on head or back. The men in their coloured clothes and black hats wheeled heavy barrows of melons or maize, which equated to turf-carrying. It was the work that made the shape. I have found it quite impossible to paint townspeople in smart clothes; they have no grace or life for me. Years later, one of my war pictures of refugees turned into masses of peasants all fleeing in one direction on Errislannan peninsula, where they must eventually drown in the sea or be crushed by the huge spiked wheel that followed them. Others were of endless columns of refugees in central Europe, but anyone could have recognized the Connemara farmer and his wife. Two of these pictures were used to collect funds for refugee relief.

When the three years at the Slade were over, I went back to the Gate Lodge, penniless but painting, and feeling that there was something to be said for the story of the 'birds of the air'. I got my Diploma with first-class honours in History of Art and seconds in the rest, and left for Ireland with everything I possessed as I had nowhere to leave anything. Then I thought of showing paintings at the hotel in Clifden for summer visitors, and sold eleven, which more than paid my debt and all my summer expenses. I was relieved, and they were mostly duds that sold. It is curious the things that people buy; always what I call souvenir pictures, never anything real.

And so I shut myself up in the Lodge to work. In spite of all the debts and mortgages on the Manor, life was lived very comfortably there. I had only to say the word and four good meals a day would have been offered. Everyone was overfed, whereas I had been weak with hunger in London; I knew they could not lay their hands on ready cash to send, so I never asked them. I found visitors very distracting. They ruined many a picture, as I had to rush at an idea and conversation can kill it dead. At last I put a string across the path with a notice saying 'Engaged', but the whispers and the tiptoeing away were nearly as bad as their company, and I did not want to turn away Uncle John or any of the local people returning from town who were tired and enjoyed a cup of tea.

During that summer, my aunts took me to tea with the Miss Blakes at Bunowen Castle about eight miles from Errislannan. The castle, an ancient fortress, is now a complete ruin and looks as though it has been for a hundred years, owing to the roof having been taken off. It was my idea of perfection. Huge rooms absolutely bare of furniture except the dining-room, where we had tea, brewed in a little room off it on an oil stove. The castle was built on a neck of land joining the peninsula of Ailbraick to the mainland, so that the towered building stood unsheltered from the fiercest gales and looked out on to both Mannin Bay and the Atlantic, which was so close that the pebbles broke the windows when a real storm was blowing. Beside it is the humpy little hill with Queen Granuaile's castle on the top, of which now only a few stones remain.

Inside the castle, the great walls of the hall still had the plasterer's trowel-marks and had never been covered in any way. I later sold a painting of one of the tower bedrooms at a London exhibition; I wished I had kept it when the place became a ruin. This room was round, with three Gothic windows; the walls were pink with a wide blue frieze round the top and the only furniture was a black iron bedstead with nothing on it. Now the castle is inhabited by a colony of choughs, said to be the largest in Ireland. I like to think of an unusual bird taking up its abode in that wild and lonely place, fluttering about the big room where we had tea in Victorian style with polite conversation. The conversations of the birds must keep it alive and their red legs add a little colour to all that greyness.

It was at this tea party that I first met Da Barnett, who became a real friend until her death in France a few years ago. She was the first person I had ever met in Connemara who thought art of the slightest importance, and who knew a great deal about it. She was kind, and sensitive to beauty of all sorts, and she loved the unspoilt country, mountains and beaches intensely. She and her husband had built a lovely house on the edge of the sea at Ballyconneely, and had made a garden surrounded by white walls to protect it from the storms. I knew the little cottage that had been there previously, and they had kept to the same level but built around it, so that it looked like a little whitewashed village from across the sea.

Da came to Errislannan the next day and we climbed the Look-out Hill together and talked. When we came down she asked to see some of my paintings, and the surprise of the aunts was almost comical as they apologized for my wasting her time. That summer I had many happy days at her home, bathing and meeting friends of hers who were staying there. These were mostly writers and painters, and it was an unknown joy to listen to intelligent and interesting conversations, with the beauty of Connemara as a background. I had hardened myself to the freezing effect of complete ignorance of and indifference to art that surrounded me at Errislannan. Da and her friends took it for granted that painting pictures was worth while and it thawed my heart and encouraged me to do a lot of work.

I saw a good deal of Da in London and stayed with her in France, but I like to remember her at Ballyconneely, where I think she was happiest. She had the courage to fly there with her son, Lord de Ramsay, in a little two-seater plane, in the days when planes were not so reliable as they are now, and they had to land on a white sandy beach. The deaf and dumb girl Mollie described this, with appropriate actions, as 'the Lord who drove a motor car in the sky'.

CHAPTER 22

The Races at Omey, and Crumpaugn Boathouse

A favourite place for the races was Omey Island, a few miles to the north-west of Clifden. The island can be reached at low tide across a vast stretch of sand, and is a barren place with only a few houses on the far side. As one approaches there is nothing to be seen but a hill and a derelict overgrown graveyard, but Race Day transformed the shore into a seething mass of people, tents, cars and bars. I loved to watch from the distant road in the morning the dark procession of horses and carts, wending its way snake-like across the pale green sea, like the children of Israel on their famous journey; the splashes made a misty path as they travelled onwards. Carts, with horses up to their bellies in the water, led the procession of lorries and riders on horseback, followed – as the sea got shallower – by people wading up to their knees. An early arrival was important as the stalls had to be erected before the invasion of visitors and their cars began.

The racehorses looked like toys as they galloped in circles on that huge expanse of yellow sand. The deep blue sea waited, foaming, at each end of the island, to sweep in and put an end to all this life, and as evening fell not a trace remained. There were no car parks or quays to litter with rubbish; the sea and the wind cleaned it all away and next day the fresh sand shone as brightly as ever and millions of cockles popped up out of the holes. I have been sand-eeling on that beach by moonlight and enjoyed the thrill of keeping one eye on the advancing tide, the other on the quickest way home.

One summer, the races were held in a field a mile out of Clifden, and I thought that if I were to go to town in my boat, I might get a lift to the course. I left the boat at the quay, taking the oars up to a house but leaving the pins in the boat, and got a lift from a kindly publican, who assured me that he would be delighted to bring me home in the evening.

For this one day, the little field was a jumble of small tents and stalls, and the same kind of competitions one would find in an English fairground, except that here everything was incredibly shabby and tattered. The competitions were run by wild-looking travelling showmen, and there were two bars, which consisted of planks laid on barrels forming a square. These drew a solid mass of men who clustered round them all day like flies round a honey-pot. The tinkers wandered about begging, with a family of dirty ragged children hanging on to the mother's skirts, and always one baby slung on her back in a shawl. The countrywomen stood or sat in groups by themselves.

There was a piper with the little Irish bagpipes, which have a bellows under one arm and the bag under the other, so that they can keep going indefinitely. Some of the men, when they had enough drink taken, would try a few steps of a jig, but mostly the pipers just played for pennies. There was a fiddler who played very well, but he looked so thin and tired one felt too sorry for him really to enjoy the music.

At the other end of the field were segregated the people who were now coming to Connemara to settle in the empty houses. They were dressed in tweed suits and wore properly polished brown shoes and sat on shooting-sticks. They seemed rather out of place when one looked at the horses they had come to watch. These were mostly farm horses that had been run round the country or along the beaches for several weeks previously, and were ridden by boys in shirts and blue trousers, some with boots on, some with bare feet. The doctor's daughter always rode, well turned out, and there was a sprinkling of outsiders with more professional-looking horses. The local boys carried heavy sticks with which they beat their sweating mounts, and if they were too far behind after the first round, hid behind a hedge and joined in the last lap, to the loud cheers of the onlookers.

I did not feel at home among the tweed-suited racegoers so retired to the side shows and found an inexhaustible supply of interesting people to draw.

When the races were over and everyone had gone, I waited for the kindly publican who had promised me the lift to town. The wind was rising and I began to fear that I should not be able to get home in the boat. At last a procession of four men appeared, with the publican slung between them. They hoisted him into the car, where his head hung over the back of the seat, but his manners were as perfect as ever. He apologized for the delay and hoped I had had a good day. We carried on a polite, if dreamy, conversation all the way to town.

I hurried down to the boat to find that all my pins had been taken. The wind was now rather unpleasant, so I broke some branches off a bush and started off, but as soon as I met the rough water, the branches broke. I was driven back on to the little peninsula of Faul, where there was a sheltered cove up which I pushed myself with an oar. Unfortunately Pateen, our boatman, had seen the boat from the Errislannan side, and when he lost sight of it thought I had gone down, as it had got really rough by that time with white horses all over the bay.

In the meantime, I had started to walk across the land, when I met a friend, a young man called Sean, who insisted on my coming in to have a cup of tea as I passed their house. His mother was so insistent that I stayed for a proper meal. I kept telling myself that no one at home would be expecting me to cross in the boat, and would know that walking would make me very late. Time passed and it was dark before Sean and I set out to walk over Ballinaboy. He was not well and I insisted on his leaving me before I reached the top of the hill. Later I wished I had not, as I thought I saw a big dog passing me over and over again. I thought of the grey ghost dog, but I suppose it was a dog making circles round me. Then I met two cars, and as the road was narrow I stepped out of the glare of their headlights and continued on my way. Later I found that these were visitors who had been sent to look for me on the other side of the bay. When they did return, much later, they said they could see my boat on its side by the light of their headlights trained on the far shore.

My aunts and Uncle John were very much upset as they ushered me to bed in the cottage spare room. After a time the teetotal Aunt Jane came creeping in with a stiff whiskey to 'set me up'. Later again, there was a tap on the door and there was Uncle John with a stiff whiskey to 'set me up'. Fortunately I had not drunk the first one, so after much persuasion, Uncle drank one with me. He needed it more than I did after standing all the evening in the window with the telescope. Whiskey was the panacea for all ills, but only in the right hands. It was the 'Devil's Brew' in the wrong ones.

I went for the boat the next day, Pateen rowing me across, and met Sean again. He had made a sail for his rowing boat as he was not allowed to row on account of his ulcer. He asked me if I would go to the castle with him for a picnic to try the sail out, so we went the following day, but the sail blew right away and we were left with a rowing boat and a contrary wind. This meant I had to row, much to his embarrassment, so we landed for a rest on Rabbit Island half-way home. Here he told me of his pilgrimage up Croagh Patrick the previous year. Sean was a very devout Catholic, and as he described it I could nearly see it all happening.

We can see the 2500-foot Croagh Patrick from the top of the castle hill, looking like a blue pyramid, almost standing in the sea. Thousands of people from all over the world go up each year; many climb the rocky track barefoot, doing the Stations of the Cross on the way. Sean went up during the night, so that he was there in time to see the most wonderful dawn. He said that the whole sky became pink with many purple clouds, and bars of gold above the sun itself. The hundreds of islands in Clew Bay looked black against the bright sea on three sides. He went to Mass in the little oratory on the top of the mountain, and said it was the most wonderful experience of his life. I was glad he had known it when I heard he had died the following year.

The next summer in Errislannan I did a mad thing that nearly cost me my life; the fact that I did not go to a watery grave must have meant I was wanted for some other fate. All my youth I had longed to go to the islands unaccompanied by a picnic party on board. I pictured coming into a sandy bay with food on board for a few days, exploring the island and talking to its people; returning to the boat for the night and lying looking up at the stars, rocked by the waves. A lovely dream and one that became an obsession with me.

At that time I was living in the Gate Lodge, but I spent my days down in an old boathouse on Crumpaugn, a round inlet of the sea like a lagoon; a very lonely place where no one ever came. The boathouse had once been plastered and had a window in it, but now it was entirely covered by escallonia bushes which had grown over the roof and enclosed it like a snail-shell on all sides except that of the slipway to the water. I had replastered one wall and painted on it a life-sized picture of a currach coming towards me in a storm, with three old women in the stern praying, and one man leaning over the side offering a bottle to a mermaid. Red devils flew about the young man but angels surrounded the old women. This had taken me some time to do so I had brought down some pots and pans to eat off and the old carriage seat from the Lodge to sit on.

My boat, *The Galley*, was moored nearby and this gave me the idea that now was the time to pack up necessities and set out for an island. My boat was too small, but now that September had come and the cottages were empty, their four long shallow lake boats were lying on the shore. There were only two oars, the others having been taken away to be repaired. I dared not ask for another one in case they wanted to know where I was going.

Some fine weather came and I started loading up. I brought the carriage seat for a bed, and a large sketching umbrella. I put in two blankets, two loaves and some cooked bacon; two bottles of beer and a few other things made up my store. I arranged with an old woman to go to the Lodge and remove my dinner each day when it was sent up from the Manor.

Then I set out with the high tide. It is ten miles to the nearest island, but there is nothing between one's boat and America, with a rocky inhospitable coast on the land side. If only I had had an outboard engine in those days! This was not a sea boat, and to my dismay the sea began to rise and break; I could not possibly anchor for the night on the far shore as I had hoped, with the white waves surging up the rocks. The only thing to do was to return to the Errislannan side of the bay behind the Look-out Hill, near the white beacon, where a narrow cleft in the rocks opened into a little gully about twelve yards wide at the top. I shot into this on the top of a wave, fending off with an oar, and, as there was a spring tide, reached the shingle, where I grounded. I dragged her up and settled for the night. A more lonely place I could not have found, and after walking about for a while I felt so cold I got into the boat. Covered in blankets and the tarpaulin, which reached only half-way up the boat, I lay and looked up at the clouds, and later the stars and a full moon. I could not sleep with the roar of the waves so close to me, and had a meal of cold bacon and beer. This made me sick. Then it began to rain and I put up the sketching umbrella, but even so I had to bail if I were not to float on my bedding.

The tide went right out of the cove in the middle of the night and I realized there was a line of tooth-edged rocks at the entrance. I missed the top of the tide in the morning and could not move the boat, so laid out all the wet blankets on the rocks to dry and waited for the afternoon tide, while all the time the sea was getting rougher and great waves surged up in my cove, going out with a sickening roar.

During my long wait I wandered along the shore until I came to the ruined cottages that the Famine had emptied for a time, though people had lived there since. It was where we had had the picnic long ago when I was a child and Charles had played houses with my brother and me. They were little changed except for a bush that was growing up the chimney, but I realized that all the people who had been there that day were dead – this was after Charles's death in 1935 – and I felt like a ghost haunting the place.

I went back to find my boat still high and dry, so filled in the time scratching life-sized figures on the round whitewashed beacon. I thought I might paint them to look like real people standing talking and frighten the distant inhabitants into thinking they were ghosts. I remembered coming there in the scarlet cloak to watch a storm and being chased by a cross bullock. I had thrown off the cloak and hidden in the rocks by the sea, while the bullock had pounded the cloak with his head and his feet. I had had to wade in my clothes round the rocks, very cold and frightened, to get home. Then I sent Johnnie Dan to fetch the cloak, which was not much harmed as the bullocks were hornless.

At last the tide came washing round the boat and she moved. I was not given much choice, as she was dragged down to the entrance before I had got the oars out even for fending off. We crashed against one side and nearly tipped over. I threw all my weight on to an oar to fend her off a rock that we were just going to sit on, when the oar broke, almost taking me with it; I was half over the side when she swung round and went such a crack on another rock that it threw me back into the bottom of the boat. A wave sucked us out and somehow I got the other oar out in time to give a good pull that carried us sideways away from the cove.

There I was with one oar and water over the floorboards; but the sketching umbrella came to the rescue. I got some light rope round it, tied the handle to the thwart and opened it up. Mercifully the wind was blowing down the bay and we moved quite fast, while I kept her straight with the remaining oar. As we got further into the bay the sea calmed down and gradually I edged her round the headland and, having no more strength left, ran her up on to some sand and waited for an hour or two. Then I landed and went across to where I knew I could get an odd oar, and with this I got her back to the boathouse. I lay on the carriage seat on the floor that night, very cold as the blankets were still damp, but from the boathouse I saw the sun rise over the mountains, the absolutely still water in Crumpaugn reflecting the flaming sky. I got back to the Lodge early before my absence had been noticed.

> How happy is the little stone,
> That rambles in the road alone.
> Emily Dickinson 1830–86

CHAPTER 23

The Charlotte Street Studio

During the summer of 1934 I was offered the post of Art Mistress at Benenden School, which later became famous with the arrival of Princess Anne. This meant that I could live in London and go down to Kent for three days a week. I was given a well-lit studio that had been the hayloft and enjoyed my work there very much. The lovely house was set in gardens surrounded by parkland with lakes and all the amenities of a fine country house: a pleasant contrast to my life in London.

Now began the hunt for somewhere to live and I soon found a studio in Charlotte Street, near Fitzroy Square, where at that time there were over a hundred studios; so there was plenty of congenial company in the cheap cafés, and friends living nearby. I had one room on the third floor with two long windows, which gave a good diffused light if left uncleaned. There was a plain wooden floor and after I had whitewashed the walls I had a good work-room. On the pitch dark landing outside was a cold-water tap, shared with the French painter in the studio next door. We both wanted to work so we never entered each other's studios uninvited, but were always ready to help out with food or paints if necessary, and went to each other's parties. The landlord was a Jew, a most kind and helpful man. I had practically no furniture, so he gave me an old painted tin trunk which held a hundredweight of coal; this sat by my fire and, with a drawing-board on top, was my only table for six years. I got out of store the old wooden-backed couch bed, a small armchair and a wooden chair, a chest of drawers and two wooden boxes. There was a built-in cupboard in the wall which did for clothes, food, canvases and odds and ends, and with all this I felt fortunate and happy, in spite of the fact that there was no bath and the lavatory was two storeys down, served thirty people and had no regular cleaner.

I found Charlotte Street the most fascinating place in which to live. At midday I went to a small café called The Dante, run by an Italian family; and after a few weeks, the father, Dante Baia Adriano, came to my table and said, 'We have said good-day so many times, now we will have a conversation.' So we did and I got to know all the family, and later did black chalk drawings of him; and of his son playing an accordion, which he needed for a poster advertising his band.

One regular customer at The Dante café was the huge Negro tipster Prince Monolulu, known to everyone on the racecourses, with his light-coloured drapery and a band round his head with three ostrich feathers in it. When King George V died he appeared with black ostrich feathers and wept real tears of sorrow.

When we had a hard frosty winter our neglected lavatory became frozen up and the situation was too horrible to describe. There was a small drain in the basement yard which someone unfroze with a kettle of boiling water and we all tipped our buckets down that. Then the kind Adrianos invited me to use theirs. Another time there was a coal strike; nearly all of us depended entirely on coal for warmth. One day when I had finished my dinner at the café, I found a large paper bag of coal by my chair, placed there by the waiter. A number of us gathered in my studio that night, and with the remains of any old stretchers or frames we could spare, had a warm evening for once.

We often had no water except what we could bring in cans from a basement a few doors down the street, where a mechanic kept a gas jet flaring by his tap. On Sunday morning there were about twenty of us there, in dressing-gowns, getting the day's supply. We had nothing but gas, but I found inverted mantles actually gave a better white light than electric bulbs so that did not worry me. One of the most tiresome things was that the tremendously high walls of the stairs and landings were dark green and must have had linseed oil rubbed into them. On a damp close day this oil ran down the walls and down the stairs in rivulets and any unfortunate visitor who did not know, and who had to feel his way up three flights of stairs in the pitch-dark, arrived covered in a treacle-like liquid.

However, the snags were more than outweighed by the advantages. One could walk all over the centre of London – to Trafalgar Square, Westminster, Piccadilly and the parks, to all the cinemas, theatres and galleries, which saved a lot of money in the year. There was a laundry nearby and a shop where one could buy French food – including snails in their shells – and newspapers, which I used to improve my French, and several cafés where food was good and cheap.

I felt more alive than ever before, there was so much to see and hear. I did not join any groups or societies as I never can find anything to say about art. Until I came to London in my twenties I had not heard one piece of good music or seen one good picture, and there they were, all for the taking and mostly free: galleries ancient and modern, museums, promenade concerts, ballet, plays, everything, and when one tired of streets there were the parks with their trees and flowers. I sailed in Regent's Park, took trips on the Thames, and rowed on the Serpentine. Here one day I saw some small children drag a sack out of the water and open it. 'It's a biby. Crikey!' they shouted bending over it. ''arry, get a copper.' 'arry ran off full of importance. Once I was waiting to see King George V go by and a small boy beside me said, in bitter disappointment, ''e allus wears that 'at. Don't he never wear 'is crown?' London speech was like listening to a foreign language after the Irish children's English with all their H's.

There was entertainment everywhere and ideas poured in, although I did have patches of loneliness and depression. I could work in comparative quiet, free from the radio which my aunts in Errislannan had acquired, and which was turned on regardless of the ugliness and vulgarity of what came out. It nearly drove me up the wall, a very accurate bit of slang that, which describes my panicky feeling when I cannot get away from the horrid voices and music that come out of that torture box. Sundays were the worst days in Charlotte Street, when people sat on their window-sills smoking and letting their radios blare across the quiet road free from its weekday traffic.

Thoughts of Errislannan made me do silly things just to feel free; such as firing all my spoons and forks across the room and letting them lie there as I thought of the baize-lined boxes they had to be fitted into one by one at home, and how when I threw them all in with the knives Aunt Jane's grieved silence made me feel as though I had committed a crime. Reaction made me enjoy squalor; sleeping in my clothes; starving until I was weak on my legs, but happy.

It was convenient to be able to take pictures to shows under one's arm, or the bigger ones in an open-topped taxi. I got them hung but sold hardly any the first few years. Then Dr Honeyman at the Le Fèvre Galeries asked me to take down a taxi-load twice and kept me on tenterhooks while he decided whether to give me a show or not. Finally he thought it would be better to put them in mixed shows and kept the seven best. Unfortunately he was then moved to Glasgow and nothing came of it. I never enjoyed seeing my pictures in mixed shows as I put them in silver frames, which suited my colour schemes best, but had to keep a few white or gilt frames for mixed public showing. Individual shows came late and I enjoyed them, knowing that all the worst pictures would sell and I would be able to keep the ones I really cared about.

I felt very fortunate to be in London; to have Ireland to love and England to live in – a sentiment echoed by most Irish writers and painters. Looking back I seem to have collected a motley collection of friends of all ages and occupations. Some were from Slade or Sark days, others just happened. No matter how much of a recluse one wants to be in order to work there are times when it is impossible and one locks the door and goes out on the town.

One good friend I acquired in the Victoria and Albert Museum; a bearded old man called John Trevor who was poring over the illuminated manuscripts when I was working on them. He always carried a magnifying glass, which he offered to lend me. He had brilliant eyes, good features and wore a black wide-awake hat and shabby clothes. A member of the Fabian Society and a friend of Havelock Ellis in the past, he had kept to a revolutionary way of thinking.

John's family had married and gone away and he lived in one tiny room in a workman's flat in Hampstead. He had made himself a chair to sleep in as there was no room for a bed with all the boxes of books that lined the walls. The one good thing about the room was the window, which looked out over the whole of London and made me think of a harbour at night with all the lights in the blackness. I learned how small a space one could live in and be happy, and how if you lived on sausages one week and fish the next, you need only clean the pan once. John had wonderful photographs that he had taken of people. The portraits of the members of the Fabian Society alone made an interesting collection; I still have the one of Havelock Ellis, a magnificent-looking man.

Then there was Jack Bilbo, one of Al Capone's bodyguards; just returned from fighting in Spain, and having written a book about that, he had taken to painting horrible nude ladies. He picked up a Bond Street dealer by his trousers and collar and dropped him in the gutter outside his gallery because he would not hang his nudes. He was not a friend but an enforced acquaintance. This strange square figure stumped up to me in Burlington House with a long stick tapping the floor, and asked me to go out with him for some coffee. I believe in doing everything once, so went. When we came out of the Kardomah in Piccadilly, he did not ask me to get into a taxi but threw me in. None of the screams appropriate to a stolen lady was forthcoming; it seemed too public a place to scream when nothing had been done.

We arrived at his ground-floor flat and he dragged me inside, whilst I still pretended that I was not frightened. When he saw that I really was a prunes and prisms miss and would not be amorous, he told me to clear up the mess from the party the night before. I refused and he raised his stick to beat me, but I managed to push the door-screen on top of him and ran. The next day he arrived at the café, but at a word from me Dante enlisted the help of the regulars, and in a body they forced him to the door and locked it. He found my studio on the day I was drawing Adriano's son playing his accordion; I recognized the tapping stick coming up the stairs and had time to bolt the door. It was as well I left for Ireland just then. Years later I saw him on television on a boat setting out to go round the world, but I expect he hopped off at Plymouth.

*   *   *

One day in Charlotte Street there was a knock on the door and, when I opened it, there on the dark landing stood the tall thin figure of Charles. I cannot describe the overwhelming feeling of joy and relief that came over me. I had done my bit and knew I should never send him away again. I had not allowed myself to see or write to him for nearly three years, but he had seen me sometimes coming out of the Slade with other students. I must have been mad to have caused us so much misery. We had suffered too much to continue our separate lives and I felt guilty for having been the cause of it.

Charles shut up his house and found a small flat in a mews near me where he could keep his car, so that we were able to go off into the country when the weather was good, and we returned to our Sunday morning explorations of London in the winter. He brought some good furniture and rugs from home and I had a busy time shortening curtains and settling things in. I was good at this because it was like creating a picture, but I preferred to live with bare boards and packing-cases myself. There could not have been a greater contrast in our shells; his all spit and polish, mine definitely a matt surface.

Charles kept an alcove in his sitting-room for one of my pictures and had a shaded light placed above it; this picture was changed now and again. After going through the stacks of pictures in the studio, he would take one away and have it beautifully framed, which was his way of helping, and in time I acquired a lot of good frames, which sold many a picture as the people with money to spend are generally elderly with houses, and one can see them considering how the frame will fit in with the furniture. I took back a picture once when the purchaser proudly described the colour of the room and the furnishings among which it would hang. Fortunately she was a stranger and just thought me mad. In Charles's alcove I enjoyed my pictures more than anywhere else as they were isolated and well lit. His work often took him away for weeks at a time and I painted on, all the better for solitude, but in what a different frame of mind, planning a supper for his return when I went to air the flat.

I made a lot of evening friends who came and sat on my floor half the night. A rag-tag-and-bobtail lot they were, but I have never listened to such good conversation anywhere else. We drank Russian tea and sometimes they would bring food, or coal or wood for the fire.

I was saving up my best pictures for a show and had no room for them, so found a furniture repository in the Harrow Road, a vast warehouse type of building, the inside comparable to a jail. One went up in a large clanging lift to different floors and the jailer walked ahead ringing his keys, down long corridors of numbered wooden sliding doors. Then he rolled one back and switched on a light in the dark windowless cavern, of which one could rent half or a quarter. I felt nervous of the jailer locking me in until I was found as a rat-eaten skeleton years later, so I watched him walk out of sight before entering. The whole place was eerie with all the much-loved and much-used old furniture crying aloud from their cells to be taken home.

One summer, instead of going to Ireland, I went to France with a friend and a haversack and we walked about, making many drawings and lying in the sun enjoying the lushness of the country in contrast to Ireland or Sussex. Then Charles had a month's holiday and we set off in his car, first to the Chilterns. He had a genius for finding nice places, generally old inns or farms, and we stayed for two weeks in one which had genuine old beams supporting the ceilings and cream roses climbing round the bedroom windows. The weather was bright and stormy as we climbed those lovely hills and explored the little village churches. We had one week on the cliffs of north Cornwall, and then gladly returned to Sussex and our downs. We found a fourteenth-century inn where we were the only guests and the landlord took trouble to make our stay enjoyable, providing wood fires in the evenings and on wet days. It was like having a home of our own without the trouble of it. It is impossible to describe our happiness, even in damp misty weather. One evening I remember sitting for hours in the car by a gurgling stream, watching the ploughed fields and trees appearing and disappearing in the fog before returning to our fire. I see that in my journal I wrote 'and so ended the happiest time I have ever had'.

While we were in Sussex I noticed that Charles looked tired, and we took the car where we would have walked all day. He said he was all right and I was only too willing to believe it. We went back to Alfriston and Rottingdean and had some of our best times. One day from Rottingdean we went up to High Barn, where I had once spent a night in a haystack. It seemed as though we had the hills to ourselves, until suddenly we were on the edge of a deep bowl-shaped valley, looking down on one of the most beautiful sights I have ever seen. At the bottom of the valley there was a farmhouse surrounded by apple trees in blossom and old red-roofed barns which were yellow with lichen. The house itself was white with a black roof and it and the trees cast blue shadows on the ground as far as the haystacks, which were bright yellow in the afternoon sun. We could see a herd of cows being driven in for milking, but no sound reached us far up on the hillside.

We sat down enthralled with all the unspoilt loveliness of earth and sky, and watched the Lilliputian figures of men and animals moving about far below. After an hour or so, we followed a sheep track down to the farm to see it all more closely. Charles leaned on the gate as though he could never drag himself away, and I noticed for the first time that he looked thin and ill. At last we turned to go, but Charles went back and stood looking up at the apple blossom. Later I knew he had felt that he would never see it again.

I think I remember it so well because it was the last time we were to be in

Sussex together and I described the day in my journal. After some weeks Charles went to his doctor. He was very ill with cancer but continued working for another six months in London before going home to see about the disposal of his house. I wrote to his French wife and she came over for a few weeks, but as she had been living in France for nineteen years and did not know the house or the neighbourhood there was little she could do. Strangely enough we liked each other and became friends.

I have always been grateful for the wonderful times Charles and I had together. He was more sensitive to beauty than anyone I have ever known. We did not need to talk as we walked through woods or country lanes or wandered by the shore; he noticed everything and introduced me to so much, but our special place was always the Sussex Downs. There we felt at home and were completely happy. I had never wanted to marry Charles as at that time I could not have lived in a proper house for long, and much preferred my Charlotte Street studio where I could work day or night. I think we were all the happier for our independence.

Charles's solicitor came down for the funeral and said Charles had sent for his will when he first became ill, but had not returned it. It was never found and so his wife sold the house and went back to France. This was not what he had planned, as apart from me he had wanted to make provision for his caretaker and some of the office staff. I think his wife did do something about this later.

When it was all over I came back to town feeling quite ill with nerves, but work and friends – and having a home of my own where I could live as I liked – helped the bad time to pass. The thing that did most good was going to Hungary for the whole of one summer. Then the war came and changed everyone's lives, mine for the better.

Some years before Charles died we had made friends with a strange solitary man called Gaston Moulinet, a Swiss dealer in prints and drawings. He had a tiny shop filled to the roof with a fantastic assortment of objects that had taken his fancy while he was hunting for prints at auctions in country houses. One evening, as we waited at his shop, an open-roofed taxi came round the corner piled high with lions and tigers, surmounted by stags' heads bearing great antlers, their glassy eyes shining. In the midst of all this was a hollow-cheeked white face under a mop of hair, with eyes nearly as big as the stags'. This was Gaston, who, leaving a country house empty-handed, had seen that the hall was decorated with trophies of the chase, and bought them all. A crowd collected in the street and the embarrassed taxi-man would not help to unload. We put the menagerie in the shop for the night and the next morning Gaston arranged them along his pavement; before nightfall he had sold them all at great profit. I regretted that I had not claimed some of his magnificence for

Charlotte Street. The oily staircase walls would have been much enhanced by the reminders of the jungle and the moors. I could have painted trees and the missing parts of the animals behind them, then the heads would have felt at home.

Gaston was the shyest and most shut-in man I have ever known, but Charles had broken the ice by taking a genuine interest in his prints and asking him out to lunch. Now when he heard that Charles was dead, he arrived at my studio with a huge bunch of flowers but gave no greeting, just silently arranged them in jam-jars; he was leaving without saying anything but I asked him to stay, and that evening made the first of a number of drawings of his head. He was the perfect model, with his very wide cheekbones, firm jaw, large eyes and long curly hair just going grey, which was sometimes pressed down under a wide-brimmed black hat, giving him more than ever the appearance of a mad musician. I did one oil painting of him, during which he thawed and became a friend.

He came of Swiss peasant stock and his childhood had been spent in a wood high on the mountains, where he had been very unhappy owing to the cruelty of his father to his mother and himself. Often he had been driven out with a stick in bitter weather at night to bring in firewood, or to feed the farm animals. He loved the forest by day, but was inordinately frightened of it in the dark; this fear of the dark remained with him even in middle age. Compulsory schooling in the valley released him at last from his father, and after school he got work with an art dealer in Montreaux, who eventually sent him to England. With no introductions, he had settled into a bed-sitting-room where no one ever visited him and no one had ever invited him to their home. And so the years had passed and he had settled into a mould of solitude.

One sunny Sunday I called for him on the spur of the moment and asked him to come to Kew Gardens with me. When we arrived and walked on the grass, he behaved as though he had suddenly woken in heaven; gazing round with a childlike joy at the flowers and the trees. He was a distinguished-looking man for all his shabby clothes and worn, unpolished shoes and I watched him with interest, relaxing and opening up in the beauty of the gardens, instead of striding, tight-lipped, along the streets, head in air, looking so tragic and unapproachable. When we sat down to have a picnic lunch by the river, at first he was silent with emotions he looked across the water. After spending long years of Sundays in his bed-sitting-room, the freedom to sit propped up against a tree and talk to someone broke down his barriers. He told me of his early life with obvious longing for the forests and the mountains, but his mother was dead and he had no other link with home. He found London as cold and unfriendly, as so many foreigners do if they make no friends at their work. He told me also of the rings formed at auctions, which being such a lone wolf he refused to join, consequently meeting with a certain amount of persecution from the dealers.

His search for prints in country houses had landed him in some curious situations. The prints were often in frames and he did not want the trouble of carrying these home, so he would hide in the gardens and take them to pieces, leaving the glass and frames tidily under some bush. Sometimes authority caught up with him and ordered him to take everything away. Then he hung the smaller frames round his neck and walked along the country roads, hanging the larger frames on gateposts, or leaving a neat pile of glass outside a garden where he thought the owner could make use of it.

When I came back from Hungary and was faced with a whole winter without Charles, Gaston was a great help. I could work while he sat silently by the fire or cooked supper for us both. One evening, later on, when the war had come and the streets were blacked out, he left about ten o'clock to walk back to Chelsea; he always walked miles across London where anyone else would have taken a tube. In the early hours of the morning, the people in the next studio woke me to tell me that my friend was asleep on the stairs. I felt very remorseful as it was bitterly cold and draughty and I had not known that it was raining. My neighbours brought him up and lent me some cushions so that he could sleep on my floor. He slept but had such nightmares that he woke everyone nearby with his shouts. Then one day he arrived decorated with sticking-plaster and I learned that during a terrible nightmare, he had hurled himself through the glass doors on to his little balcony. Something was very wrong and the cause I think was just loneliness. He was always late for any appointment and had come to live without time in that clockwork city. The sun was his only watch as it had been on his native mountain farm.

I felt very bad about leaving him and was glad to hear he had found a nice woman to work in the shop, who became a friend. But Gaston was never intended by fate to know happiness, for one day I read in the paper that this woman had been murdered in the shop by a mad black man with a sword, and Gaston was the one to find her. Poor, poor Gaston! His nightmares must have been worse after that. He never answered my letters, and by that time I was married and settled in Cornwall.

CHAPTER 24

Hungary

In Errislannan in 1937 I met an Hungarian Jewess from Budapest, who told me that Hungarians were very keen to have English girls as guests – with all expenses paid – because they wanted to learn English. She knew of one who had a château on the banks of the Danube eighty miles south of Budapest. This sounded exciting and I wrote to Szitanyi Marietta that autumn, who replied at once asking me to go to her for three months in 1938. She said there was a garden room that I could have as a studio, so when the time came I packed large canvases and set off with high hopes to Victoria, little realizing that I would have to pay an extra six pounds for my luggage.

That night at Calais, a porter took me along some dark narrow streets to a disreputable-looking house which turned out to contain a bar with the most hideous-looking female behind it. It was so dark that only her nose and chin showed under a mass of untidy hair. Her enormous bosom rested on the counter. The porter explained that I wanted a room for the night, and although I backed away he had my luggage, which he carried up the stairs. The woman followed and took me into a dirty room with a basin on the floor catching drips from the ceiling. I put the dressing-table across the door and lay on the bed in my clothes, not expecting to sleep, but I did.

The next day at Frankfurt, I missed my train to Vienna, so took the next, which meant that I was behind schedule all the way, and people were supposed to be meeting me.

I was enthralled by the magnificent scenery as the train followed the vine-clad hills and castles of the Rhine, and went through forests, villages and mountains. There was too much to see, and after a time I felt that I could not take in any more. Mercifully, before we got to Vienna, everyone left the carriage except a very tall Englishman, who suggested that we make the most of the space and have a lie-down. This we did, and were grateful for a whole seat each on which to stretch out.

When we arrived in Vienna he got a taxi and took me to the address I had been given. He waited to see that all was well and then said goodbye. I was sorry to part with him since he had been so kind, and I did feel a long way from home.

The maid who opened the door could not speak one word of English and her mistress was out, so our conversation was limited to signs. How do you sign that you want a bathroom and lavatory? I nearly gave up until I saw some hinges in the wall of the hall and discovered a door which led to what I wanted.

My room was light and airy with a polished parquet floor and innumerable snowy curtains and hanging embroideries. The sheets were of a linen so fine it was like silk, and I was thinking how fortunate I was to be there when I saw a bug walking across the floor, and another one on the wall near my bed. I had so far only seen pictures of them, and was sick with horror at the thought of what I should look like if bitten all over by the morning. The painter Leo in the studio next to mine in Charlotte Street had drawn them on the walls most realistically to frighten me, and described their habits. I tried to stay awake, but knew nothing more until my hostess stood by my bed in the morning with a cup of coffee.

I left the next day for Budapest, not expecting to be met as I was so late. It was nearly midnight when the train drew into the dark station. Some men had been annoying me in the carriage and I was quite frightened at the thought of getting out with them. They surrounded me, talking and laughing as we went down the platform, but at the van they all got out musical instruments and I realized they were a band. I think they were laughing at my nervousness. Then to my joy Radisics Alice, Marietta's sister, greeted me and I knew at once that all would be well. She took me home and was most kind and welcoming. I was so thirsty that when she offered me a drink, I signed to the maid that I should like a very long one, thinking of something like orange squash. The girl brought in a tumbler of a drink that I thought was strong, but foreign. I was shown to my room, I saw the bed, fell on it in my clothes, and knew no more. The next morning poor Alice was most upset and explained that the maid had not understood, and had given me a tumbler of their special blend of cognac and apricots, one small glass of which I learned was enough to make me dizzy.

Alice saw me off on the little steamer that was to take me the eighty miles down the Danube to Doonafoldvar. This was a fascinating journey as we glided along between forests with no backgrounds, maize fields, and plains that faded into a blue distance; then more trees and little villages. My companions were mostly peasants with baskets and sacks. One large monumental woman opposite me fell asleep, so I could make a number of drawings of her, and later I painted her in brilliant colours. There were some beautiful dark gypsies on board and I heard for the first time the tzigane music.

We arrived at a wooden quay that appeared to be in the midst of the country, but this was Doonafoldvar, and there was a neat little woman in black waving to me. Marietta had come to meet me in a four-wheeled trap drawn by two American trotters, and driven by a coachman in livery with a top hat swathed in black ostrich feathers. He sat at attention, his whip in his right hand, which he used to swipe at anyone who was not quick enough getting off the narrow cobbled road into the dust at the sides, so that we could sweep by behind the high-stepping trotters. We drove six miles along dusty roads in the blazing sun between fields of maize, pumpkins and streches of vineyards. Marietta gave me a scarf to put over my face when we passed another carriage, as the dust rose up like a thick cloud and obscured everything for some time after we had passed.

When we reached the drive gates there was a beautiful, almost life-sized crucifix on one side with a flowering creeper covering the base. Then we entered a different world of trees and green grass and shady verandahs. Water was sprayed from the river to keep this oasis green in the parched land. The long low house was cool and airy, with marble floors and all the doors open to encourage as much draught as possible. How grateful one came to be for darkness and iced drinks.

Marietta was the only person who could speak any English and I spoke only French. All her friends spoke German, so they made up for this by smiling and bowing to me most graciously, all through dinner parties and picnics. I replied in kind until my face ached with smiling and my neck with bowing. One fearful party went on until two in the morning with the main body of guests playing cards, but the two ladies who did not play were entertained by me in another room. I found a gramophone and we smiled at each other over it hour after hour, and not once did their charming manners fail.

It was extraordinary how keen they all were to be like the English, due partly to the influence of the Duke and Duchess of Windsor, who had been staying in Budapest. They wanted English clothes, English music, English magazines; and were very keen to learn the language – hence my arrival, though the girl of seventeen with whom I was supposed to speak English cut down her lessons to one hour in the mornings, and it was with her mother that I spent most of my time.

The food was delicious but too rich for me. I cannot describe the meat as it seemed to be covered in rich sauces. The pudding course was often a cake about two feet long on a tray, full of rich things and layers of cream. It was considered impolite not to have a second helping of everything, and so I suffered. There were great piles of grapes and lovely melons, and always tender white cobs of maize, which came in piping hot, but which one dipped into the glass bowls of iced water on the table.

Their civilized veneer was only skin-deep, as I discovered when one of the workers' hens pecked at Marietta's tomatoes. She took down a gun and went tripping down the garden in her high-heeled shoes and shot them all. She then hung the birds on the man's fence, and he had no redress. It was like being back in feudal England.

The estate workers lived just outside the garden, round what looked like a village green, in thatched cottages with white, pink or mauve walls, in the shade of the acacia trees. They had decorative bands of the most beautiful colours and designs along the outside walls, and all kinds of decoration on the inside, which was freshly painted each year.

In the evenings, when the sun was setting, the people gathered on the green, sitting on the carts, and sang with tremendous vigour, music that sounded lovely to me listening from the garden. The women sat doing their embroidery, their heads bent over their work, and the men, in bright trousers and shirts, played and sang, while the cream-coloured bullocks munched in the background under the trees. The women embroidered aprons and skirts in bold designs, or did very delicate stitching on blouses and pillowslips: lovely work that would be sold in Budapest, or go into the daughters' wedding chests. These chests were painted like the priceless coffers one finds in a museum.

Near the house was the well, backed by a row of enormous sunflowers. One tall pole supported another high in the air, with a jointed stick at one end that went down into the well, and was balanced by a weight on the other end. A simple device that could be used anywhere, but nowhere save in Hungary could you get it combined with such beauty of action. The women wore many petticoats, which stood out like bells and swayed as they walked or leaned over to lift the buckets of water. Their head-dresses were starched and their blouses tight and trim. A group of these women would be gossiping by the well, washing clothes in one trough, while the bullocks would be drinking at the next, all to a backdrop of towering sunflowers.

The estate was nearly self-supporting; there was the wheelwright's shed, where the lovely bullock carts were made, and the great barns and stables housing the twenty farm horses, where a man had to sit on a corn bin every night on guard, the discomfort making sure that he did not fall asleep. The same thing applied to the long cow-sheds, and the sheds for the sixteen bullocks, which were used for ploughing and taking the carts in to market. I saw it all in the height of summer, but tried to picture it when the long winter closed down, and the wheels were taken off the carriages and replaced by sleighs. The men then lived in fur coats and hats and tall leather boots. Those flat endless plains must be a wonderful sight in the snow.

The friends who came most often to the house were a couple who had been a monk and a nun, but had run away to get married. They had two good-looking sons of about thirty, who were very kind to me and took me sailing, and danced with me in the evenings, teaching me their violent dances on the stone verandah, the beat hammered out on the hard ground with their heels, just as in the Irish dances in the little kitchens at home. I learned only a few words of Hungarian, such as the greeting which means 'I kiss your hand.' I tried this out on the maid when she brought my morning tea; she went off into fits of giggles so I gathered you used it with discretion. I was warned not to use it to any woman younger than myself as it was a sign that you thought they were older and due for respect.

My studio was a whitewashed room in the garden with no furniture in it, which was just what I wanted. My sketchbook was filling up with drawings and soon I got several good models to sit for portraits. Hans, the coachman, sat like a statue. He was a fine-looking man who had led a most respectable life, but that summer he had just come out of prison for killing a man. Their form of defence was to carry a stone on a string up their sleeve. If in danger they swung this round their heads until it hummed. Unfortunately the other man had been too drunk to hear the hum and the stone hit him on the temple, killing him.

Hans was a good coachman, who always kept his horses in perfect condition. They were so well trained that one day, while he was in a shop in Doonafoldvar and they were frightened, they set off for home, keeping to the middle of the road as though he were there with his long whip to clear the way for them. They arrived at the hall door and stood the appropriate time for passengers to dismount, then swept away to the stables to await the return of their master, who wept on their necks before putting them away.

Our mornings were spent by the river, bathing and fishing with grasshoppers for very small fish. Swimming meant going with the swift current about half a mile, lying on one's back drifting along, enjoying the coolness, until the mill came in sight, at which point one made a determined swim for the bank. These mills were like two black wooden arks, joined together by a large water wheel. If you were careless and got caught in the current you went into the wheel, so we took no chances.

At one place near the mill the women assembled to do their washing in the river, leaning from a little wooden stage. I thought of the steamy kitchens at home and the hot water required, whereas here they produced snowy-white clothes and head-dresses out of the brown water and had a happy social life in the sunshine while doing it.

We shared the riverbank with herds of long-haired pigs, who played like children, enjoying the cold water. Their swineherds sat under the acacia trees, carving things out of very white wood, or playing a pipe as they sang. They looked exactly like an eighteenth-century French painting, with their wide-brimmed black hats on the ground with their crooks, their coloured trousers and shirts and masses of black hair. Their easy attitudes as they leaned against the tree trunks, the background of the bright water, and the cattle grazing on the lush green grass, all made one feel that it must be only temporary, it was too good to last. But I have proof that it was real, as one of the swineherds carved me a cigarette-holder with my name intertwined among the flowers, and I have it still.

In the villages, the swineherd blows his horn and the owners of pigs or cattle open their gates. Then there is a rush of pigs along the pavement as they go for their daily outing down to the river. The same thing happens in the evening. At the sound of the horn, every door opens in the solid wooden fence topped by sunflowers, and each pig finds his home.

On market-days, Marietta kindly arranged for me to go into town about six in the morning to Doonafoldvar so that I could sit drawing or watching the people from some shady place. The long full dresses and the graceful walk of the women, often with large baskets on their heads full of ducks or hens, or piled up with green melons or scarlet paprika, came into my pictures for years to come. In the market among the stalls were huge piles of melons, and everyone seemed to be making their dinner off a large luscious dripping slice and a cob of maize. Others sat in the gutter throwing grapes into their mouths. I say throwing because they swallowed the grapes, skin and pips, at the rate of about one a second. I learned to do this too and found that they made a good meal for a hot climate.

The gypsies sat on the ground looking romantic and beautiful, among the wooden basins and troughs they made by hand. They were not popular, in fact they were regarded just as we regard the Irish tinker. They were very musical and generally had a fiddle which they played to us in the beer gardens. Unfortunately the craze for things English, affected even them, and in Budapest I heard one playing an English song with disastrous results. Their dance music, curiously like the Irish, goes like lightning.

The afternoons were spent in the coolest place one could find; for me brief spells in the ice-house. This was a deep cavern dug out of the ground, with a very thick thatch going to a point in the middle. It was filled with ice during the winter, and there were steps going down and shelves at different levels on which all the food was stored. The entrance had to be kept carefully closed, but the dark coldness at the top of the steps was a most refreshing thing.

In the evenings we played tennis or went for walks by the river or along the fields, when it was like walking into infinity; it was all sky, and at night, with the stars out and the frogs croaking, I could have stayed for ever. Radisics Alice, who had met me in Budapest, came to visit and we became friends. She could speak good English and by that time I was feeling quite depressed by the lack of conversation.

Over the centuries the Danube had changed its course and cut its way into the sandy cliffs near the Szitanyi estate, so that we often pulled bits of Roman pottery and other objects out of the cliff while we were bathing. Marietta had a good collection of Roman burial urns, bowls and pitchers. I was given a bowl from the first century by a man called Auriel, who was working with the excavators from the Budapest museum. He spoke English and we became friends, which involved a state call on his parents. He wore the gold ring given by the University of Budapest to the most brilliant student of the year, and was a charming companion. We later wrote to each other until the war broke out.

Auriel's home, although very old, was built on the open-plan method for the sake of coolness, but in each room were the enormous tiled stoves reaching nearly to the ceiling, which were lit in the winter. We sat down to the most enormous tea I have ever had to face. Course after course was brought in, but there were little jugs of rum in front of each person to put in the tea, which helped it down. Then came the lovely evening drive home, mile after mile, by the river and through groves of trees. I sat beside Hans on the box, so did not have to talk and could enjoy the tremendous distances and the colours of the evening sky.

It was a happy, interesting time and I love to remember the long drives along the Roman roads by the Danube, the only sound being the clop of the horses' hoofs and the rustle of the maize leaves slithering against each other. I liked the formal afternoon calls on Marietta's friends, when everything was done in such a ceremonious way in the large shady interiors, with their Turkish and Mongolian hangings. In the vast barns attached to these houses, the peasants from other provinces camped for the harvest. Their elaborately embroidered dresses and fourteen petticoats were hung from the roof over their beds of straw. They wore plain pink or blue dresses for field work with a crisp handkerchief on their heads.

This wonderful summer drew to its end and I had arranged to spend the last week in Budapest with the girl who had told me about the Szitanyis the year before in Ireland. When Marietta heard that I was going to stay with a Jewess she was horrified and tried to persuade me against it. I could not see any reason for this and so they agreed to take me to the end of the street where she lived, but would not come any nearer in case they were seen to have any connection with a Jew. They were staying in Budapest during this week and we arranged to meet at a restaurant for lunch. When the day came I waited for Marietta and saw that there was only one table with three places vacant; the fourth was occupied by a Jewish man. Marietta called the proprietor and told him to order the man to leave, which he did – and was well scolded for letting him come in in the first place.

I enjoyed my week with the Jewish family, who took me to see a lot of the beautiful city of Budapest. I found that they were building up a store of money in England against the day which they knew was coming. They had brought many English girls to Hungary and paid their fares. The English girls then paid the money into an English bank for them. I hope they were able to leave Hungary in time to enjoy it, but I fear the war brought tragedy to all the people I knew there. I had no answer to my letters to Marietta or Alice or the Jewish family, and I know that the Russians advanced across the river just where the Szitanyis estate had been.

The day came to leave and I arrived at the station to find that my canvases could not leave without a permit from the curator of the gallery. This meant a long delay and everything had to be unpacked in the hall of the gallery, while my friend indicated in pantomime that I was only an amateur. This meant one more day to swim in the lovely lakes on the island and bask among the rose trees between bathes, so I was glad of the extra time.

The journey back to England was uneventful. A large bottle of the apricot liqueur, decorated with flowers, was given to me at the station. This helped to make the journey convivial, but as only one man, a priest, could speak English the others expressed their gratitude for the drinks with the usual dozen bows and smiles I had come to dread, but they were all very friendly and pleasant.

The young priest sat next to me and we found that we had a great deal to talk about, and when we got to Vienna he took me round sightseeing, as he knew the city well. He was on his way to a boys' school in Belgium and wanted to improve his English, so he wrote to me for a few years and I sent him magazines.

One very foreign thing happened on the journey. A woman in our carriage took her little girl out into the corridor and let her use it as a lavatory. At Frankfurt attention was called to this, and soldiers appeared from nowhere and jumped into the train as though they were going into battle. They shouted at us and accused us of making the mess. The woman never batted an eyelid and denied all knowledge of it. Such a frightening issue was made out of such a trivial thing that we were quite relieved when the train started moving and the soldiers had to get off, still shouting and shaking their fists at us.

I arrived home, my mind full of the friends I had made and all the lovely things I had seen and hoped to see again, but two years later came the war, which destroyed so much of that loveliness, and the friends are no longer there to see.

CHAPTER 25

Autumn in Sark, and War

In the September before the war, 1938, I found a different-coloured Sark and a healing one, which I needed after the loss of Charles. I quote from my journal:

> ... dark much earlier, a cold wet evening, but it is perfect inside ... am sitting in front of a bright fire of drift wood and gorse, though Hannah has put coal in for me. The flames are up the chimney and the kettle steaming on the hob, the lamp light reminds me of the winter. Bathed down the valette, not a soul in sight. No boats in Harbour Gosslin as a storm sank them all, but they are now round at the other harbour after hard work getting them up. The sun was shining this morning as I went out to my rocks. The grass was cropped close by Elie's horses and the sheep. The hawthorn hedges were a deep scarlet with patches of brilliant hip berries; old man's beard and yellow convolvulus leaves; purple patches of sloes like grapes. I will gather some tomorrow for Hannah to make sloe gin and some blackberries for myself. There is something special about the fruits of the earth in such places, so lavishly given for birds and humans.

I stayed on my rocky seat for hours watching the sea currents and the gulls. The white foam cast out by the race formed patterns I wanted to paint as it swirtled rhythmically into the deep blue and green water. A hawk hovered on the Saut de Juan; a few rabbits clung to the side of the 200-foot cliff side; grasshoppers perched briefly on my knee, ants with wings like ladybirds were busy round me and, above all, surrounding me like a dome, was the blue sky with flying clouds making swift shadows on the sea. I went down for a swim and enjoyed the brightly coloured stones, then gathered wood for my fire. Collecting my sack, I climbed through the hole in the hedge and went shopping.

This involved strolling through the fields, through more holes in hedges, past the duck pond, on which reposed my models. These quacked and came to me for bits, or stood on their hind legs twisting their heads into their feathers, or squatted, heads buried in their backs, all making perfect shapes and colours.

If I wanted meat, which was seldom, I looked for the piece of paper nailed to a tree saying when a beast was to be killed, with a large space underneath for you to write your name and which piece you would like. First come first served, it was all in writing who would get the titbits. A woman called Frankie came hurrying by in black hat and long blue apron with her shopping basket, returning to her solitary cottage, but she is really a man whose mother had wanted a daughter and brought up her son as such. At the fancy dress dance he appeared as the most angelic golden-haired choirboy in surplice.

Sybil Andrews and Cyril Power came in the afternoon, dripping from head to foot and cold. We had tea round the fire and good interesting talk. They were both good artists, engaged on three-colour linocuts for the London underground. In the winter I used to go to their studio in Hammersmith on Sunday mornings and listen to the Dolmetschs and others playing violas da gamba and other ancient instruments. One man made and repaired violins, and he told me that inside some German ones were engravings and poems where no one would ever see them. Some words he had found in one remained with me: 'When I was alive I was silent, now I am dead I sing sweetly.'

One evening I went out to see a red sunset and found on a grey stone wall a row of tall foxgloves with yellow leaves at their feet. The sunset turned one side of them the brightest scarlet while the other remained purple. This became a larger than life painting, very violent with the sea below and the rushing purple bars of cloud above. Another painting at this time was born in Hungary but carried out in Sark. A woman at a well, her great bell of starched petticoats and stiff angular arms in front of the big well wheel. This was in different pinks, but needed a sharp note, which was supplied by a Sark blackbird. When this went on tour it was bought by a man who got my address and sent me a photograph of it in his frightful sitting-room, over a tiled fireplace topped by revolting bits of sculpture. I could have wept and wanted to ask for it back, but was too hard up to raise the money. I do not enjoy selling pictures.

My journal again:

Monday. Stormy wet day went down to the beach enjoying the rain on my face and the wind flapping my hair, the screeching of the gulls and the boom as each wave hit the blow hole. Two boats out to save their pots in the ink-blue sea. The cliffs were frightening hanging over the beech heavy with ivy, which is like a nightmare crawling steadily over the island. Hannah keeps cutting it as it has reached my cottage and is climbing over the hawthorn hedges and the walls. First the pale green grasping fingers, then the stick-like stalks and below almost on sea level the great trunks many years old. This is why I painted the island as a green circle in a grey sea with bare ash trees like a candelabrum in the centre.

Tuesday. Edwin and Mary Hayward arrived today on their honeymoon. Very stormy. They were in the little *Joybell* and the engine gave out for half an hour while they drifted in among the rocks near Herm. A bigger boat would have been wrecked. The north passage being too rough they were landed just below here and had to carry all their luggage up 300 feet of cliff path. In spite of it being the honeymoon they cowered over my fire and said they wished they could stay there all night.

* * *

I had been in Errislannan for two months when war was declared. With no radio or newspapers it came as a surprise and I did not know what to do. I felt that I wanted to go back to England and join in in some way, and realized that I could not stay in Errislannan with no money at all. The news was brought by the postman and the visitors began to pack; as their cars disappeared over Ballinaboy a lonely emptiness settled down over the whole place. Then the first ship of the war to be sunk by the Germans, the *Athenia*, went down off the north-west of Ireland and some of the survivors were brought in to Galway. Our doctor went down to see if he could help and brought back with him a man who had lost his wife and small son. This made the war real to us all.

That afternoon I went down to old Johnnie Dan the shepherd's house, where he was in bed with his last long illness, but was expecting me to finish my portrait of him. We did not feel like it so we sat and talked. When I told him about the war, in great distress he said, 'God Almighty, no country will be left out of this and there'll be no victory for the destruction that will be in it.' Then he turned to the Mona Lisa over his bed, which he thought was a picture of Saint Anne, and, whispering a prayer and crossing himself, said, 'I'll be gone myself but the boys! Oh God all the boys!' He seemed to know intuitively the way the war would take and time proved him to be right. People like Johnnie seem to have an extra sense, acquired by sitting day after day looking out at the earth and sky as Johnnie had done for fifty years on the Look-out Hill, minding our sheep and cattle.

I felt when I left a fortnight later that nothing would be the same again. In 1940 Uncle John died suddenly, leaving Aunt Jane and Aunt Edyth terribly alone in the house. Mercifully, as I said goodbye, I did not know that I was looking at my much-loved uncle for the last time. During the long journey to England, a large war picture rose in my mind, and before I arrived every detail was ready to put down; I could hardly wait to unpack my paints, buy a large canvas and start. A gas mask had to be got and food bought, but by day and night I worked until the painting was finished and it is one of the best things I have done. At the end of the war, having seen London during several blitzes, I do not think I would have altered anything. It got good notices in several exhibitions, but it is not a subject anyone would want to hang on their walls.

I went down to Benenden as usual, returning in the dark on Wednesday nights. Sometimes there was a dim blue light in the carriages, sometimes none, which made it possible to see the country nights and the long beams of the searchlights. I enjoyed these dark journeys, which helped me to paint, but was uncertain as to what I ought to do. I felt that I should be doing war work, but was too old for any of the Services, and wondered if I could do something about camouflage or map-drawing. To this end I went to the Air Force Headquarters in Kingsway, where a very supercilious girl in uniform sat at a desk, looked me up and down and said, 'You've come to the wrong place, the Labour Exchange is more in your line.' She turned away to deal with the next one and there was no getting past her. Too late I realized that I should have dressed myself up in suitable clothes; perhaps some thick brown shoes would have inspired confidence. I put some on before going to see the Land Army, but that was no good because they wanted a doctor's certificate, so I rather thankfully returned to my red cloth sandals and cloak.

In May 1940 I went to Sark as usual for the Easter holidays, and it seems incredible now to think that we were allowed to take up shipping space. I left Sark ten days before the Germans arrived, not because we thought they were near, but because term was commencing. My friends the Skeltons arrived as I left, to settle up their farm, but they were caught by the Germans and, not being Sarkese, were told to report at the harbour in the morning for deportation to one of the camps. Major Skelton spent the night writing lists of everything he wanted Elie de Carteret to do for him, and of everything that was to be given to his friends. Then, in the morning, he and his wife went up to the cliffs and took poison. He died but his wife did not, and she was not found for a day and a night. The Germans made Elie look for them and he remembered a place where they often sat, and there he discovered them. She was in a terrible state as it had been raining all night. Elie took her up in his arms and carried her away. She was ill in Guernsey for a long time, but eventually came back to Sark. The poor de Carterets had loved them both dearly and had worked for them for many years, and the tragedy has cast a lasting gloom over that part of the island.

One day, coming back from Benenden in daylight, the train drew in to a small station and I saw that the opposite platform was covered with the bodies of soldiers, lying or sitting propped up against the walls in the most terrible state of exhaustion; covered in mud, their clothes in rags; some seemed to be unconscious. They had just come from Dunkirk. Two very young officers in torn dirty clothing were staggering about trying to look after the men. Any that could walk were bringing cups of tea to those who could not get up. It was a terrible sight and shaming to us civilians sitting there in comfort. The train moved on, and I am sure that picture will remain with us for the rest of our lives.

In Charlotte Street the authorities decided that our coal-hole under the pavement must be our air raid shelter, so they replaced those fascinating round iron lids with square ones and decreed that we should sit under them and wait for the tottering old house to fall on top of us. We should have been a queer collection. One French painter and his Belgian girl; one German woman (later interned); one Swiss woman; one English shoemaker; a Scandinavian sculptor and his girl; two Jewish tailors and me. We did not use it as we thought it better to be on top of a house than underneath it, but the house next door was the one to get the bomb. Ours lost all its windows, but stood.

I was in London for part of the 1941 blitz and it was amazing when one emerged in the morning to see the ruins covered in snow. It was like a shroud draping the houses and the sad bits of furniture that still clung to the walls high in the air. The cold blue light and the silence of the snow froze one's mind and nothing seemed to have happened. I walked round one of those garden squares lined with trees, a statue in the middle. The black branches held the snow, and the marble figure of a seated man looked a dirty yellow. Crowned with a white coronet he gazed unblinkingly at the ruins, the only unmoved witness of the night's horror.

While one raid was going on, I was sitting in a blacked-out train in Paddington Station while the roof was rattling down onto the platforms. When we finally drew out into the country and a dim blue light was turned on, only a row of white faces appeared, as they were all sailors and their blue did not show in the faint light. They were returning to Plymouth and all agreed that it was far safer at sea.

In June 1941 I received a telegram from Benenden telling me that the school was being evacuated to Cornwall and asking me to go with them. I felt rebellious at the thought of leaving London, but with no money there was no alternative. So reluctantly I packed my best pictures, an easel and paintbox and stored my other belongings, hoping to return before long. I little thought then that the most important part of my life was about to begin.

CHAPTER 26

Cornwall and Marriage

On the long journey, as the train went cluckety-cluckety-cluck, cluckety-cluckety-cluck, endlessly, dreams and pictures to paint rose behind my closed eyes. I always find the solitude of trains – particularly at night – a time and place for inspiration. This time I was tired after packing; sad at leaving my studio and my friends; going into the unknown on the strength of a telegram saying 'Come.' I knew nothing of the future save that I was to get out at Newquay Station, so I shut my eyes and drifted towards the gilded years of childhood.

I was running through the sunshine and storms of our lives on the farm in Warwickshire, which depended on horses: a worrying and precarious form of livelihood. The winters I remembered from the nursery window: snowflakes falling against grey skies, covering the garden and trees, and my brother and I tobogganing down the long hill. I saw my mother skating along the frozen canal pushing my sister's pram, looking as though she were flying through the white fields. I saw the picnics in cowslipped fields, the mill cottage and our explorations in mysterious woods and their green light. Then we were walking to school, fixed in a timetable like flies in a spider's web, until summer released us and we bounced up and ran again through the sunny days at Errislannan; running, running from the lake or garden to the stable yard; running along the Candoolan road to the sea; climbing over the Look-out Hill or riding on donkeys to the bog for turf.

Then came the black misery of living when Donald went to boarding-school in Suffolk. My mother and I had driven him there in a trap from my great-aunt's house and left him standing in the doorway as we started our homeward tearful way, but soon a little figure came scampering along the road and hung on to the back of the trap. Huge brown eyes were fixed on Mother in utter despair. I stared at the pony's wobbling hindquarters till we took him in and turned again for the town. This time he ran in to the black doorway and we cried all the way home. I spent that evening in the harness room with old John, the coachman, who had been with my great-aunt for sixty years when she died. I polished harness and an old saddle until they shone.

I loitered through the landscape of early teens, the weather grey lit by bursts of sunshine between long, rain-falling days, until at sixteen I was held in Errislannan for four years of loneliness and poverty. Then came release and London and a grown-up world in which to run about. Charles, my childhood love, was there and the sun always shone, till Donald was killed and my father and mother died. Then Sark and the Slade built up for me a new world of light and space. Charles was still there. How much happiness he gave me and how much of the beauty of England he showed me. Then he died.

Deaths are like stepping-stones, it seems to me. One nearly falls into the rushing water at each one, but fear of falling makes one reach the far bank. Hungary helped this time with its new interests, the burning heat and the wide landscape, and the Danube swirling by. Switzerland, France, Belgium, had all granted me respite, but I always saved my fare back to Errislannan, and nearly every summer, and sometimes in the winter, I hurried back over Ballinaboy Hill as though I could not wait to arrive. It had become the perfect place again now that I had the Lodge to live and work in, and freedom to come and go.

Now the seven fruitful years in Charlotte Street were over. It had been a home, too, and saw some of my best work. Sark was hidden by the war, but someday I would go back to the Fregondée. I scribbled away in my journal as the train went cluckety-cluckety-cluck, carrying me away to Cornwall, which at first sight I hated, but came in time to love.

> I'm just a country boy,
> Money have I none,
> But I have silver in the stars,
> Gold in the morning sun.

It was June 1940 when I found Benenden School settled in the Hotel Bristol, a vast hotel on the sea-front at Newquay. It was a far cry from Benenden's own lovely gardens and playing-fields in Kent, but they were making the most of the sea and beaches. On first viewing the place my heart sank and I dived into a pub for a whiskey to keep my spirits from oozing out through the soles of my shoes, but I was lucky enough to find a large room in a farmhouse on the hill above Porth, about a mile from the school, overlooking the sea and Trerelgue Island. I found I could work there and was reasonably happy.

When the summer holidays came I went to St Ives and wandered all over the town looking for somewhere to stay, until providence took a hand and led me to an hotel overlooking the sea, where I met my future husband, Roger Bent, who was staying there with his mother. Their family home a few miles away was too big to live in without help, and his five brothers and sisters had left home for good.

Roger took me to the top of Trencrom, a high rocky hill, in his old Alvis car with the hood down on a hot sunny day, and we spent the afternoon talking; it was love at first sight. It is difficult to describe one's husband, but I must put down a few things that mattered. He had had polio when he was a child and it had left him very crippled, so that he could walk only short distances with the help of two sticks. People seemed to forget this in his company and saw his magnificent head with its mop of red curly hair and his cheerful kindly face. He also suffered greatly from asthma, but he rose above all his handicaps with a courage I have never seen equalled, and he was admired and soon loved by everyone he met. He was a very good driver, which saved him from a housebound life. He used the car as legs and took it over fields, up rough hillsides and along sandy shores, without a thought as to whether it would bring him home again.

We fell deeply in love and when I returned to Porth wrote long letters to each other until the Christmas holidays, which I was invited to spend with Roger's family in Lelant near St Ives. At that time they were staying in a lovely little stone house in the village belonging to the Ranee of Sarawak, whose son was a friend of the Bents. There were also many china animals and glass trees, some of which I wove into a composition, a 'pinkish landscape with sea'; this always remained Roger's favourite painting and we never parted with it.

Roger was driving Home Guard instructors all over the county, day and night, and sometimes I could go with him. One snowy night he had to meet one of them on Trencrom Hill at midnight, so I braved the cold, and with chains on the wheels we made it to the top. There we waited an hour with no heating and the wind whistling through the canvas hood, but the scene in the snow was beautiful in the moonlight and we were together, so we enjoyed it.

Another term separated us, but Roger came up to stay at the farm and at other times we met half-way on the old slag heaps at Chacewater. Then Easter and, with his mother's blessing, we went to stay on Cape Cornwall near St Just, from where we could look down that wild Atlantic coast to Land's End. The Cape is a small, very steep, pointed hill of rocks and heather jutting out into the sea; there was only one house on it, in which we stayed, but while we were there the Germans emptied two lots of bombs on to the hill.

I had had to spend a night in St Just while waiting for Roger, and had chosen a pub in the square and gone to bed very early. I was woken by a fearful bang and saw the window quite red with flames. Another bang, then more, and by this time I was on my way downstairs in my nightdress. The lights in the bar had gone out and the men were suddenly silent. I cowered in a corner of the hall listening to the heavy breathing of the landlord as he groped his way along until he met my form, which puzzled him. Then, 'My God it's the lady upstairs!' and he dragged me into the kitchen, where I spent an hour under the table with the landlady and her children; the landlord being careful to wrap me in a table-cloth before lighting a candle.

I had no sleep as early the next morning, with every window in the square shattered, the glass was being swept up, which made as much noise as the bombs. Roger arrived and we drove the mile to Cape Cornwall and settled in. Here Roger could climb the rocky hill to the top, pulling himself up with his hands and a little help from me, so we spent our days there or down on the shore as near to the waves as we could get, for we both had a passionate love of the sea. It was a time of perfect happiness.

The bombing of St Just brought back the disaster of twenty-one years previously, when thirty-one miners were killed in the Levant Mine because the machinery had been neglected and the 'man-engine steps' crashed to the bottom of the mine. It was the last example in the world of that primitive method of lifting the men; they stood on two-foot platforms every twelve feet down until the moving pillar stopped in front of them with another step to stand on and a wire to hold. It was a terrible thing for such a small village to lose its best men; we heard about it from a survivor.

We came back determined to get married in spite of the fact that Roger had nothing and I had only what I earned. His family had taken it for granted that he would always stay at home with his mother and not want any money. I thought of my Uncle John and how it had been taken for granted that he would never marry because he was lame, or want any of the things that other men want. Roger's family were delighted at first because they thought I would take their place and stay in the family home with Roger's mother, but when I refused and said that we must have a home of our own, even if it were only one room, there was great trouble. Until the day before the wedding we did not know if Roger would get his allowance of £3 a week left him by his father, but the priest finally persuaded his mother and all was well.

Meanwhile I had been staying for six weeks with some great friends of Roger's, the Kennards, in a deep wooded valley near Cape Cornwall, where Roger was able to visit. It was a beautiful stone house with a big room in which I painted a large picture of our Connemara shepherd's funeral. My bedroom window faced across the valley and had roses climbing up all round it and here Roger and I discussed our bleak financial future. On paper it was impossible for us to live, but the Kennards were kind and helpful and encouraged us so that we were very happy except for the antagonism of my future mother-in-law, who was determined that we should live with her.

A priest came several times to give me instruction in the Catholic faith, but I became more and more nonconformist as I listened to the fantastic doctrines he propounded. The Kennards were followers of Rudolph Steiner and everything about themselves and their home was good. I remember Mrs K. coming up through the wood in trailing draperies, bearing on her shoulder a pitcher of well-water; we all got boils and I thought the well might have had something to do with this.

The wedding day came and I took a last walk along the shore, and then the hired car came to drive us the twenty miles to St Ives, along that lovely coast road through Zennor. I sat in front with the driver in my home-made wedding dress of pale green, with a handkerchief on my head. Roger was to be in his usual tweeds. Mr and Mrs Kennard sat in the back holding on to their two pet goats; these had to be taken to a farm on the way and it seemed a good opportunity to deliver them.

Catholic churches are not decorated for mixed marriages, but a kind church worker looked up a saint for the day before and decorated the church with blue hydrangeas, which she then conveniently forgot to remove, so it looked very pretty. When the service was over, Roger and I drove off into the country for a breather before facing the wedding breakfast. I removed my stockings and other signs of civilization so we arrived late and the champagne had started on its way. I did not know anyone except the Kennards, and no one was introduced to the bride, and I hated every minute of it. We soon escaped, got into our oldest clothes and dashed for the car. We had a happy drive up the north coast, stopping only to have a picnic tea on the heather overlooking Watergate Bay. Then we went on to the little village of St Mawgan, where we stayed at the Falcon Inn. We always remembered our gorgeous four-poster bed with its golden curtains and golden eiderdown – the greatest luxury we were to know for many a year.

Roger was a devout Roman Catholic and loved St Mawgan with its beautiful chapel surrounded by trees. The convent of Lanherne was next to it, and for ten magical months we had a room in the convent farm. We could hear the nuns, who never spoke, tapping about on the other side of the high wall; the sound must have come from pattens or nailed shoes as they went to the garden! There had been a fire in the convent and all the village men, young and old, piled in to see the interior of the mysterious place and were well questioned when they returned. Any goods taken to the convent were put on a turntable so that the nun inside was never seen. I found it frightening to think of those human beings over the wall shut away and wondered if it were really voluntary and what made a young girl decide to put away her natural life.

My first picture was of a huge magnolia grandiflora with its plate-sized cream flowers that grew up past our bedroom window; to our delight one day we saw a pure white cat asleep on one of the branches. My paintings were stored in a damp old coach-house where I could not paint, so we did not feel we should settle there.

For one month after the wedding we had the car that Roger had always driven, but his mother had paid for it and so she took it back and kept it in her garage, unused as she could not drive. Roger never complained but I felt bitter to see him deprived of his legs and the joy he always felt at exploring new places. We had one bicycle and evolved a method of both riding it, Roger sitting on the seat and me standing on the pedals. As we were on a steep hill and surrounded by hills, he had to walk up the worst parts with the help of two sticks. The kind policeman asked the men in the pub to warn us to get off if we saw him coming as it is against the law for two people to ride one bicycle, but they knew Roger could never get out without it. Once we went ten miles with our weekend luggage in the basket. Roger dreaded my beginning to laugh as this generally meant our downfall, so he guarded the conversation as we spun happily down the hills and loitered up them.

There was a kind of Civil Defence organization in the village and we went to the meetings to see the people. The moving spirit – not a good description – was an ex-nurse, very plain, thirtyish and unattractive, a sadist by nature, who became grotesque with pleasant smiles as she told us that in the event of poison gas we were to go down to the river, take off all our clothes and submerge. As the river was only a few inches deep running over stones and rocks, this seemed to Roger and me an hilarious idea, and I nearly got round to painting a picture of the local worthies wading in the nude under the trees. No provision was made for bringing this orgy of bathing satyrs to a satisfactory close, so we used to look at the river and people it with panic-stricken villagers splashing up and down in torment at the sight of each other deprived of their natural protection.

Before we left St Mawgan, the Mother Superior of the convent sent for us to ask if I would repaint a statue of Our Lady in a grotto that was in a bad state of repair. We were shown up to her room and behind two iron grilles sat a black figure, entirely covered in veils. It was all very eerie talking to that black pyramid, but did not last long and we turned to go. Roger caught his foot in the carpet and sat down, mercifully below the level of the grille as we both collapsed into laughter. I felt so weak I could not help him up, but eventually he managed to rise and we backed out of the room as though we were leaving royalty.

I found the statue was made of plaster of Paris and rotting with the damp, but it was pleasant working in the ivy-covered grotto with St Bernadette kneeling beside me. Behind was Lanherne chapel and convent, all enclosed by trees and an atmosphere of holiness that was almost tangible. Roger felt happy and at home there.

Those ten months, surprisingly, were the most bomb-free of the war for us, sandwiched as we were between the airfields of St Eval and St Mawgan. I was still teaching the Benenden girls in Newquay, so went in by bus from Monday to Wednesday, coming back in the dark on Wednesday night. Roger was very lonely confined to the house while I was away, and I used to see him in the light of the headlamps, waiting for the bus, propped up against the wall cold and exhausted, so I hoped it would not be late. He counted the hours until it arrived, unable to wait in the room, and I found that he had had fireless mornings in order to have a good fire for me on my return. We explored the woods nearby and gathered sweet chestnuts, and went for many an expedition, and in the evenings sometimes Roger played the old piano and the farmer's family came in for a sing-song.

I realized this could not go on, and when we knew a baby was on the way we were lucky enough to find a studio in St Ives, where Roger had lots of friends. So we got a van and packed ourselves, our belongings and my pictures into it, and set off to make ourselves a home.

CHAPTER 27

St Ives, and a Homecoming

We were tremendously excited at the thought of our first home, which was a large studio with a skylight, at the top of a house owned by a fishing family whose boat was called the *Blue Bell*; so the studio was called the Blue Bell also. We spent four extremely happy years there. The window faced the sea and that lovely coastline with Godrevy lighthouse some miles away. We watched naval boats, barrage balloons, landing craft and fishing boats turned to silver by the searchlights. Many a time the lifeboat left by day and night, the ropes pulling it across the sand, staffed by men, women and children.

Our only table was a narrow one that had been in Roger's bedroom, and we sat looking out at the sea while we had our meals. We bought a huge bed from the policeman for two pounds, and got an ottoman for five shillings. We had a dark chest of drawers with no back and three legs from Roger's garden shed; a friend gave us a bed-chair that was comfortable for Roger, and I had one out of his old nursery, and with an unpainted cupboard with a working top, we were fully furnished. We had no kettle for weeks until another friend gave us a huge one, and a few weeks later we obtained a rusty old frying pan.

The widow who owned the house had several sons. William, who lived below, was a carpenter who did beautiful work and made model boats up to museum standard. He came and mended our furniture and cut the high rails off the bed, making shelves that would hold a morning cup of tea. I made a patchwork quilt on the machine out of all the pretty bits our friends gave us, which made the whole room look bright and cheerful. There was a lavatory in a cupboard in the corner. This used to flood with black muddy water after a heavy rain-storm, although it was two floors up from the street. When we heard the gurgle, we rushed with a board and suitcases to block it up, but even so it sometimes came out of the cupboard.

Then there was a cold tap, and a hole in the floor – not under the tap – for the water to drain; it went down a pipe and across the yard in an open gutter and so reached the sea. A galvanized bath, pierced at one end and with a piece of hose-pipe attached, made a sink, and the water could be guided into the hole.

One day out on the island by the gas works, two German planes came over so close to us that we were looking at the pilots' faces. While the bullets were sweeping the beach and the island, Roger said 'Lie down!' but I considered because they were overhead that we made a smaller target standing up. As we argued about this, a bomb went straight into the gasometer which exploded with a roar and sheets of flame shot into the air. Metal was thrown all over the town, even as far as our studio door. A big pile of coke slithered down on top of some men and we thought they must be killed, but actually it saved them from the flames and heat.

My baby was on the way and this bombing was rather a shock, but Roger went off on his bicycle and got oil for our little one-burner round oil stove. For the next three winter months, we cooked and heated all our water on the little stove and had the gas fire taken out, to find a pretty little high-up grate behind it. We were very pleased about this as it was much warmer and we could supplement the coal with wood from the shore and a friend's garden.

Neither of us had done any cooking, so Roger got books from our domesticated friends and studied them. He became an excellent cook; it gave him something to do and left me great freedom to get on with my work. I began to show pictures in the galleries and sold quite a number, which eased our situation. People were horrified to see Roger riding a bicycle, but he had been doing it since he was a child and it was a tremendous help now that we had no car. We managed very well with the bicycle in the town and soon had the pram to take all the picnic things to the beaches.

When the baby was nearly due, I painted a lot of postcards of our studio, washed by the sea, a stork flying over our roof with the baby in its beak. Roger had only to fill in the sex and weight and send them off to all our friends and relations as soon as he heard the news. They were already stamped, and in his excitement he posted them all without writing anything on them. My poor aunts thought the worst must have happened and it was a long time before they dared to write and enquire. In the event we had a son we called Donald, after my brother.

When I left the nursing home, we went to stay in St Ives for some weeks with a dear old friend, Mrs Dow. This was a godsend to us as we had help and advice on how to cope with a baby. I had never seen him bathed, as there were so many air raids at that time that the babies were kept under a table in the basement. Mrs Dow was like a grandmother to us; and then there was Pietro, the manservant, who had come back from Italy with her thirty years before; and Susan, the Irish cook, who had been with her for over twenty years and was the mainstay of the household.

A friend lent me a very large studio next door to the Blue Bell where I was able to paint on large canvases. It was so near that I could keep an eye on

Donald's pram, and Roger could sit on the balcony looking over the sea and the Lambeth Walk, that great feature of the St Ives harbour, an endless source of entertainment to us as everyone used to look up at our window and wave. I had my first individual show in this studio and sold seventeen pictures, which kept us for half a year. From then on I had a show every two years as well as the annual Show Day, which was a good time for selling as people came from London and all over the south of England. I missed the London exhibitions, but it was too expensive to crate the pictures and send them up.

We were fortunate in that the carpenter who lived below our studio had a little girl called Pamela who was the same age as Donald. They were brought up almost as brother and sister, spending their days together from the time their prams stood side by side in the yard. I used to put her in the other end of the pram when we went to the beach for the day, where Roger was happy lying on the sand making a centre for all the children who were alone on the shore. He was always surrounded by children, who left their clothes and sandals in his care while they bathed, and gathered round when I came down with the picnic. We kept a supply of biscuits and bottles of water for them, and dug enormous castles in the sand. They were very happy days in spite of the war, which prevented us going to Ireland.

The coastline between St Ives and Zennor was a great place for wreckage and we found many useful things. Once great blocks of paraffin wax came in and I was given large blocks to carve. I had not considered what the material was as it was streaked various lovely colours from the sea: it looked more like alabaster than anything. I was longing to start and wondered if a little heat would help to get rid of the corners before starting on a head. I was about to apply a taper when Faust Lang, the wood-carver, came in. He rushed at me and knocked the block to the floor, shouting that the house would go up in flames. I think he was exaggerating. The authorities tried to reclaim some of the wax but they were out of luck and it lit fires in the little farms along the coast for many years. One night tons of new wood came in to the Porthmeor beach and the streets became alive with running men. The town turned out with anything on wheels; women with prams, bicycles and carts. Again the authorities tried to claim the wood, but they might as well have saved their breath as to try to take a gift from the sea off a Cornishman. The locals just walked past their tormentors, deaf and blind, and one could see how all the tales of wreckers and smugglers could have been true. The next day, Roger and I sat on the island, enthralled, as we watched the processions, silent, with heads down, carrying away their loot through the narrow cobbled streets to all the little net lofts and cellars.

The Cornish have amusing ways of showing their dislike of anyone. They will make up a song about the supposed crime or ill-doing and then, with tins and trays and any noisy thing they can find, arrive at night outside the victim's house and sing. Another form of pillory was performed in our street. They disapproved of something one of the shopkeepers had done and we were woken in the night to hear an object being dragged along and the sound of many feet. In the morning a large boat was in place across the doorway of the shop so that no one could go in or out. It was there until the next night when after payment someone agreed to move it. And in their strange processions, the men dressed as women and the women as men, all wearing masks; a loud band preceding them and torches lighting their way.

When Donald was three, we were dismayed to hear that we should have to give up our studio to the son of the owner, who was coming back from the war. As Roger's mother had died and he could raise some money on his inheritance, and I had sold a number of pictures, we bought a large block of buildings in the middle of town for £1500, and by letting off the greater part of it managed to keep enough for ourselves. We missed our beautiful view terribly and there was no garden. The sitting-room used to be a shop and had a very nice arched window set in deep stone walls. It was once the coach-house for the Exeter Coach and the little buildings at the back had been the harness rooms; the bookshop next door still had the stalls for the horses in its basement. Upstairs we had one long bedroom, and by making a hole through a wall we had a huge studio with four windows and a pillar supporting the roof in the centre. This was a good place for parties as well as painting.

Before we had been in our new home for three weeks, we let it, furnished, and set off for Ireland for the first time since the war. I did not know how Roger would manage the journey without being able to lie down often, but he was quite comfortable and loved travelling. There was no food on the trains in those days, so soon after the war, so we booked rooms and took three days over the journey. Later we found much easier ways of going and from then on spent four months in Errislannan every year, the tenants of the St Ives house paying for it all.

In Clifden a taxi was waiting instead of the horse, much to my relief. The longed-for day had come and Roger and Donald were with me in Errislannan. We got out of the taxi on the top of Ballinaboy and had a long look round. Roger could hardly speak, it was so much more beautiful than he had imagined, although I had tried to describe it to him for years past. Then we descended the hill and found people waiting to welcome us at the Lodge gates. We bumped down the drive, exactly as my mother had done all those years ago with my brother Donald, when she brought him to show to the family. There were the aunts, beaming, so much older than I remembered them; sadly there was no Uncle John, but it was a glorious moment. They already knew Roger from his letters and now took him to their hearts and he became part of the family; the deep affection between Roger, Aunt Jane and Aunt Edyth made for much happiness in the years to come. They were full of admiration for Donald, who stood and stared at them, and were sensible enough not to rush at him and kiss him as many people did. He certainly was a beautiful child, with pale gold hair and big blue eyes.

Everything was exactly as it had been when I left six years before, except that instead using the Lake Room, the aunts had turned out the Mistress's room and arranged it for us, with the famous patchwork quilt on the canopy bed and a small bed for Donald. Flowers everywhere gave the old familiar smell, and a big turf fire in the bedroom made me realize I was home at last. The beautiful furniture, the silver candlesticks and lovely rugs, were a welcome change after our Spartan existence, and even the framed texts, decorated with flowers, which I used to find so irritating, now seemed charming period pieces. The huge bed with its curtains and canopy covered in realistic flowers made us feel that we were reclining in a rustic bower, but the ancient base of wooden slats on chains, the hair mattress overlaid with a vast feather mattress, into which we sank almost out of sight, was overpowering and Roger's asthma became very alarming. We managed to change it for a hard one from the next room. Our clothing looked very funny in the enormous mahogany wardrobe which must have held crinolines and mantles and beautiful dresses when it was brought down from Dublin about 1832; I am sure it had never been moved since then.

As there was no car in Errislannan until 1950, one of the men thought out a scheme to make Roger mobile. Someone had sent Aunt Jane a large heavy hospital chair which she never used, so Stephen Duanne made two boat-hooks into shafts which he fixed to the chair, and lent us a docile donkey to go with it called Belinda. With some cut-down harness, and a cushion for Donald in place of a saddle, we were provided with a most delightful form of transport. Donald rode the donkey, Roger was comfortable in the chair and I walked alongside. There were long reins so Roger could drive himself and only twice tipped over. This conveyance carried all the picnic baskets, rugs, cushions, etc. when we went to the beach daily, and once took us the six miles round Errislannan.

There was a farmer's family of four children, the Conneelys, who lived near the beach, Candoolan, and who became our special friends. Years later the father was to build up our house, the Quay, after the Manor was sold. When we were seen on the road, four little figures flew barefoot towards us, over the walls and rocks as though they did not need the ground under them. Several other children would come and we spent the day fishing in the rock pools for shrimps and fish for Donald's cat and kittens. There was a long strip of sand between high rocks which made wind-breaks and seats, but it was the multicoloured pools which were our chief joy. Sometimes we found the little by-the-wind sailors, like blue boats washed in, and sometimes the rocks were silver with fry, driven in by mackerel, which we gathered in buckets and which were very good to eat. Occasionally I discovered the violet snail shells with the animals alive inside them. These are carried across the Atlantic on the Gulf Stream by means of a plastic bag, formed of air cells about two inches long, and when you pick them up they squirt violet ink on your hand.

Country children do not bathe, so they all went into the sea in their clothes for the first time, paddling and playing in the foam of the great waves. It was years before I could get Donald to go into the sea without at least a shirt and shorts on, because the Conneely children did not do so. Later we did entice them into bathing togs of a sort, much to the relief of their mother. They were so sure-footed on the rocks and knew so much about the shore that I was very glad to have them looking after Donald, and sometimes he spent the day in their house, happily eating potatoes and drinking milk that he would not touch at home. They were all very musical and taught us many Irish songs as the procession wound its way back along the road from Candoolan: 'If I Were a Blackbird', 'The Hills of Donegal' and 'The Rose of Mooncoin' among others.

Irish children do not sing children's songs or play with toys; they learn to sing from hearing their parents sing far into the night, and toys seem superfluous when there are real things to do about the farm. Their father, Martin, played the fiddle and the melodeon and sang very well; the eldest boy was a genius with the fiddle when he was older. They all played the two instruments and Micky was in great demand playing for the dances a few years later. We gave him his first tin whistle and soon he was playing the rapid elaborate dance tunes they all know. Donald, inspired by this, also bought himself a recorder in town for half a crown.

Martin was a fisherman-farmer and had a currach in which he sometimes stayed out all night. Once he and a friend had been out and by the morning were feeling very thirsty, so they drew in to shore to find a well. They saw a woman coming down to the boat with two mugs of buttermilk in her hands and she seemed to be walking on the water. They were so frightened that they turned and pulled away as fast as they could go. It is well known how unlucky it is for a woman to go down to a boat when it is going out and they thought this might be a fairy woman.

Micky had an unquestioning faith in the spirit world all round him and had many tales to tell of strange happenings. He introduced Donald to the idea of spirits when a funeral went past the Lodge. If you are not going to walk a mile with it you keep out of sight, but Donald wanted to see it. The coffin was strapped to the roof of a Volkswagen car with five people inside, and the bumpy road made it slither about in a most alarming way. Micky took Donald to hide in the rushes so that they could see it all, and as the corpse passed told him to bless himself 'in case anything would happen.' 'She can see you now and it would be dangerous not to show respect to her.' The discussion went on at home and Donald became upset at the thought of the corpse being left in the ground all night.

Once, that first year in Errislannan, I saw him standing on the Manor lawn in the rain of a stormy day, dressed in a little black mackintosh and sou'wester, looking up at the trees swaying in the wind. I went to join him, but as I drew near I heard him singing a lovely song with the trees. He has always listened to music with an intentness unusual in a child, a trait he inherited from his father.

That first summer, we stayed in the Manor for a few months, but with some elderly cousins arriving we thought it would be nice to make our home in my old Gate Lodge. With help from the aunts we refurnished it, settled in, and for years to come it was our summer home, and we would go down to the Manor for Sundays and often during the week.

The Lodge had no water supply, so a bucket of spring water was brought up with the milk every morning. For everything else I fetched buckets of water from a turf cutting, or rain-water from a hollow in a rock. I took the washing down to the bog and dipped the bucket into the brown water that is so soft and makes the clothes so white. Then I laid them on the heather and gorse to dry, and at the end of the day brought back a bundle of clean clothes smelling of heather and lovely scents of the grasses and mosses. It was a great happiness to have a washing day out there, with the mountains and the sea to look at and the fresh scents around one's feet.

On the south side of the Lodge was a half-door, which opened on to a grassy yard protected by a long thatched shed on one side and a high stone wall on the other, with a sycamore tree spreading lichen covered branches overhead. There were little woods on each side, with grassy glades, a low wall, and then a long stretch of bogland before the smooth green hill of Joe King's farm rose out of it like an island. His little white house and his cattle moving about always gave us something to watch as we sat by the fire in the Lodge with the door open.

We had our meals in this yard and sometimes slept out there on moonlit nights, oblivious of bats skimming by and the odd snuffle of a donkey or bullock on our faces as it wondered what we were doing. Roger spent many hours outside the little wall where the scarlet and purple fuchsia bells hung in thousands and the great dragon-flies, yellow or kingfisher-blue, whirred up and down, alighting on one's arms or legs with a gripping of their feet, or paralysing one with their formidable eyes. A loose stone wall provided endless hiding-places for birds and field-mice, who poked their heads out like curious neighbours wanting to see without being seen. We had a toad who seemed to make it a permanent home, and sometimes a stoat popped out and sat up like a squirrel until frightened, when it disappeared into the wall to reappear a long way away. A patch of mint, left by the Kings twenty years before, still flourished and was a help to our cooking. The flat stones on top of the wall held our washing-up basin, or we did carpentry or the vegetables out there in the sunshine. The wall was a useful and beautiful adjunct to our lives, and gave needed shelter to the animals from Donald's 'Pussy' and two or three kittens, who danced a continual ballet round the house or up the tree, or lay asleep on the thatched roof of the shed.

To my joy I found that my boat *The Galley*, which I had had since I was sixteen, was still in good order and had a second pair of small oars, so down to Crumpaugn we would go in the donkey-chair, Donald jumping off the donkey and into the boat before we had tied up Belinda. At first he rowed about with a long rope attached, as he was only three, but we soon saw that this was not necessary and that he could take her out in the lagoon by himself. We could all fit in and had a glorious time rowing to other beaches, and across to the castle if the sea were really calm. We bathed, and caught shrimps, raked for cockles, dug for razor-fish and went sand-eeling by moonlight, returning at four in the morning to cook them for a party.

Sometimes the dark beach was transformed by the silver fire that sparkled and shone in the wavelets one made paddling along, and it clung to the seaweed and rocks and one's wet legs. Only once have I seen this on land and that was when I was coming home in the dark from Mollie and Annie's house across the bog. The fire sparkled only where I had put down my feet, so that a trail was marked out behind me. Once I heard that it was seen encircling the Kings' barn on the edge of the cliff, so that Lizzie ran out and was saved from falling over the cliff only by her son Michael Angelo. At another time a tall pillar of fire was seen to be moving round a farm at night after the farmer had died, and was accepted as his ghost. The little corpse lights that move between the graveyard and any house where someone is being called were also believed in by the older people. St Elmo's fire has a lot to answer for; near the sea, where the spray flies inland, it accounts for many a ghost and much fear.

I resumed my old habit of going off in *The Galley* in the evenings fishing for mackerel, which were a great help to our food supply. Sometimes we cooked them on my return, on the red coals, and they were best like that. *The Galley* also resumed its Saturday morning shopping expeditions, with Roger and Donald accompanying me. Roger would lie happily on the grass by the quay in Clifden while Donald and I went to town. On our journey back we stopped at Rabbit Island, which Donald had claimed for his own and where he buried a treasure under a cow's skull when he was six, saying he would not dig it up until he was thirty. He landed every year to put a flag with a skull and crossbones on the highest point of the island.

At the Lodge in the evenings our neighbours used to visit us, and the men, if they were alone, would sing to Roger, who soon picked up the tunes. One night two of them went on singing until two in the morning without repeating themselves. Sometimes Martin Conneely or Michael Angelo would bring their fiddles, or Joe King would come and sing or dance a jig, the beat of his iron heels making its own music on the stone floor. Even Belinda the donkey stood in the yard with her head in at the door as though she liked the music, but if we were alone she came right in and stood with her head to the fire between our chairs.

The Lodge windows face the tall silver gates across the road, which are set in heavily built stone pillars, separated from the road by curving stone walls. This leaves a wide open space roofed in by old trees that meet overhead and make a continual rustling, which mounts to a roar when a storm is blowing. One night I woke to hear a curious sound of breathing, tapping and shuffling, outside the window. I looked out at a grey and white moving mass of something dotted with vivid greeny lights that moved and blinked. I went out in my bare feet as silently as possible and saw dozens of donkeys pressed together; the moonlight striking through the trees lit up their eyes and waving ears and moving white legs; the silver gates and grey walls, all dappled with the moonlight, made a background. Then I trod on a snail shell and the tiny noise brought all the heads round in my direction. Some went one way and some another, their unshod hoofs thudding on the white road, until, in a few seconds, a complete silence fell and the moonlit space was empty.

I have never before or since seen a concourse of donkeys; perhaps because the Lodge was dark and empty through the winter they had made it their meeting-place. The shining lights from the eyes are due to the coating of the inner wall of the eye with guanin, a metallic lustre of gold or silver which catches and reflects any light in the gloom and brightens dim images on the retina of the animals, so that they can see better than we can in the dark.

For the next few years we lived at St Ives in the winter for Donald's schooling and my work and exhibitions. Then in May or June we set off for Ireland and I tried unsuccessfully to give Donald lessons. Later, from boarding school, he joined us by air. The journeys were now easier for Roger and he enjoyed them in spite of the long platforms and the horrors of the customs sheds with all their stairs. People were always kind and friendly to Roger and we came under his mantle, but to travel from Cornwall to western Connemara every year was a great undertaking. He had courage and a childlike capacity for finding everything an adventure.

When we arrived on Ballinaboy Hill we always stopped to look down on Errislannan with sighs of relief. All my life I have fed on the thought of that long tongue of land enclosed in its bubble of changing skies. Once we arrived to see a strange effect when a thick sea mist lay down below us on the land and only Joe King's semicircle of hill with his little house and its fields of Noah's-Ark cows was brilliantly clear, as were our Lodge and artificial-looking trees growing out of the white carpet. From above we could see the smoke rising from the Lodge and would find Annie Angelo's laughing face at the gate and supper ready in front of a huge fire. She always brought back Donald's well-loved Pussy, with kittens – her own or other people's – and they settled in as though we had never been away. One first night there were no kittens, but before morning Pussy had rectified this and a nest of young were squirming about on top of Roger's clothes on his chair. A stray dog, cat, kittens, some chickens and the donkey made up our menagerie, not to mention the bullocks who noisily snuffled and munched our grass and stared at us over the wall. Only a half-door divided us from the animals, so life was never dull. I could not paint in the Lodge now that the family filled it, but I had plenty of time to draw and think out what to do when I returned to my studio.

It was about this time that I painted a series of four 'Holy Mountain' pictures. It was my way of expressing the essence of Connemara. First thought of in colour, the composition came of itself while I walked about and was perhaps all the better for the enforced delay in execution. These paintings can only be described through their subject matter – mountain, bog pool, solitary tree, sometimes people, and always the sea under changing lights. Unfortunately the first was sold before the others were finished and I wished I had kept it. Money never compensated for a picture, but I enjoyed the end-of-term cheques at Benenden, and payment for small models, which for me were hobbies.

In Errislannan visitors were always asking me for lessons, which I would not undertake, but I gave occasional advice to children if asked. Others badgered me to give serious criticisms of their horrid little water-colours. One conceited young man I had refused to bother with left half a dozen at the Manor in case I changed my mind. While I contemplated the daubs, a large car drew up at the door, and out came Lord and Lady Moyne (better known as Bryan and Elizabeth Guinness), six children, a governess and a cat; in the back were a Shetland pony and a goat. He sympathized with my dilemma and gave me some useful advice: 'Look at the perpetrator with an admiring smile and say – "You really have got what you wanted."' A subtle way out. They were staying in Da Barnett's at Ballyconneely, that perfect low white house with its enclosed garden by the sea.

At both sides of the Lodge were narrow meadows which could be saved for hay. I used to cut them with a scythe – very tiring until I got back my skill of olden days – and Donald and Micky raked them over until it was time to make the hay into cocks. Then the donkey-chair came into its own when we laid planks across the arms and converted it into a hay cart. It took many loads down to the barn, with Donald leading the ass and the men unloading it for him on arrival.

During the days on the white sands of Mannin Bay we collected many bones, sometimes whole skeletons of cows, horses, or the delicate spillikin-like frame of a rabbit or bird, and skulls; all cleansed and bleached white by the sun and the blowing sand. This became a great interest for Donald and Micky who went seaching for them while Roger and I lay sheltered from the wind by the small sand cliffs. We looked across the deserted, white shell-laden beaches to the pale green sea, which farther out turned to navy blue broken by white wave-tops, and beyond to the brilliant blue mountains dappled with dark blue shadows as the puffy white clouds sailed across them.

There is always something to find after a sou'wester: glass balls, buoys, coconuts in their husks from Mexico, fruit, bits of lobster pots, good for firing; cabin parts, bones, dead birds and animals. Once we found a baby seal, still white, lying as though asleep at Candoolan when we went to bathe. We searched the sea wondering if the bereft mother were among the waves watching us with those doglike eyes. With some of the driftwood we found washed up on the shore I made furniture for the Lodge, as we had nothing but beds and strings for hanging clothes. When finished we all helped to paint it like Hungarian wedding chests, with bright blues and reds and elaborate small decoration, which gave great scope to the children. It looked very gay against the whitewashed walls.

There is always something to find after a sou'wester; glass balls, buoys, coconuts in their husks from Mexico, fruit, bits of lobster pots, good for firing; bits of cabins, bones, dead birds and animals. Once we found a baby seal, still white, lying as though asleep at Candoolan when we went to bathe. We searched the sea wondering if the bereft mother were among the waves watching us with those doglike eyes. With some of the driftwood we found washed up on the shore I made furniture for the Lodge, as we had nothing but beds and strings for clothes. When finished we all helped to paint it like Hungarian wedding chests, with bright blues and reds and elaborate small decoration, which gave great scope to the children. It looked very gay against the whitewashed walls.

As we paddled in the green transparent sea, Roger said that he had never known such joy and such beauty. I felt the same now that I had his companionship, which transformed the same beaches that long ago had not seemed at all desirable because of my freezing loneliness.

The great event of the year was the Sports Party we gave every summer for the twenty-four local children and the few remaining orphan boys. We said three o'clock, but by midday we could see heads popping up over the stone wall and large brilliant eyes watching and waiting for the curtain to go up. If there were visitors in the cottages their children came too, but they were too well fed and slow to compete with the skinny barefoot Errislannan children, whose diet was soda bread, potatoes and tea.

The eight orphans hovered round the Lodge, silent, over-clad, too frightened to take off clothes or shoes. They clustered round Roger – always a magnet for children – and somehow he persuaded them to join in the easier sports while he kept the tea and drinks going. How different they were to their predecessors, the happy independent orphans I had known long ago at Ballyconree, until the terrible day in 1922 when the Republicans turned them all out and set fire to the building, and the orphans watched the only home they had ever known be completely gutted. The eight little boys who came to our sports were housed in Glenowen, the D'Arcy dower house, which had been the girls' orphanage. It was impossible to get good kind matrons and the boys were so repressed and miserable that it filled Roger and me with fury, and we implored Aunt Jane to send them to Dr Barnardo's. She would not do this until she was too old and ill to fight for their retention any longer. The family had always been involved, as secretaries or members of the committee, and she was very upset to hear that the home and the Protestant school in Clifden were no more.

Once we had two of the small boys in the back of our car. A woman with three children stood on the pavement in Clifden, and one orphan tugged at the younger one and said, 'Look, Jimmy, *that's* a mother, see?' Jimmy peered through the window until the family were out of sight.

To return to our sports day: for children who had no toys, every present was exciting. We found that it was better to lay out the prizes on our bed and let them choose, and everyone had some little thing to take home. The toughest little boy chose a girl's paper sunshade and used this for weeks. As they rode to school, two or three on an ass, we could see the sunshade coming along, and even on the bog it was planted on a turf stack until the owner was ready to ride home. When we let the big kite go free, the Errislannan children were off like arrows to catch it. Walls, ditches, banks and bogs; nothing turned them aside. Once to my horror the kite caught in the highest tree and when I arrived I found the tree decorated with children like a crop of brightly coloured apples. The visitors' children were always left behind. It was a great day if fine; if wet, the children crowded into our tiny kitchen or played cards sitting on the Elsan and the turf in the shed, but the food and the drink were just as good.

CHAPTER 28

The Connemara Pony Show,
Seaweed Harvest, and Dances

In 1950 a friend of Aunt Jane's gave her a saloon car, a Hillman Minx, and the apple store was cleared to receive it. The excitement was intense as we saw it arrive, and Roger drove it down from the Lodge to the house; henceforth he became a very happy chauffeur. He taught Martin King to drive, so that he could take over in the winter. Martin, whose family lived at the point of Errislannan, had been with my aunts for many years. A very quiet and exceptionally kind young man, he became a smart well-groomed chauffeur and an excellent driver. He had worked on the farm and in the garden, and later came to live in the house so that he would be there if needed in the night. He looked after the two old ladies and drove them all over Connemara.

We did not give up the donkey-chair, as it was too far for Roger to walk to the stables, but *what* a joy it was to be able to go to town without getting wet. Roger loved being able to go to Mass on Sundays to the monastery, and we all went off for glorious days to the white sands on the far side of Mannin Bay, which had been accessible in the past only by boat. Roger could drive right on to the beaches and look at the most beautiful view of all: the white sand melting into the pale green sea, in which – often black – cows and bullocks stood or lay on the shore, making just the right contrast of colour; all backed by the mountains.

The aunts looked and felt like queens in their first car; driving along, beaming at everything. They loved driving round the mountains and to faraway places and returning calls, which they had never been able to do before with only a horse. Unfortunately the habit of never passing a walker on the road continued and they stopped to offer a lift until the car was tightly packed. The many potholes in the roads made this very hard on the springs, but all was happiness within the vehicle. There was one fly in the ointment as far as Roger was concerned. Aunt Edyth sat in the back seat flanked by her two large stinking dogs, one of whom rested his nose trustingly on Roger's shoulder and licked his face. This stopped when I explained that it was bad for his asthma, but the car never got the better of the smell.

The day for the Connemara Pony Show arrived, and the two aunts and I set off in the new chariot, with only four faces showing above the entries of flowers, vegetables, chickens, butter, eggs and a mass of other produce. When we arrived at the gate, through which no cars were allowed to enter, a man, with great temerity, brought this fact to Aunt Jane's notice. Her eyebrows went up and her voice rang out: 'Nonsense, Jimmy; drive on, Martin,' and on we went to the centre of the field, which is on a little rise, so that we could see everything and enjoy our lunch watched by all the envious people perched on shooting-sticks or sitting on the wet grass.

The Pony Show was the great event of the year in Connemara. People came from all over Europe to buy Connemara ponies, which are cream or pale grey with dark manes and tails, and small heads and bones. The show ring was roped off, but the rest of the field was crowded with mares and foals and ponies of all ages. The young ones were often frightened at this first introduction to crowds and noise after wandering loose on the mountains, bogs and beaches all the year. Many had been on the road since early morning or even the evening before. They generally travelled in groups, a very tiring walk for their owners, as the foals regularly broke away, and the whole caravanserai would come to a halt while one man chased the truants back on to the road. When they arrived on the show ground there is nowhere for their owners to rest, and some have to face the long trek home if their animals are not sold.

Many years before this, we had gone to the show in the open carriage and been even more entertained, as it was easier to see and talk to people from a roomy open carriage than a car. The Maharaja Ranjitsinhji, the famous Indian cricketer, who had been living at Ballynahinch Castle for some years, was once asked to open the show. Surrounded by his native entourage, he beamed upon us all and finished his speech with these words:

'I feel I understand you people so well, because you are like my own dear people at home!'

We all clapped and registered approval, but an old man from Doonloghan turned round and said loudly:

'What the hell are ye clappin' for? Isn't he tellin' ye ye're like a pack of dirty niggers?'

Aunt Jane reprimanded him, saying that they were very nice clean people. This unwise speech brought forth a torrent of poetry in a loud clear voice:

'Miss Janey, those heathen never let a drop of God's water come near them. They wash in barrels of oil. Oil that comes from the stinking whales that do be coursing up and down in the deep sea. They may have as many jewels as the stars in the sky, but where will the heathen be when they come to their end? I tell you it's a terrible thing to have such people set up on high!'

Aunt Jane racked her brains to think which religion the Prince might belong to, but all her knowledge of India came from Aunt Eva, the Zenana missionary, and was not very helpful where the 'heathen' were concerned. Aunt Edyth, always on the spot, offered the man a drink, which he quickly swallowed, promising that when next she came to Doonloghan with the boat he would have some fine lobsters waiting for her. I am indebted to Aunt Edyth and her infallible memory for this story, but the 'barrels of oil' were common knowledge as Prince Ranjitsinhji sent his nieces to the local convent school, where they cleansed themselves with oil instead of water.

The Prince was a well-known sight in those years, tearing along the narrow roads in his old Ford car, or accompanied by a retinue of six servants in native costume as he fished the famous Ballynahinch river. One man held an enormous coloured umbrella, one the landing net, others all kinds of comforts, and one often held the rod until the last moment, when the Prince rose and landed the salmon. A strange sight it was in those lonely dark-coloured boglands. How surprised the previous owners of Ballynahinch, the Martins, would have been. They were ruined by the Famine and poor Humanity Dick Martin, the last to live there, died in poverty in France, after founding the Society for the Prevention of Cruelty to Animals. I have spoken of Maria Edgeworth's visit there in the 1830s and her description of the dreadful state of the castle. Now it is all in very good order and turned into an hotel.

To return to the Pony Show: apart from the ponies, round the field were stalls of garden produce, eggs, cakes, vegetables, etc. and cages of poultry, ducks and turkeys to be judged. There were beautiful lengths of hand-woven tweed from the Millars' mill, and an exhibition of vegetable dyes used by the countrywomen for this occasion only. I expect a packet from the grocer coped with most of their dyeing. They advocated, for instance, the use of the root of a water-lily as a black dye, but I was never to see some brave countrywoman leaning over the side of a boat pulling one up.

A great deal of drink was consumed and later in the day there was dancing and entertainment, but by that time we had always gone home. The visitors drove away in their cars or retired to their hotels, and the inhabitants of Clifden and the farmers from faraway places took over. Boys and girls rode their bicycles in to the dance in the parish hall, and we would have known nothing about it had it not been for the soft swish of tyres passing the Lodge in the early hours of the morning.

*   *   *

We met the poetical fisherman from Doonloghan again when we went to get lobsters and picnic there. He was old and his currach lay up on the grass; it was decayed but would never be used for much-needed firewood: it was part of his life. It was a joy to hear the lovely speech of a man who had never left home and could not read; listening to him made me doubt the benefit of education when I compared his cadences to the ugly voices and ugly thoughts of the masses.

Doonloghan is an small, isolated quay that in the past we had reached by sailing across Mannin Bay from Errislannan. It is on that incredibly rocky coast that reaches out to Slyne Head lighthouse and is protected by a reef which takes the full force of the Atlantic, the foam rising up like a white curtain against the sky. The ocean outside is often inky blue, while the sea inside is light green as it comes up over the white sand. One day, when I was alone on the beach, I thought I was seeing one of the four horsemen of the Apocalypse as a large white horse came splashing towards me with two dark figures on its back, their legs dangling to the water. The horse held his head high and his mane and tail stood out stiffly. He drew nearer and nearer and eventually rose out of the sea and came up the beach; the two men had been gathering seaweed on the reef and headed for home just before the tide cut them off.

From the quay a few currachs fish for lobsters and crayfish, and for some years the seaweed industry came into its own and gave them a little prosperity, but it was hard gained; cutting and gathering was very heavy work and the men were cold and wet most of the time. They cut weed or gathered fresh wrack washed up by the tide and partially dried it on rocks and walls before taking it by ass or horse cart to the nearest road, where a lorry collected it. The most profitable weed was the long ribbon type growing on long stalks, which were also valuable. This they cut at low spring tide, or by using long poles with cross-pieces with which it could be pulled up from a currach. This was bleached and made up into piles like haycocks and once brought in £18 a ton.

This was a help to the few fishermen left in the lonely coastal areas of rocky fields and poor soil, who had no harvest but that of the sea and small patches of potatoes. In 1970 the Ballyconneely seaweed factory closed down, but the weed is still collected and taken to Cashel, where they have modern equipment and work on a big scale. I remember as a child seeing the little stone circles on the beaches where weed was kept burning for three days for the production of kelp, which was used for iodine. Now the factory treats the weed and sends it away by ship or lorry in liquid or powder form to be made into an extraordinary range of things. Its chief use is as a fertilizer, but it has now proved to be a storehouse of valuable chemicals essential to modern industry. It is the main source of agar and is used in cosmetics, ice-cream, chocolates, jellies, films, as a wood preservative – even, after much treatment, in the making of typewriter rollers. It is used in laboratories as a culture on which bacteria are nurtured by research chemists, and a factory in Scotland specializes in making it into the cherries eaten in cakes.

Then there was the short carrageen moss that we all gathered off the rocks for ourselves and laid out on the grass for three weeks, before drying and storing for the winter, when we used it for blancmanges, soups, hot drinks or jellies, or put it in the babies' bottles. My aunts thought the green seaweed called sloak a great luxury, but it was difficult to get and required an exceptionally low tide.

Because of the rocky ground, life would be hardly supportable without the seaweed which was so abundant round our shores. It produced the rich green grass and the good potatoes and provided man, ass and cart, with work to do when the turf was gathered in. Days of solitude made a man work independently and use initiative, surrounded by bog, mountain and sea, becoming wiser and more mentally alert and able to turn his hand to everything, from playing a fiddle to building a house, from constructing a loose stone wall to fishing from a currach, cutting his hay with a scythe or his corn with a sickle, cutting his turf for all his heating and cooking, or driving an old car into town. And added to his many skills, he was generally an entertaining conversationalist.

*   *   *

One summer Glendowie, the cottage by the sea with the thirty-foot room, was empty, so we thought that we would give a dance. Invitations were not given. It just happend that one walked round Errislannan the day of the dance mentioning casually to everyone one met that there would be a dance that night. Then as darkness fell about ten o'clock, figures of every age could be seen wending their way along the road or across the bog, all going in one direction. Everyone was welcome.

For our dance Aunt Jane cooked many loaves of soda bread and we got butter, jam and pounds of tea from town. The dancers were taken into the bedroom in relays throughout the night, where a table was laid with bread and jam and endless pots of tea were kept going. On the dresser in the kitchen there was always a bucket of spring water and anyone who was thirsty took a cup and drank. When the night came Roger went down to the cottage first and I tied Belinda to the big gates, while I loaded the donkey-chair up with the food, oil for the lamps and a few bottles of beer for the players only, as was the custom. Generally Michael Angelo and Martin Conneely played the fiddles, and two or three others passed round the melodeon.

I was just getting ready to go when I saw some boy visitors coming up the drive with the 'Giddy Ass' and opening the gates. The Giddy Ass was the fierce jackass who was always breaking away during June and July to range the countryside. He had killed a number of foals and done endless damage, but he was a splendid worker and fast in the cart for the rest of the year, so nothing was done about his temper. This evening, the moment the gates were open, he fell upon our little ass with horrible squeals. A frightful scene ensued as he attacked her; the shafts being in his way he roared and stamped and the chair turned over. I ran out with a broom and beat him as hard as I could, and the boys at last came to their senses, got sticks and helped until eventually we were able to keep him at bay and I pushed Belinda inside the gates. Then we righted the chair and patched up the harness with boat-ropes.

Donald, aged three, came with us and went to sleep in a bedroom until midnight, when he joined in as the dancing became wilder and wilder. We did sets and half-sets most of the time. These sets are rather like the English Lancers, danced by four or eight people. They all include the spin and the big circle spin, when people are often thrown against the wall. A wonderful night it was, with Roger in a comfortable chair enjoying every moment of this, his first dance. We kept the doors open, and when not dancing went out and sat on the sea wall, looking in to the dimly lit room alive with music and movement. That night there was phosphorus on the water, covering the seaweed and rocks with its blue silvery fire, so we went down the steps and dabbled our hands in it.

There was always a lot of solo singing at the dances. We would all sit on the floor around the walls, while the singer put down his head and went through the words of his song to make sure he remembered the countless long verses. Then he sang, still on the floor with his eyes on the ground, with no one looking at him until he was finished. There was always a dead silence and rapt attention for the singer, and the men nearly all sang well in rich deep voices, or else danced a solo jig. There was never any applause. Roger thought they might like to sing together and they tried to please him, but he soon saw his mistake and never suggested it again.

One summer I went with Annie Angelo, as a spectator only, to a dance in the new hall at Ballyconneely seven miles away. As at Mass, the sexes were segregated by mutual consent, the women sitting round the walls on the pews that had once been in the Protestant church. The men, of all ages, as they entered took up positions against the wall, as close to the door as possible. This standing mass of men, mostly in dark blue suits, gradually formed a triangle, the apex reaching out half-way across the floor. The band started up but no one moved, until, after two or three tunes had been played, the bandmaster harried them into action. Then the men made a dash across the floor and seized a girl. They danced sets and half-sets, interspersed with a waltz and quickstep, but as soon as the music stopped the women retired to their pews and the men to the bar or back to their places against the wall. It was after midnight before things began to warm up, helped no doubt by some drink. The priest came and stood by the door for a couple of hours to show his approval, since the hall had been built to entice the young men and women to stay at home and marry, instead of leaving for England, as was now the pattern. He had not been there at the beginning of the evening so it was not due to him that the men were so immobile. The dances were quite different in August, when the less inhibited visitors were not so shy of their partners.

One dance was held in Errislannan in a new house with no furniture, to which I went alone. The owner, John Manion, could not bring himself to leave the house where he had been born, which was in the middle of the bog. We had a lamp on the shelf, and planks on stones round the walls to sit on. In the middle of the night Pateen, our boatman, came running in breathless to say that Donald was covered in blood at the Lodge. He led the way home over stone walls, rocks and heather, and I followed, given wings by my fears. All the boys followed; one carrying his bicycle in case he had to ride to town for a doctor. In the tiny bedroom, by the light of a candle, Donald's bed and himself seemed entirely reddened from a violent nosebleed, and poor Roger was distracted. He had heard footsteps on the road, but when he went out, there was no one to be seen. He shouted and by a miracle there stood Pateen at the gate. The 'footsteps' had been those of the Giddy Ass, who, seeing the moonlit night, had broken out of his stable, but had given himself away in his search for love by stepping past my aunts' window in his four new shoes. Aunt Jane woke Pateen and sent him after the ass, so that he appeared like an angel in answer to Roger's prayers.

The bleeding soon stopped, and the boys crowding into the little room, full of sympathy, did much to soothe Roger and Donald. The only one to benefit from all this was the Giddy Ass, who had got his night out and was possibly miles away by then.

CHAPTER 29

The Bishop and the Baptist

Once a year our Bishop of Tuam, Achonry and Killala came to Errislannan to take a service in the church, and Aunt Jane, with smiling bland effrontery, always arranged that he should stay at the Manor the previous night, despite the ill-concealed fury of the Rector, who knew that every facet of parochial and diocesan life would be presented – before he had had a go – from Aunt Jane's unassailable position as manager of the church. After all, it had been like a private chapel since her grandfather had caused it to be built, and the remaining members of the family caused a parson to come five miles every Sunday to take a service for them, either in the church or their drawing-room. Aunt Jane chose the hymns, played the harmonium and was guardian of the communion plate. Aunt Edyth cleaned the place and put flowers on the Holy Table. Uncle John for many years applied paint and repairs and lit the fire behind our pew. The only financial support came from the tenants in *our* cottages, who were forced to attend by Saturday night visits from the 'ladies' bearing presents of flowers and eggs, and leaving with a smiling reminder of the time of the service next day. The tenants groaned as they donned their Sunday clothes, but often put £1 on the plate.

Before the Bishop's visit there was chaos; the aunts moved out of the Mistress's room so that the Bishop and his wife could be sunk in the deep feather bed. The canopy and curtains allowed little air and the window cords had been broken and plastered with paint for many years, so that a piece of wood had to be carefully put in place if more air were required. Cowmen, protesting at doing domestic work, carried the carpet out to be beaten on the damp lawn; blankets and curtains were draped over damp escallonia bushes; the furniture and silver were polished by an army of girls who all had to be fed, and the Rockingham tea service had to be washed and laid out in the servants' hall. All available men, who should have been at the hay, were turned on to scuffling the drive, so that everything looked very nice for weeks afterwards.

The Bishop was known to have a weak digestion, but Aunt Jane turned a blind mental eye to this and her eyes glistened as she thought out a gargantuan feast to do him honour, and before dinner the table would groan under its load of cream-filled cakes and scones for tea.

One year a grey day dawned and rain fell, turning the drive into a quagmire. Roger and I set off from the Lodge to meet the Bishop at tea-time in mackintoshes and sou'westers, driving the donkey-chair. As we got to the narrow part of the drive, the Bishop's large car purred up behind us. After all the preparations he had become like a celestial figure and we were overcome at the thought of holding him up, but we could not move to one side as the chair would have turned over in the mud, so with urgency I addressed the ass, but she put back her ears and shortened her step, and I could not beat her under the eye of my heavenly shepherd. We tried to smile friendly apologies, but this is impossible in a sou'wester, as your head turns but it does not. Roger, being an RC, was more of an interested spectator and was much amused as we plodded on in front of the purring car.

At last we reached the half-way gate and let it pass, but as I was shutting it another car arrived and five unknown young people waved as they sailed by. They turned out to be the children of old friends and filled the hall with loud cries and laughter, obliterating the ecclesiastical atmosphere of gaiters with their jeans and shorts and happy burbling.

There were not enough Rockingham cups to go round or chairs to sit on in the dining-room, where tea had been laid so that all the massive cakes could be enjoyed by the Bishop. The young people helped with these, but poor Aunt Jane's plans for settling the diocese could not even be discussed. She was red in the face and tired after the day's cooking, but smiled and remembered all about the young people's parents and made them feel welcome. I had done my usual bit by cutting masses of flowers in the dripping garden. It was like being under a shower gathering sweet peas and sprays of blossom, or moving between raspberry canes filling and eating cans of fruit, but it was a pleasant way of making myself feel busy and helpful. I enjoyed doing the flower table in the drawing-room, forming a pyramid five feet high with fresh flowers whose sweet scents drowned some of the smell from Aunt Edyth's wet dogs drying themselves on the chintz covers of the chairs.

After tea the girls and boys were sent up to the garden to feast on strawberries, raspberries, red and black currants and loganberries, and were then ushered into their car, while Aunt Jane went back to the kitchen to produce the Bishop's banquet. Roger and I harnessed up the ass and retired to the Lodge for a rest before returning to the Manor for dinner and several hours' talk about old times, as everyone in Ireland knows stories about everyone else's family running into many generations. Those left behind remained static in the same houses and seem to have remarkable memories, and of course the Bishop and his wife knew everyone. Especially interesting were the stories about the old people remaining in Achonry, Co. Sligo, where Aunt Jane and

Aunt Edyth had spent so much of their childhood and where my father had started his horse trade and farming at Knockadoo. The Gore-Booths were still at Lissadell, the O'Haras at Annamore, the Coopers and many more still there.

Getting ready for the Bishop had been hell but his visit roped in a congregation so that the church could not be closed, as the parson wished. People came from all over Connemara for this great day at Aunt Jane's request. Da Barnett brought three carloads of her guests from Ballyconneely – four of them Roman Catholics – twenty campers were enlisted with the promise of tea afterwards, and so the congregation filled the church as it had done in the days long ago.

While my aunts were alive, the whole congregation came down every Sunday in August to tea and cakes at the Manor after the morning service, and one prayed that it would be fine so that they could walk and talk outside the house. It was chaos if rain fell and they all crowded in and their cars destroyed the lawns. Aunt Jane, crimson from exhaustion, sat in the drawing-room in the Nelson chair and held court, and many a friendship was formed among the visitors who came to Connemara every year. Roger loved these gatherings and if possible sat outside enjoying meeting all the people. He never forgot anyone who had been before. I stood in the dark pantry washing up dozens of cups and Donald played hide-and-seek with the children in the wood or up round the stables. The young people generally went out in the boats, and the old place saw again the happy gatherings described in the diaries of a hundred years before.

Soon after the Bishop's visit I was looking out of the Lodge window one morning and saw a bearded man in dark dress lean his bicycle against the silver gates and start tidying his very dishevelled clothing. His tie hung down his back and one of his sleeves nearly hung off his coat, but he did not look like a tinker. Just then, Aunt Edyth came hurrying up the drive to catch the post. At this time she was about sixty; a stout little body, but with a cadaverously thin face and enormous eyes. She had washed her hair, which was grey and scraggly, and left it loose to dry in the wind, and she was wearing a Japanese kimono and gumboots. She welcomed the stranger in her usual laughing way and invited him to breakfast; then hurried on to the letter-box. This letter-box was now a sober green, with none of the amusing decorations of flowers and animals that Great-aunt Alice used to paint on it. When Aunt Edyth returned to escort her guest down the drive, he looked at her sympathetically and said that he was sure he could help her.

I was intrigued by all this and followed them down to the house. It emerged that he thought Aunt Edyth was mad; when speaking to Aunt Jane he referred to her as 'your poor sister'. Realizing this, Aunt Edyth began dropping curious remarks and did a little dance in the hall, leaving her hair over her face. Then we went into breakfast and he said a long grace, thanking the Lord for bringing him to the Silver Gates of Heaven, where that poor woman had welcomed him in. Aunt Jane plied him with bacon and eggs, while he told us that he was a Baptist minister and had found the Irish very unresponsive. He could not understand that modest Roman Catholics would not be bathed by him in pool or sea or proclaim their sins out of the confessional. He said that the boys of Ballyconneely had been very unsympathetic to his message, but we heard later that they were about to baptize him in the sea and were swinging him out when the priest stopped them. He had barely escaped with his bicycle and had flown up the Errislannan road for safety.

After breakfast we had to go into the drawing-room and kneel down and be prayed for in turn by description as he did not know our names. Aunt Edyth gave out little cries to cover her laughter when her turn came and Aunt Jane said 'Amen' to everything, and 'Thank you' when her breakfast was praised. Her eyes were tightly shut, but her laughter tears were trickling down her cheeks. It was balm to the poor man to see us all kneeling under his upraised hands. I glanced up to see him looking out of the window at the lake, so butted in with 'It is not safe for bathing.'

Before he left, Aunt Jane spoke to him in her special voice reserved for priests, nuns and ministers 'not of the faith'. She impressed upon him that the Church of Ireland is much older than the Church of England and founded on St John; that it is 'Catholic' and the usurpers were the 'Holy Romans'. Every year he sent Aunt Jane a letter and a large packet of pamphlets, and every year she sent him a subscription to cover postage, so somewhere in the annals of the Baptist Church we are probably his only converts.

CHAPTER 30

Post-War Sark, Roger and Connemara

When Donald was nine, our doctor advised sending him away from St Ives as he was spending too much time in bed with colds on his chest. During the winter neither he nor Roger was getting enough fresh air. We had to sleep in one small bedroom, and our sitting-room had no chimney and only the large arched shop window, which did not open. The front door opened straight into the room from a busy shopping street and was not much help. We heard of a prep school for Downside high up in the Mendips and with the aid of grants we sent him there; the cure was instantaneous.

Meanwhile Roger and I were left absolutely desolate without our boy. The house felt so empty it was like death, and we could not bear to go on the beaches, so we arranged that Roger should visit his sister for three or four weeks and I would return to Sark. It was sad to realize that Roger could never come with me to Sark since he would not have been able to manage the boats or walk as far as the cliffs, but he enjoyed lying in his sister's garden by the sea and visiting all his old haunts in Cornwall. In some ways we became even closer because of our letters, in which one can say so much more than when one is in daily contact. I had missed the lovely letters he used to write when we were apart before we married, but now I collected dozens of them again.

And so I returned to my island and Elie and Hannah de Carteret were just the same and thought out all kinds of treats for me to make up for the lost years. I might have left my cottage only yesterday; Hannah had remembered how empty I liked it and cleared it out. The Germans had burned all my canvases and my two easels, but Elie made me a new one. I will not write about all the troubles and horrors of the occupation and the deportations. They provided an unending source of conversation, but among the stories were some that appealed to the island sense of humour. For instance, one day when Elie had removed the lid of the cesspit to clean it out, a German officer and a soldier came up the field to Hannah's back door. After a conversation, the officer politely saluted and stepped sharply back, and still saluting sank up to his armpits in the cess. His man quickly wiped the laugh off his face and Hannah hid behind the door to laugh; Elie helped the man out but although they wiped him down he was a sorry mess. The best thing that came out of the troubles was a magnificent pair of German field-glasses given to Hannah when the Germans were leaving. They were so sure that the British would steal their watches, glasses and so on that they gave them all away to anyone who had been kind to them in the last days, when they were starving and grateful even for a cabbage-stump to make soup. Hannah's kind heart could not harden itself against the young German boys who were skin and bone with hunger.

The Queen had been several times to Sark, as had many other members of the royal family. An old man called Charlie had the honour of driving Her Majesty up from the harbour in his carriage with the farm horse in the shafts. He then had the royal coat of arms painted on three sides of the carriage, and always sent the Queen a telegram when anything important happened, as he considered that she knew him best.

How interested she would have been to see the perilous operation of the firing of the seven cannon when she was returning from her Australian tour. The rusty old cannon, given to Sark by Queen Elizabeth I, are on high cliffs all round the island. Their stands have gone, so they are wedged into the ground and propped up on pieces of wood. Elie was in charge of no. 6 on Little Sark so we went to see the fun. The procedure was as follows:

A muslin bag about a foot long made by Miss Cheeswright, the local artist, is filled with gunpowder. This is rammed down the muzzle, then a sod of turf is rammed down hard. Then a rounded pebble off the beach, then more turf and more pebbles and so on. A little powder is sprinkled into the lighting hole and a piece of rag soaked in methylated spirits is laid on top, kept in place by a stone. A match is put to it and hey presto!

The bang deafened us and the pebbles flew out to sea. One day they will surely burst the cannon. Thirty people gathered round to cheer, including one old man in the scarlet coat of the Sark Militia, enveloped in a shawl. A tractor with trailer brought us back from Little Sark, merrily singing and throwing our bottles three hundred feet down into Le Grande Grève as we passed over La Coupée. Sark seemed strangely the same in spite of the war, but I was warned to keep to sheep tracks or paths as there were still many trip-wires left attached to mines by the Germans; there were a few tragedies, but the mines mostly went off when the commons were being burned.

I could not settle down to work for a week or two, but suddenly I felt free and was able to paint, being tempted out in the early morning mist at five o'clock seeing only the tops of trees on the hill rising out of the cloud that filled the valette. The sea was always sounding and the cuckoo singing as the phantom shapes came and went. The sheep and lambs looked identical with my models of long ago as they bleated their way along the grassy paths or posed on perilous rocks. Part of the way was like a corridor with flaming gorse on my right and white hazy blackthorn on my left, and through the gap was the sea and the little islands of Herm and Jethou.

I worked in a frenzy, knowing that my time was short. Ideas poured in and there were no real interruptions. Sometimes I took some hours off to go for a gossipy ramble with Hannah. If only I had had a tape recorder, as she told me about the inhabitants of every house we passed, all in her soft Irish voice in the way that an Irish tale is told. I wrote some of them down but it was not the same thing.

Although Sark had changed so little in the ten years I had been away, I had changed, and felt rather like a ghost; seeing perhaps more, but feeling less about what I saw. Previously I had been completely absorbed into the cliffs, the sea, the flowers and sky, but now I suppose most of my heart was with Roger and Donald, who were never far from my thoughts, and I was no longer single-minded. I was very happy and much more efficient in all that pertained to painting and living, but I recognized the difference. My previous self could not have made a home for anyone. I had lived from day to day with no plans, and like the birds of the air I had been housed and fed. Now I knew about such things as rates, fire insurance, income tax and the rubbish turned out by constant radio and all manner of things, and for each bit of knowledge I think a painter pays out of his diminished power really to paint. I was exceptionally lucky in that Roger took on so many of the chores such as cooking and encouraged me to work, but without such a husband I think marriage would be the end of a woman artist.

And so we established a pattern which lasted for years, of Roger going to his sister in May and me to Sark. Then we returned to St Ives, got the house ready for letting and went off to Ireland, Donald following us each July.

*   *   *

It is seldom that one finds a place where one can look freely round in all directions and see nothing that is not beautiful with a beauty that will endure: Roger found this place in Errislannan. He thought it and its people perfection; he found serenity. He was able to explore the whole of Errislannan, and to visit the people who came to see him, because Mickey Duanne (the boy who fell in a fit at Anne Gorham's wake long ago) brought along an ass cart full of hay to take him on a round of calls. He was very comfortable on the hay and it became his favourite form of transport, except when a wheel came off and rolled into the ditch. To travel at donkey pace was the equivalent of walking; a joy he could not remember. In this cart, or the donkey-chair, he could go slowly along the narrow lanes between the loose stone walls full of ferns and wild flowers, the verges rich with heather, loosestrife, ragwort, harebells, scabious, daisies, honeysuckle and much more. In the chair Roger had the reins and could stop to look at something more closely, or pick blackberries and talk to passers-by, who always stopped to talk to him.

After living in Cornwall, where Roman Catholics were heavily outnumbered by members of other religions, it was a joy to Roger to be among his fellow Catholics, and to be able to take Donald to Mass where he would be among his friends. So far in England Donald had not been to church, but now that he was three I knew that I should have to let him go with Roger. One Sunday, the first summer at the Lodge, he wanted to come to church with me and cried when I turned him back. I felt sad and angry at having to do this, but in the middle of the service a small figure in a black sou'wester and mackintosh, his face stained with tears, crept along the floor and into my pew. When the music started and he peeped over the top to see Aunt Jane pedalling furiously at the groaning harmonium, the tears vanished and he made a dash towards it. Then, thinking he might be caught, he climbed up into the pulpit and his little face appeared over the top, from where he surveyed us all. Reassured by the smiling faces, he came down and wandered past the chancel looking at everything, stopping and turning round as small children do before they have been to school and learned to conform. He finished up at the harmonium, watching Aunt Jane pulling out the stops. Then he pulled one out with such force that it came away in his hand. Delighted, he ran away with it and out of the door. This was the only service he attended in the church of his ancestors until he was grown up.

I have never quite decided whether it is the country or their religion which makes Irish people so much more aware of the things of the spirit. I think it must be a mixture of both, for it is impossible in a place like Connemara not to believe in God, and the other world is almost tangible. I quote a few lines from Robert Gibbings' book *Lovely Is the Lee* because it is so typical of the kind of thing one would have heard from the older generation of Errislannan women. An old woman told him of her husband's death: '"I'm going now, Mary," he says, "and I'm very thankful to you, Mary," he says, "for all you have done for me, and when I see God I'll ask him to be good to you," he says. Them were his last words, and then he shut his eyes like a child and goes straight to Glory.'

Roger liked seeing the expressions of faith in all the houses, the Holy Water, the pictures and statuettes and the ever-burning red light; all things that were taboo among his Protestant friends. When the first car came to the Manor he could go to Mass in Clifden, Ballyconneely, or in the school at Ballinaboy, but he liked best of all going to the Chapel of the Monks on the lake at Ardagh.

There was a little white road that he loved, which came to an end in the bog, with stacks of turf on each side, providing shelter from any wind. He could leave the donkey-chair and lie in the heather, which was soft and springy, and watch the changing colours of the mountains to the east, or the sea and islands to the west. There is much of the big bell heather, St Daboc's Heath, which grows only on west coasts and ranges from rich purple to deep rose; sometimes we found clumps of the white variety. Always the bogland provided strange little plants and insects to see, and the deep turf cuttings reflected the sky in a darker tone.

The turf is cut in the early summer in long deep troughs, the ledges on which the men stand being about a yard wide. The long narrow blade of the turf slane cuts downwards, each sod being formed by one cut. These are thrown up on to the heather to dry. Then the women and children come and spread them out for more drying, and finally they are footed into little stacks of five or six sods to shrink, until they are put into creels by the children and taken to the nearest track, where a stack will be built. The stacks are made with the sods placed neatly side by side on the top, the slanting edges pointing a little downwards, so that no rain can enter. These stacks may be left all through the winter, but in August dotted all over the bog were groups of children with asses and creels, taking home their turf. Generally there would be one small child riding on the tail of the ass, and the others following, hopping from rock to rock, which gave them the appearance of dancing, they were so light and graceful in their bare feet. We knew them all, as in term-time they came into the Lodge to play with Donald on their way to and from school. Often they had collected a few donkeys on the road, and two or three children would be riding on each one. Donald joined them and they hoisted him up between them and sent him home when he had reached his walking limit. Now with the holidays, they were free to bring home the turf and spend their days on the bog, roasting potatoes in the turf fires, helping them down with milk from any cow that happened to be near.

This bog road finished at the foot of a high ridge, the far side of which dropped down more than a hundred feet of sheer rock to the salt lakes and the sea, with more coastline beyond the sea stretching out to the lighthouse. The ridge had always been a favourite haunt of mine at sunset, as nearly every house on Errislannan could be seen from it. Looking down on those little houses and knowing the history of each, and visualizing the interiors with the family gathered around eating their evening meal, may have prompted this book. It seemed such a pity that all should pass away untold.

CHAPTER 31

Night Falls on Errislannan; Roger's Death

Since the seventh century when St Flannan had built his shelter near the spring well, the one permanent feature of the Manor was the lake. It had seen so many facets of Aunt Jane's and Aunt Edyth's lives from when they were children playing in Paradise, running across the meadows with Aunt Jane feeding her hens in the wood and Aunt Edyth trailing her line round the lake from the boat. Now, in 1955, it saw them both old and tottery, with shawls round their shoulders and walking-sticks, emerging to speed their parting guests with cheerful smiles. The garden had become neglected; the flower-beds under the windows were sad wrecks and everything was coming to a standstill. Each year when we returned from England I realized it could not go on much longer.

We were moving from Cornwall to Dorset when a letter telling of Aunt Edyth's death followed us after a week's delay. It must have been the ultimate tragedy for Aunt Jane to be left alone, the last of the seven. I could not leave Roger by himself in a strange place where as yet we knew no one, and that year for the first time we had no house to let to pay our way to Ireland. When Donald came home for the school holidays I left him to look after Roger and dashed over to see Aunt Jane for the last time in Errislannan. She had a nurse she disliked looking after her, but friends were kind, especially the Ruttledges, who later had the task of clearing up the incredible confusion at the Manor – the accumulation of over a hundred years of letters, deeds, clothing, furniture and many other things.

It was obvious that Aunt Jane could not live there alone, and so she accepted a kind offer from her friend Miss Barrett – who had one of the best nursing homes in Dublin – to have a room there. In Dublin Aunt Jane found that she had a host of friends who had known her in Errislannan and who paid her visits. I am sure she was happier than she would have been in Errislannan without Aunt Edyth, now that she could hardly walk. She settled down to write a most amusing journal about the family, and I have used it to describe the family in the Sligo days. Unfortunately it was never brought up to date.

While in Errislannan that final time, I spent a most absorbing day in the attic of Drinagh, at Great-aunt Alice Heaslop's home. Everything that I could take away had been given to me by her daughter Viola, but I did not want anything except the silver that was to go to Dublin with the Manor silver and be sold. I never received a penny as it all went to pay the Errislannan debts. I went up to the attic, where the rain had been running down the walls for years leaving them green and covered with fungus. There stood the ghostlike remains of Great-aunt Sarah's Everard harp, the strings lying on the floor in a tangle; the gilt frame all to pieces but still standing. There were many trunks of clothing belonging to three generations and Irish lace in rolls, gone quite brown. There were shelves of beautifully bound leather-covered books, boxes of china and glass; silver candlesticks, two silver trays and a beautiful Sheffield-plate tea urn. I had only one day and the rain poured down. I was alone in that house full of ghosts, remembering my brother and me as small children on a donkey at the door. I thought back to my aunts' childhood when the Rector's family, the Erwins, had been their great friends. I thought of my Great-aunt Alice and her two daughters, who had used the attic as a studio and written their poems there; how they had played the violin, the harp and the piano in the drawing-room below.

There in the cold damp attic, with no sound but the rain outside, I was filled with panic at the thought of how the family had been wiped out while the house still stood, an empty shell, the furniture frozen in its place, but with no fires, no welcomes. The musty smell was suffocating as I crept fearfully down the stairs and rushed out of the house. Later I sent a man to collect the silver and told a woman to take anything she wanted and to make a bonfire of the rest.

The auction at the Manor in November was a fiasco, as all the big dealers were in Westport that day for a more important sale, and knowing that most of the really good silver and furniture had gone to Dublin. The auctioneer was so late starting that it had to go on into an unadvertised day and many were the tales we heard of how the auctioneer's friend stood next to him and everything was knocked down to him before other people could bid. A leather purse of 'coins' was sold for 10/- and it was full of gold sovereigns – a family collection.

I had many letters telling me how tragic it was to see the Manor stripped and the furniture bundled away on carts and lorries in the rain. The mud and muck all through the house was indescribable. My little green boat, *The Galley*, lay on the lawn among the other boats. I was glad it had been impossible for me to be there. I would have had it sunk at sea.

Those were terrible years, 1955–8, when the Manor was empty for the first time in one hundred and forty years. The windows were boarded up, and damp and storm did their worst. In England I was always conscious of it and on stormy days and in the night I seemed to wander through the empty rooms and feel almost physically the cold of the passages and kitchen with no fire in the great range that had warmed the whole house. I joined the other ghosts that must have wandered round the walled-in garden and the stable yard, and followed the green path to the well. As month succeeded month I found the drag of Errislannan almost unbearable at times and longed to be free to go back.

At this time I came to know Mrs Ivor Bond and her sister, whose family home was Tyneham, that lovely unspoilt valley on the Dorset coast leading down to Worbarrow Bay with its village and church. During the war the whole valley had suddenly been evacuated to make way for an army firing range. I got permission to go down to paint the beautiful Elizabethan house, the last painting done of it before shells went through the roof and it became a ruin. I often found myself alone in the ghostly valley early in the mornings, as I climbed over the barbed wire fences keeping a wary eye out for unexploded shells. It was the only place I felt at home and I wandered round the deserted manor house full of sympathy for it, always conscious that that was how Errislannan was then, empty and deserted, and I could grieve in solitude away from friends and relations. I saw how houses die; the weeds, the creepers, the fallen stone, the gradual take-over by nature, the tameness of the birds. A common expression used in Connemara of an empty house is 'The rooks are flying in it now,' and you know then that it is doomed.

On Christmas Day for years we went down with friends to Worbarrow Bay through the Tyneham valley, lit a huge bonfire of driftwood on the beach and watched the sun set over Portland. Returning, we would find Roger asleep in the car, glad of a rest after a tiring day.

At last Errislannan was bought by a man who had known it as a child. Donal Brooks was a London surgeon, and he and his family of six children made it their holiday home and brought it back to life again. They worked the farm and bred Connemara ponies so it looked much as it did in the last century when there were many ponies round the lake and the ivy had not covered half the house. Aunt Jane had the happiness of knowing all this before she died as the Brookses kindly went to see her in the nursing home and took her Errislannan flowers. She died just after Christmas in 1958, and I was able to go to the funeral in Errislannan as Donald was home for the holidays and could look after Roger.

In Galway I was met by Mr Millar, the weaver, who was then over eighty, and we set out on the fifty-five-mile journey to Errislannan, hurrying along trying to catch up with the hearse. When we came to the mountains we met a severe storm of hail which lay on the ground like snow, making the road invisible and the lakes an inky blue. At last we saw the dark shape of the hearse through the blinding hail, just ahead of us, and followed, thinking of the brave cheerful little person who was being hurried home through the storm, to lie with her loving and united family in Errislannan. She had told me she was absolutely certain that in the after-life people would recognize each other, and so she must have been glad to go. The undertakers were in such a hurry that we lost sight of the hearse again, and some of the Errislannan people who had come five miles in order to follow the corpse on their bicycles were completely left behind.

I arrived at the church to find every wall and hedge lined with people, and as it was a long time since I had seen them, the women came forward and kissed me and the men waved their greetings. I lingered a little to look at them which annoyed an old clergyman, who seized my arm and hurried me towards the church that Aunt Jane had served so well all her life. When the service was over I met the new owners of the Manor, Donal and Stephanie Brooks, who kindly invited me to lunch the next day. I went and walked through the familiar rooms again and sorted out a few things that Aunt Jane had left for me in a locked room. These included the family portraits in large gilt frames. I had to cut them out of their frames with a knife and roll them up, and the Brookses brought them to England for me. Above all their many kindnesses, they offered us the use of the Lodge for holidays, and so for two years Donald, Roger and I fitted into our beloved Lodge, but it made me too sad watching the silver gates with no welcoming aunts at the end of the drive, and feeling that I could no longer wander about inside them, round by the lake or over the Look-out Hill. Also Donald was now sixteen and even with bunk-beds the tiny bedroom was too small for us. It was an unhappy time; the end had really come and I realized what it meant when the three, Uncle John, Aunt Edyth and Aunt Jane, who had always made a home for me, lay together in the churchyard.

*   *   *

It was in 1960, while feeling that we should not be happy at the Lodge any more, that I walked along the shore of Mannin Bay and suddenly noticed the ruins of a little stone house on a rock out to sea, with the waves lapping nearly all around it, cattle inside and a small stone quay making a protected harbour. I remembered as a child seeing an old fisherman sitting at the gable, but when he died the roof fell in and the walls became a shelter for cattle. I had often sat on the rocks by the house and entered the grass-grown kitchen, with a tree growing up the chimney, and woven dreams of having such a place of my own. It faces Errislannan across the bay, only a mile from home. Suddenly I stopped, looked, and from feelings of deepest gloom, my spirits soared as I realized that the ruined little house could be ours. I ran and scrambled over the hill to the Lodge, where it did not take five minutes to persuade Roger and Donald that it was the ideal place for us, and we bought it that very day.

At first we pictured just a new roof and floor, windows and doors, with the cow-shed as a bedroom for Donald. As it turned out we needed many tractor-loads of stone to heighten the walls and make a driveway in for the car. Three of the Errislannan fishermen-farmers I had known all their lives came to do the building with only a few scribbled notes from me. Reluctantly we had to leave for England as Donald's term was beginning. When we returned the following spring we could hardly believe our eyes, the men had made such a wonderful job of it. The interior looked twice as big with all the grass gone and the walls whitewashed inside and out, with red doors.

When we could tear ourselves away we went on to the Lodge, where Annie Angelo was waiting for us as usual with her broad smile, a huge fire, supper waiting and Donald's cat with kittens. We sorted our things our during the next week and when we heard that the calor gas cooker, table, beds and chairs were installed, we moved house. The men had put in a high barrel roof of unstained wood which looked splendid, with skylights in every room, which let in the sun and kept the house warm and dry.

It had been a ruin for thirty years since Jack Larry died aged ninety. He and his father before him had been fishermen-tailors: a pair of scissors on his tombstone in Errislannan commemorates this. It was known as the 'Céilí House', where neighbours gathered in the evenings for talk and music, enjoyed no doubt by the cow tied up opposite the fire, where now our kitchen cupboard stands. The little house perched on the rocks with its quiet quay and harbour is a lovely sight and causes hundreds of tourists to stop and take photographs. It has frequently been seen on English television and even included in a book called *The Cottages and Castles of Ireland*.

I shall never forget our first morning, when waking early I saw from my bed a pink sunrise framing the whole range of blue mountains, reflected upside-down in the calm sea. I had to wake Roger and Donald and we breakfasted outside, feasting on the sight of sea within a few feet of us and distant mountains. Cows and a donkey munched alongside and all kinds of sea-birds flew about. Every neighbour passing along the road waved a greeting. That evening we put our supper table out on the little patch of grass on the west side where the sea, yellow with sunset, nearly came up to us. I walked by the shore on cushions of sea-pinks; herons rose lazily from the rocks or fished in front of the windows. Seal Rock was often decorated with seals which we could watch from the door; peewits swirled about our heads afraid that we might tread on their almost invisible nests with the four large eggs. Little ringed plovers never ceased running about to entice us away from their nests. So much of everything, not to mention the mussels, cockles and shrimps which were there to eat.

That first year Donald and I were tempted to go fishing off the rocks and I slipped and broke my leg below tide level. Poor boy, he was only seventeen, but he got two broomsticks for me to use as crutches, brought the car as near as possible and got me home. All very difficult on such rough ground. The doctor said that I must go to Galway Hospital, fifty-five miles away, for an X-ray, so we all set off at seven next morning in the old car, which was on its very last legs. We staggered along in third gear, finally stopping at the hospital to put me down; the car gasped as far as the garage, where it gave up the ghost. I sat on a bench in a draughty hall from ten o'clock until four except for the interval in which a plaster was put on my swollen leg, which later that night back in Clifden had to be removed.

Meanwhile Donald had searched Galway for some conveyance that would get his two crippled parents home. He found a car which we bought for eighty pounds. It had doors tied up with string and nothing worked except the engine, but at least it took us home. Then began the experience of being killed by kindness. The calls began at 8 a.m. and went on until 10 p.m. and in Ireland one cannot turn anyone away. After three days of this I was almost unconscious and the ambulance was sent for. Poor Roger was sure I was dying as I was placed on a stretcher and carried away to the local hospital. I slept for days and eventually returned in plaster able to hobble about, and we began to enjoy ourselves again. My family had been busy getting old furniture in town and painting it up pale yellow, which looked lovely against the whitewashed walls.

We realized that we must have a boat and decided on a wooden currach for fishing and working lobster pots. To this end we drove to the island beyond Carna to see old Patrick Cloherty, who had helped to build the *Dreadnaught* in the Errislannan barn yard at the beginning of the century, the boat in which we had gone for all our island picnics He was now over eighty and the boat he made for me was his last. He built it in his kitchen during the winter with only an adze; a really beautiful fifteen-foot currach, every line a curve. When it was ready, but not painted, my builders set out in a turf trailer behind a tractor to bring it home. In Carna they celebrated and, full of good cheer, climbed into the new boat and sang and rocked their way over thirty miles of country road. On arrival they threw her into the sea and set out on her first voyage. They caught thirty mackerel by way of baptism, and she has been a wonderful source of pleasure and fish ever since. Roger was comfortable in the bow and we all landed on those white sand beaches, lazing away the sunny days until the tide forced us home.

My first success from the currach was a seven-pound lobster. It happened one Sunday that the Bishop was gracing Errislannan with his presence, so having put out a lobster pot, I donned my Sunday clothes and polished shoes and went to church. The Bishop, friendly and affable as always, preached a long sermon while I began to suffer torture at the thought of the tide ebbing inch by inch, leaving the currach high and dry. The service dragged on as usual and the hymns were heartily sung by all those visitors' Sunday hats to the breathless harmonium. At last the end came and I hastened, smiling and bowing towards the door, but the Bishop was there before me and clasping my hand he enquired at length after my husband and son and reminisced about my holy aunts.

Extricating my car with difficulty, I rattled to the top of Ballinaboy Hill to see the currach just drying out. I raced home and ran down the shore regardless of my only pair of shoes; jumped in and with a mighty shove got her floating. There was no time to unpack the engine so I rowed out to the pots, and was rewarded by hauling up seven pounds of glittering monster. After one near miss from its claws I decided to return home and seek the assistance of the fire tongs to retrieve it from the pot. We had six large helpings of lobster.

That second summer was perfect, with everything more comfortable and no accidents. For the first time we had a garage of our own which Roger could reach alone, and this made him quite independent. We had our meals on the table by the shore and the sea-birds and seals were a constant joy: we never ceased to glow with pleasure in our new home.

On the day we left, all the neighbours came to carry the boat up and to say goodbye. They stood in a group waving and Roger smiled his beaming smile at them. Little did they think that they would never see him again. The following winter of 1962/3, in Dorset, we were snowed in for seven weeks, and Roger died suddenly in February, three weeks after Donald had gone to Sandhurst. He was buried in the snow in frost-hard ground by the river in Wareham. Another stepping-stone, and the worst, had to be negotiated. Although his physical presence with its crippled limbs and asthma had left us, I felt that his strong spirit lived on and that he looked after us as he did in life. Supreme courage, joy and cheerfulness, unselfishness and kindness, with an intelligent awareness of people's needs, were his characteristics, and we were specially blessed in having lived with him.

The ice that winter which changed our lives also sank my boat in Dorset. I could see it at the bottom of the river in a frozen shroud. When the thaw came I sold it as I could not enjoy the river any more. I was helped by the hundreds of letters expressing so much love for Roger, and by Donald, who was a tower of strength, although that first term at Sandhurst must have been terribly hard for him.

After three months I had to go back to Ireland to see to the rebuilding of another house we had bought the previous year and in which we hoped to have friends or tenants, but I could take no pleasure in the prospect and soon sold it.

> The years like great black oxen tread the world,
> And God the herdsman goads them on behind.
>> W. B. Yeats

The loss of a loved husband and daily companion is like a flood that sweeps away everything but the muddy ground. The earth grows green again but there is no real joy. One strange thing was that I lost all desire to paint. Grief is very tiring and though I listened to friends recommending work and entertainment I had no physical or mental energy to do more than feed and clothe myself; a solitary drive or walk was misery so I became very house-bound. I covered a few canvases with paint to keep my hand in, but they were poor and soon disposed of.

The sixties were quiet for me but full of travel and adventure for Donald. After Sandhurst he joined the Royal Irish Fusiliers and went to Germany, exploring Europe on his leaves. This was followed by a tour of duty in Africa and Aden. Sailing was his chief interest and he crewed in many ocean races, including two 'Fastnets'. Friends came to stay with me at the Quay and I went to stay with the Moores (my godchild's parents) in the Hebrides. Here we visited uninhabited islands in a rowing boat and had an exciting and danger-ous voyage home in a storm which later that night rose to force ten. We found a dead storm petrel which I had seen skimming the wild green sea among gannets and which had flown into a wall.

I made one strange sortie to Holland with a friend, bowling along in a coach with twenty assorted sheep. As their life stories unwound behind me I longed for a tape recorder. It was not my scene but a splendid distraction. We left the flock and returned to my old haunts of the twenties in Bruges; even to my old pension with the bedrooms in the garden. Everything was remarkably intact within the walls of the old town after forty years and the war. It was like walking the familiar ways in a dream and as I looked at the office in the Belfry where I had worked, I remembered the telegram arriving there telling me that my brother had been killed, and the brazen way I had lectured to tourists about art when I had not even been to the Slade.

In May each year I returned to my cottage in Sark and walked the unchanged paths along the cliffs, until Hannah de Carteret died in 1970 and I felt that my thirty years of intense happiness and painting there had come to an end.

Nineteen sixty-six saw the fiftieth anniversary of the Easter Rebellion which was celebrated all over Ireland, but many recalled with bitterness the divisions of families and the loss of so many lives. Ireland is now a country of the old. The steady drain of emigration continues and the little farms revert to bog. The hillsides are patterned with walls and potato beds; the house walls still stand, roofless, while the young generation who grew up in this clean sea and mountain air live in squalid lodgings in England, working in factories or on building sites. Very few return and marry, and then only because there is a farm waiting for them. This means that a trickle of children is collected in a minivan and taken to school miles from home instead of running and jumping along the roads barefoot, two or three on stray asses, to the isolated school on the top of Ballinaboy Hill, as they did in the 1950s. Asses and creels and ass carts are still a common sight coming down from the bogs, but who will cut turf – the life-blood of every house – in the future? The cities are different: Dublin and Cork prosper and expand, becoming more foreign every year.

Life goes on fairly unchanged here. The seaweed factory that promised so much for the area has closed down and the weed has to be taken many miles to Cashel. The factory stands a gaunt shell, the fate of many an industry started in this kind of environment, be it Scotland, Ireland, Brittany – all the west coasts. The Frenchmen still buy lobsters at Cleggan, a few miles up the coast. I go there often now as I am painting a picture inspired by the dark stormy sky and harbour.

I remember the darkness of that terrible storm in 1927 in Errislannan, such darkness that one man thought he had gone blind. At Cleggan it wiped out the whole fishing fleet except for one currach with five men in it. Twenty-seven were lost. The last survivor, Festy Feenan, now aged ninety, who lost his son in one of the other boats, said the sudden darkness and storm came with no warning when they all had their nets out. Some boats were thrown in the air and tipped the men out among the nets. Festy tried to cut his nets and shouted to the man next to him to hand him the knife but he could not reach it. This saved them as the nets acted as a drag until they were thrown up in the middle of a sandy beach, south of the bay. Festy could not believe his eyes when he saw a man step out into sea only up to his knees. There were stories of the Virgin appearing on the water and also of a boat full of dead men following, but Festy knew nothing of those things.

He sits, now quite blind, and recalls how seventy years ago Cleggan Harbour had a hundred sailing boats, Nobbies, bringing in fish and how the Norwegian ships called for them, but then the price fell and the fishing died away except for the few currachs. The Norwegians took the fish salted in barrels, but that is no longer done except by families for their own use. I remember the single street of Cleggan, dead and ruined after the disaster, the most desolate place one could imagine, but now big, brightly painted boats are coming in from all round the coast and the harbour is a cheerful and prosperous place lined with cars and people.

CHAPTER 32

Return to the Islands

In 1971 I returned to the small islands about which I wrote earlier. In those far-off days of my youth it was rather a perilous undertaking as it took quite a wind to move us in the old *Dreadnaught*. Now, with unbelievable ease and with no preparations, my god-daughter Helena Moore, aged thirteen, and I drove in my minicar to the deserted harbour at the point of Errislannan, where we embarked in Michael King's new, home-made, nineteen-foot currach. In these days of shifting population and fibreglass boats there was something especially good about being in a boat built by a man who had lived in that place all his life and had built his boat with the help of a friend, exactly as it has been done for hundreds of years. The only difference being that we were propelled along by a small outboard motor, but the four narrow oars were there for when the petrol ran out.

When we drew near Turbot Island it seemed just the same. There was the lovely white sand beach and little stone quay, with fifteen black, beetle-like currachs either floating or turned over on the beach. We heard that fifteen more were away at Slyne Head and Doonloghan after lobsters. Instead of shy children dressed in long grey tweed dresses hiding behind rocks, there were a dozen boys and girls in bright bathing suits or dresses, who came to watch us. The men looked much the same as before, but came forward to help moor the boat. Helena and I followed the only lane on this enchanted island and it led us to the west coast between stone walls and masses of wild flowers which lined the way and turned the little fields white, yellow or purple. Patches of cultivation were fitted in between rocks until we came to the wild green Atlantic, which sent curtains of spray high into the air. Helena, tall and slim with her long hair flying behind her into the wind, leapt from rock to rock, deafened by the sea, full of unconscious grace and joy, while I sat enthralled by the beauty of everything – the sea, the purple and white sky, the lichen-covered rocks.

Soon an old woman dressed in black, driving some cows, approached me full of curiosity as to where I had come from as, thanks be to God, there is no way for visitors to go to those islands yet. When I told her that I had been a

Heather of Errislannan she took my hands with many blessings, and said she remembered our boat and Miss Edyth and Darby Green and Pateen. She reminded me that it was her father, Pat Mullen, who had guided us into High Island fifty years ago and more. The cows went home and we sat on a rock talking. She had ten children and had never left the island except for the shopping trips to Clifden by sea. She even remembered my little green boat coming into the quay along with theirs – 'It was a little dote, but dangerous.'

The island remained enchanted as we wandered back to the quay, facing the blue mountains across the sea. At that time Turbot had twenty children, but only three girls of marriageable age, who swore they would not marry an island man as they wanted to leave. By the end of the decade it was empty, the people housed on the mainland, and the island was left to the sea-birds as were so many others; a perfect unspoilt place.

Now when I cross Ballinaboy Hill on to Errislannan and go down past the church where my family lie together in rows, past the silver gates of the Manor and the Lodge, to where one looks across the lake, I find that hardly anything has changed since my childhood. The woods still surround the house; the Look-out Hill and the sloping meadows are the same. The same families still live in the same houses, but behind the Lodge, Joe King's house is in ruins and we should have missed him; there will be no light on that hill any more. He was old but ran the farm unaided until the day he died alone in his house; the noise of the unmilked cows brought a neighbour, who found him dead. I remember the many times he came squelching across the bog carrying buckets of precious water for us at the Lodge.

For two nights he was given the last proper wake on Errislannan. Johnnie Dan's daughter, Norah Christine, and Annie Angelo arranged it. Joe was liked by everyone and people came from miles around. He was dressed in his blue suit with collar and tie and slippers, laid on the bed on a white sheet, and as everyone arrived they went to the room to say a prayer for him. Then down to the fire, where whiskey was served, and plates of cut tobacco for those with pipes and plates of cigarettes for others. They talked and sang till midnight, when the Rosary and prayers were said, followed by tea.

Then the wake games began. They got straw and plaited it and sat round in a circle on the floor. The straw was passed behind their knees while one in the centre made lunges to get it. The game became violent as they fought for the straw. The one caught with it had to take a turn in the centre. The kitchen must have become very warm by this time and Norah Christine said she was black and blue after the games. Rough hide-and-seek is often played, and whacking on the door and whacking the furniture and chasing in and out and under the beds, to chase away the evil spirits.

The wake games have their origins in pre-Christian times, and the players would be horrified at their behaviour on any other occasion, but after a lot of drink they let themselves go. At other wakes, under the direction of the Borekeen, they played weddings, with a faked priest in a straw stole who married the couples. Other games were 'Making the Ship', the 'Bull and the Cow', 'Hold the Light', and 'Drawing the Ship out of the Mud'. The wake games were played only in the houses of solitary old people with no one to mourn them, not where there was real grief, but even there it was felt right to cheer up the mourners. Wakes are now an excuse for a party as the dances in the houses are discouraged, much to the loss of the old people and children who all used to join in.

Looking at that graveyard, which is fuller now, I remember some of the funerals in the old seventh-century one next to it, where the rusty iron gate still hangs askew among the nettles as it has done all my life, but now a beautiful white May tree, blown by the west wind, forms a perfect arch over it. I remember a corpse with no coffin, wrapped in a sheet and laid on a plank with the toes standing up, and preceded by a boy with two sticks tied together to make a cross; and another funeral when there was no priest and the people stood round saying the Rosary while the grave was being dug. This was interrupted by a frantic whirr of flapping wings and squawks, as one of our dark sinister Muscovy ducks flew low over the grave, almost touching it. The voices died away and I saw all heads turn as they watched the duck and crossed themselves against the ominous thoughts that came to them.

Still looking across the lake I remember the daffodils, and how, each year, their fluttering yellow frames the house. They grow along the lawn's edge; they surround you as you go to the well for water, they crowd closely along both sides of the drive. They rise, a sheet of yellow, up the wood behind the house, and even in the lake they shine when all else is dark. We used to pick thousands of them almost in bud and keep them in buckets in the servants' hall ready to be bunched for the Dublin market. It was a cheerful time; all the boys and girls were roped in to help and great was the talk and laughter as they learned to bunch. Uncle John packed the crates far into the night and then in the morning the blue and red ass cart, drawn by the Giddy Ass, came to the door and the golden cargo was loaded up. They set off over Ballinaboy Hill in all weathers, hoping to catch the train, but they did not always succeed. When flowers began to be flown into Dublin from abroad, we could not compete. So, unmolested, they grow and multiply. Even through the years when the Manor was empty and, I thought, dying, the yellow flowers kept up their display, giving way to the bluebells and narcissus, when the woods turn blue; and snowdrops, violets, primroses still grow under the feathery moss.

I continue along the road to St Flannan's cottage, where we spent many summers of childhood, on towards Candoolan, our favourite beach, which is absolutely unchanged. I can see the ruined house of Mollie and Annie, the deaf mutes. Annie stayed in her father's house down by the sea until her death in 1977. I had tea with her once a year, and well into her nineties she remembered names and dates better than myself.

The land does not change here, only my family has gone, but it will be remembered with great affection for a long time. After the auction Mary King, the cook, wrote, 'I do feel lonely for Miss Jane, may God help her. She was good to everyone. To see the Manor, it would make you lonely, only the four walls and no one around it. Many a good Sunday dinner I cooked in it, but never again, those days are gone never to come back. I do miss the dear old Manor, there was always full and plenty in it.'

Looking back over one hundred and forty years or so, the Manor housed a remarkably affectionate family, with no dark shadows or quarrels between them, with the exception of an occasional affray with deaf and eccentric Great-aunt Alice Heaslop, which accounted for much of the trouble. Now a new era has started and a large family has brought back life and happiness to what was always such a warm and friendly home. The house and stables have been repaired and dozens of Connemara ponies roam the Look-out Hill. The quay at Derrygimlagh is only a mile from Errislannan so I often go to see the people I have known all their lives.

As an autobiography cannot be neatly finished off with the death and burial of the author, this seems as good a time as any to bring the story to a close. I can still take my boat out fishing alone, drive the car and travel, but realize that I have begun to look back with interest for the first time, a sign of old age. My paintings have built two houses and provided a comfortable living, my son is happily married with two children, and I am deeply grateful to the 'Almighty who took this family by the chin and kept the head from drowning', to use John Smyth's phrase from the seventeenth century.

I write these last words at the quay, looking across the sea at Errislannan, only half a mile from where it all began, when I ascended Ballinaboy Hill five months before I was born, and was home for the first time.

Connemara, Sark and Dorset, 1978

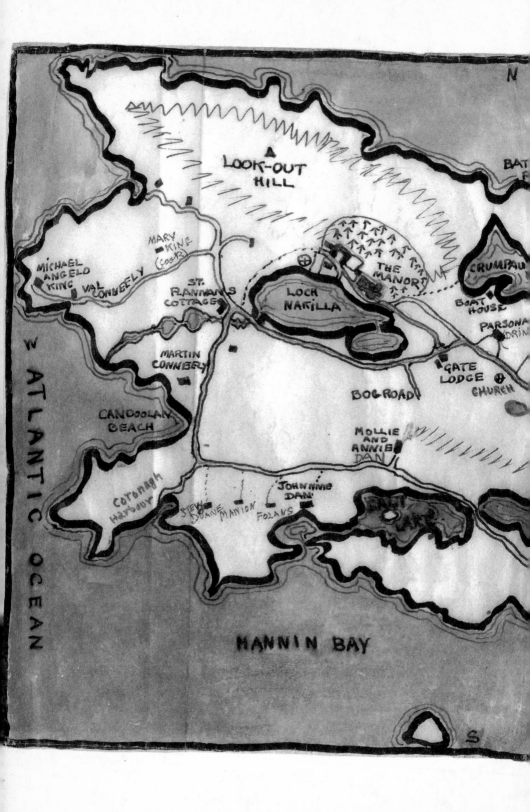